Author's Note

Cast

I have tried to dispense with too much formality in this book. Titles are so stuffy! Where possible I have used first names and not Duke, Duchess, Earl or Countess. So the main cast of characters reads Sophie, Edward, their children Louise and James, Charles and Camilla, Anne, Andrew, Diana, Fergie, William and Kate, Harry and Meghan. I sometimes use Prince or Princess and the first name, as in Prince Edward.

The Queen mentioned so often in this biography refers to the late Queen Elizabeth II, who was basically the Queen for almost all of Sophie's (and my) life. Her late husband is Prince Philip. It would be confusing to call him the Duke of Edinburgh when Edward has now been given that title.

I recall that when I wrote a biography of the current Princess of Wales I called her Kate, because that's how she was known when the world first noticed her. I suspect she will be popularly known as Queen Kate when William becomes King.

Sophie

Sophie

Saving the Royal Family

SEAN SMITH

SPHERE

SPHERE

First published in Great Britain in 2025 by Sphere

1 3 5 7 9 10 8 6 4 2

A CIP catalogue record for this book
is available from the British Library.

Hardback ISBN 978-1-4087-2420-0
Trade paperback ISBN 978-1-4087-2421-7

Typeset in Bembo by M Rules
Printed and bound in Great Britain by Clays Ltd, Elcograf S.p.A.

Papers used by Sphere are from well-managed forests
and other responsible sources.

Sphere
An imprint of
Little, Brown Book Group
Carmelite House
50 Victoria Embankment
London EC4Y 0DZ

The authorised representative
in the EEA is
Hachette Ireland
8 Castlecourt Centre
Dublin 15, D15 XTP3, Ireland
(email: info@hbgi.ie)

An Hachette UK Company
www.hachette.co.uk

www.littlebrown.co.uk

To Penny

Contents

Introduction

My first reaction was that she must have been misheard. Did Sophie Rhys-Jones, the Brenchley Belle as I once called her, really refer to Her Majesty The Queen as 'Mama'? For many years, I hadn't taken much notice of the Countess of Wessex, as she was in 2019, until she made the speech at a Buckingham Palace reception.

I had to watch a recording to reassure myself that she had not been misquoted. I was struck by several things. First, she looked very elegant, poised and at ease in the company of the Queen, who was ninety-three at the time. Second, it was very hard for the Royal Family to receive any media attention that was not connected to Harry and Meghan, whose emotional programme, *An African Journey*, had been broadcast the previous week. Thirdly, she spoke in a clear, easy-to-listen-to manner, not in an overly posh way that strangled her words before they left her mouth.

The Palace reception for two hundred guests was in support of the Queen's Platinum Jubilee Trust and, in particular, the promotion of care and medical help for those with sight problems throughout the world.

While the throwaway reference to 'Mama' (pronounced *Ma-Mah*) guaranteed some much-needed coverage for the event, it was what Sophie said next that made me sit up and take notice: 'Mama, when I have returned from my travels, I have been so proud to share with you the work I have witnessed and the care of so many people working so hard to save and cure sight.

'Each time you have listened and been eager to hear how the work is going, and each time I have been stunned as you have shared with me your deep knowledge of each of these countries, not top-level observations, but personal experience, demonstrating to me time and again the real affection you have for all people of the Commonwealth and why that affection is so abundantly returned by them to you.'

Was she saying that she always popped in to see the Queen for a cuppa and a catch-up when she returned home from a trip? Sophie's home was only ten minutes down the road from Windsor Castle so it would have been very easy for her to drive over. I made a mental note to find out more about what Sophie had been doing for the past few years.

It didn't take long to discover that she was just back from a trip to Kosovo, in the Balkans, where she had given a powerful speech in support of survivors of conflict-related sexual assault. This didn't sound like a subject for ribbon-cutting at the local fête. Sophie declared, 'We must shift the blame from victim to the perpetrator. If the stigma goes unchallenged we are merely perpetuating the offence, over and over again. So I say there is no place for stigma in our world today ... no one should have to feel ashamed ever again.'

Wow, this was great stuff that the whole world needed to hear. Who knew that Sophie was the voice of reason and global compassion? At the time I was writing a biography of the Duchess of Sussex called *Meghan Misunderstood*, a fair and unbiased account of her remarkable life and experience in the UK, but I thought Sophie might be a great subject to return to at some point in the future. She seemed to become more fashionable and beautiful as the years passed. But then the Royal Family became beset by tragedy, unhappiness and serious illness.

Prince Philip, the Duke of Edinburgh, died not far short of his hundredth birthday. We will never forget the picture of the Queen, dressed all in black, including a mask, sat alone in the chapel during those Covid days – an iconic image of melancholy and sadness. Then the Queen herself left us the following year, in September 2022. Just as we were getting used to a change of pomp and circumstance, both Charles, the new king, and Kate, the queen-in-waiting, were diagnosed with cancer.

This was taking the notion of a slimmed-down Royal Family to ridiculous lengths, it seemed. There was no Prince Andrew, who had been brushed under the carpet as a national embarrassment; there was no Harry and Meghan, although the daily media obsession with them showed no signs of reducing. They were only a working royal couple in the UK for less than three years.

The old faithfuls – the Duke and Duchess of Gloucester, the Duke of Kent and Princess Alexandra – are all pushing eighty or ninety. Camilla, the new Queen Consort, turned seventy-eight in 2025. The redoubtable Princess Anne is also well into her seventies and she needed a break after being kicked by a horse that gave her a nasty concussion.

And then, just as I was thinking that the Royal Family as we knew it when the late Queen was alive was slipping quietly away, I saw a picture of Sophie shaking the hand of President Zelenskyy in Kyiv in April 2024. How did that happen? Once more, she came across as a woman of considerable substance as she championed a cause about which she felt so strongly. She met survivors of war-related sexual violence, visited a mass grave and gave a speech in which she declared,

'Rape is used to demean, to degrade and to destroy, and we have to get better at trying to prevent that from happening.' Can you imagine any politician being able to deliver those lines with such power and grace?

So how did Sophie get to this point in her life? How did she travel a path that took her from being a fun girl in rural Kent, a sociable London PR representing Mr Blobby, to a fête-opening fringe figure of the Royal Family, and then become arguably its most important asset? It was time to find out.

PART ONE:
THE BRENCHLEY BELLE

1

Pretty, Bright and Fun

As a child, Sophie Helen Rhys-Jones was like the quintessential Enid Blyton heroine of the classic *Malory Towers* boarding-school books for girls. Brought up in a beautiful part of the English countryside, at school she was popular with both teachers and her classmates, had lovely, supportive parents and was brilliant at sport. Nevertheless, even Enid Blyton might have thought twice about a storyline that had Sophie falling in love with a charming prince or becoming the bestie of the Queen of England. But Sophie's world is one where fantasy has merged into a breathtaking reality.

She was not originally from rural Kent, the county where she was raised, but was born at the Nuffield Maternity Home in Oxford on 20 January 1965, just four days before the nation went into mourning following the death of Winston Churchill. She was given the middle name of Helen in memory of her father's sister, who, tragically, had been killed in a riding accident five years earlier.

At the time of her birth, her father Christopher, mother Mary and elder brother David lived in the pretty village of Ickford, in Buckinghamshire, but shortly after Sophie was born, they moved to the equally desirable Brenchley, about six miles from Royal Tunbridge Wells. Christopher, who had placed the hyphen in the family surname, was an overseas representative for a tyre manufacturer, so it made sense for him to live nearer to Dover and Folkestone for business trips abroad.

After a couple of years in a small house in the centre of the village, the family moved to the quaintly named Homestead Farmhouse, a very comfortable, four-bedroom, seventeenth-century thatched farmhouse along Palmers Green Lane, a quiet road on the outskirts of Brenchley. These days this would be London commuter country, just an hour – hopefully less – from nearby Paddock Wood station, which connects directly to Charing Cross, and the location would mean there would be little change from a million pounds for the house.

Homestead was a typical weather-boarded Kent house, with whitewashed walls and bits of buildings stuck on the side, almost as an afterthought. In winter, Christopher made sure there was a large pile of logs crammed into the sun porch at the back. Inside the house, the rooms were furnished in a comfortable, unflashy, middle-class sort of way, with simple wooden furniture covered in faded chintz material. Pride of place was given to a splendid old Welsh dresser adorned with brightly coloured plates. The family did not realise it when the children were growing up, but it would prove quite useful as Sophie became famous that the house was difficult to spot from the road, being tucked away at the end of a footpath. Best of all for Sophie was the inspiring view from her bedroom, reaching out across acres of trees and rolling fields.

Until he finally settled in Kent, Sophie's father had led quite a nomadic life. He had been born in the state of Sarawak, Borneo (then a British colony), but his father returned home to be headmaster of St Peter's Preparatory School at Lympstone, in Devon – the village that would later be the scene of Prince Edward's unhappy experience in the Marines. Christopher attended the well-known West Country public school King's Bruton, in nearby Somerset, and when he left he spent a lot of time travelling in Africa before settling on a career.

One of his oldest friends from his Sarawak days was his step-brother, the actor and dancer Thane Bettany, who *Doctor Who* fans will recall played Tarak in the long-running TV series. Thane, the father of the award-winning actor Paul Bettany, was a supportive godfather to Sophie and a welcome guest when the Rhys-Jones family settled in Brenchley.

Both Christopher and Mary fitted well into village society and were considered very sociable. One of their friends, local farmer Michael Noakes, observed, 'We always tease people that you have to be here for twenty-five years before you are accepted. But this is not so. If you mix easily you are accepted straight away. Christopher and Mary were popular pretty early on.'

It helped that Christopher enjoyed outdoor pursuits including sailing, shooting and fishing, as well as having a love of nature, which would all have a lasting effect on his daughter, who liked nothing better as a little girl than donning a pair of wellington boots and tagging along with her dad. He also enjoyed the indoor pursuit of a good gin and tonic, which had always been *de rigueur* in Brenchley society. Years later, when Sophie dropped the bombshell that she was going out with Prince Edward, her father memorably remarked, 'It was the first time in my life that I needed a gin and tonic before ten o'clock.'

Christopher had first met his Irish-born wife-to-be, Mary O'Sullivan, a bank manager's daughter, on a trip to Gibraltar. She was working as a secretary in South Kensington and living on Sloane Avenue, so, in some ways, she was an original Sloane Ranger – a path that Sophie was to follow when she left school. In fact, Sophie was not the first member of the Rhys-Jones family to come into close contact with a prince. Her mother once danced with a dashing Prince Philip at a society ball.

When Christopher and Mary moved to Kent they were determined to do their very best for their children. They worked hard to pay for private schooling for Sophie and her brother David, who is two years older. For many years Mary worked as a secretary for Lambert & Foster, a local estate agent in Paddock Wood. To make some extra pennies she also advertised her secretarial skills locally, offering to type reports, letters, theses, CVs and book manuscripts, and this work made all the difference to the family's finances. Freelancing also meant she was available to run the children to and from school. Sophie's childhood friend, Janie Stewart, whose father was a local vet, recalled, 'She was a proper "mum" figure. She would always have chocolate biscuits in the house!'

Sophie and David went to the Dulwich College Preparatory School in Cranbrook, about nine miles from Brenchley along typically high-hedged Kent lanes. Local legend has it that Queen Elizabeth I once spent a night in the original building. The prep school had been separated from the famous London public school when the pupils were evacuated during the Second World War. After the war, the older pupils moved back to the main school, but the juniors remained in Cranbrook. Sophie was four years and nine months old when she started at the junior part of the school, called Nash House. The fee for each term was £29.7s, which in predecimal days was quite a tidy sum for her parents to find. A big circular driveway led up to the school and was clogged every morning with Volvos dropping off little ones at Nash House.

Sophie was in a class of twenty boys and girls, split up into little groups according to their activity that day. When they arrived in the morning, they were sent out to the playground, an open field that was quite the biggest that young Sophie had ever seen. At one end, there was a sandpit, and some tree houses and climbing equipment that Sophie loved. Janie Stewart remembered those happy days: 'We would meet up with all our friends and play. We would go out and run around and fight the nasty little boys. After that, we would be called in for a drink of milk in those quarter bottles with straws, which was quite disgusting. We sort of had lessons, counting and stories like *Brer Rabbit*. In the afternoon we might have another story and then we could either play quietly or we could lie down on one of the camp beds and have a nap. It was nice having a kip in the afternoon. Sophie was quite a good little girl but she was easily led by the naughtier girls. I well recall a rebellion, for instance, when we locked ourselves in the Wendy house. We shouted that we weren't coming out. It was a proper house with a lock on the door and three children could get into it together. After that it became quite a problem with children locking themselves in the Wendy house, so they had to take the door off.'

Although Sophie and her friends were very young, they spent the entire day at Nash House; it was considered a proper school and discipline was quite strict. If a boy or girl was naughty, they had to stand in the corner with their face turned to the wall, which must have been frightening for a small person and not something welcomed at all in educational circles today. At an early age Sophie decided this was not for her and punishment was a dish best avoided. She had a happy knack of escaping at just the right time, leaving her friends to face the music.

At this early age Sophie developed her lifelong love of

water. In summer, all the children would jump into the shallow pool and splash around happily until it was decided that they could swim properly. Then they were allowed to go down to the big pool with the older children. Sophie was the first in her year to receive this accolade and be given a proper costume, and since then she has always excelled at swimming.

Sophie was seven when she moved on to the next stage of school – where the girls and the 'nasty little boys' were split up. The girls moved to a building called Little Stream and had to wear a uniform, which, as all parents know, is a major hidden expense. Sophie's long clothing list was a typical one: navy raincoat, grey felt hat with hat band, grey blazer, tunic, blue jersey (school colour), blue blouse (school colour), grey knickers, grey knee-length socks, brown walking shoes (lace-ups) and two overalls. In winter she needed a pair of grey woollen gloves, school scarf (optional) and a navy duffel coat with red lining (optional). For the summer term she had to wear a school summer dress, cardigan and white ankle socks.

Everything had to be bought from S. Simmonds & Son, the school outfitters in Calverley Road, Tunbridge Wells. Mary Rhys-Jones, who had been taking on yet more freelance commissions to meet this expense, took Sophie along to the shop to be kitted out. Sophie could never understand why she was not allowed to wear jeans to school. Her mother's work was not yet done, because when they returned home she had the tedious task of sewing a name tag saying *S. Rhys-Jones* into every single item. The other drawback of the move to Little Stream was the dramatic increase in school fees to £95 a term.

Sophie's special gang at this time comprised Janie Stewart, Sophie Douglas and Tracy Foreman – whose home in the village of Headcorn the others loved to visit because her wealthy parents kept horses, and the girls would hang around the stables making nuisances of themselves. They also enjoyed watching Janie's father at work in his surgery treating cats, dogs and hamsters. Best of all, though, was when they would stay over at each other's houses. Sophie loved the midnight feasts: it had to be midnight even if they had already fallen fast asleep by then. Each feast was planned like a military exercise, with the girls tiptoeing downstairs to raid the larder and sneak back to bed armed with goodies like Coca-Cola, crisps and chocolate biscuits. The mothers, who were not supposed to know what was going on, always made sure they got in extra supplies. Sophie's mum, who was very jolly and down to earth, found these furtive feasts highly entertaining.

Summer was a magical time in rural Kent. When they mowed the grass of the school playing field Sophie and her gang – the Famous Four – would make a camp from grass cuttings. Then they would lay out a showjumping course for themselves and imagine it was Hickstead, the famous equestrian centre. Their summer dresses had little bow ties at the back, which they untied and pretended were reins so that they could play 'ponies'; the girls would charge around the field shouting 'whoa' and making clip-clop noises. It was an age of wonderful innocence.

Horses were definitely the goal in life for the girls and, sadly, Sophie was the only one of the four friends who, growing up, never had a pony, which meant in the very competitive 'horsey' world she was stuck on a lower social rung; it would be many years before she jumped up several divisions. She did join her friends cycling around the country lanes, though, in a more sheltered time when it was still considered safe for children to enjoy that innocent outdoor pursuit. Sophie and her pals had very little contact with boys apart from seeing them across the field playing rugby and cricket while they took part in hockey and lacrosse.

Sophie was quite tall for her age, with long, light brown hair, which turned blonder under the summer sun. She had to tie it back for school – yet another rule that would mean a trip to the headmaster's study if disobeyed. That never happened to Sophie. 'She wasn't exactly a goody-goody but she was definitely a nice girl that everybody liked,' recalled Janie Stewart. 'She wasn't really rebellious like the other three of us might have been. She would toe the line. She would never come in with her socks all wrinkled down and her cardigan half off and her hair all over the place. She would always look clean and scrubbed and neat and tidy. The teachers liked her as well. She was pretty and bright and fun and giggled a lot, but she was never vulgar or over the top about anything.'

Away from school, Sophie was beginning to develop interests that would remain with her far longer than anything she learned from textbooks. She had a family connection with the world of theatre and dancing, and it was this great love of the performing arts that would later help to turn the head of a certain prince. Her early inspiration was her godfather Thane Bettany and his wife Anne Kettle; he had been a member of the Royal Ballet. From the age of four, Sophie was coached ballet by Pearl Westlake, the elegant ballerina and wife of Derek Westlake, a fine dancer and long-time manager of Sadler's Wells in London. These ballet classes were held at the beautiful Brenchley home of June Bowerman, also a gifted ballerina, who had taught Princess Anne and Prince Charles. She recalled Sophie as being a 'very beautiful girl'.

Sophie's regular partner at the classes was another local girl, Sarah Sienesi, who would prove to be an enduring friend, her first flatmate when she moved to London and her very first lady-in-waiting when she became a fully fledged member of the Royal Family. The only problem at the dance classes was that one of the girls would have to lead. Usually, it was Sarah, but the result was invariably the same: both girls would be reduced to fits of giggles. During the summer months, June Bowerman would put on little shows in her back garden, which parents and most of the village would come along to support. Mrs Rhys-Jones was hugely proud of her daughter, especially when she appeared as Cinderella, with Sarah as the fairy godmother. Sophie's mum could be seen in the audience wiping away a tear.

During one less-serious performance, Sarah and Sophie, dressed in hideous purple outfits, had to dance to Michael Jackson singing 'Rockin' Robin'. All went well until the record player began to slow down and, as the youthful high notes of the pop legend became a rich baritone, Sophie and her friend danced slower and slower while trying to keep a straight face. The audience roared their appreciation. Sophie has never lost the ability to have fun, a characteristic from her young days and one that she still has when royal decorum is not required.

The only part of those early performances that Sophie did not like was wearing all the stage make-up. She found it very cloying on her skin, and this aversion to cosmetics continued into adulthood – she always preferred to wear as little make-up as possible. Sophie managed to reach Grade 4 in dancing, which was quite respectable for a non-professional. The most memorable exam was when Sophie was nine and travelled to a school in Maidstone for her test. One of the other little girls suffered a bad attack of nerves and left a puddle on the stage just where everyone had to run round in a circle. The whole session became like a circus, with all the little girls getting to the puddle and suddenly leaping into the air and jumping over it. Sophie found it hilarious.

One of the perks of dance lessons was the regular trips to Sadler's Wells in Islington to see real ballet at first hand. Sophie developed a lifelong love of these trips to watch the classic ballets. She still loves it – especially if she and her husband can slip off unnoticed to the Royal Ballet in Covent Garden. She was particularly proud to lend her name to the prestigious Countess of Wessex Studios, the new home of the Central School of Ballet in Southwark. She has been the school's royal patron since 2003.

Pursuits like ballet and drama that demanded self-expression were a particular strength of the schoolgirl Sophie, much more so than traditional subjects. She was a bright and vivacious child who might have been best described as a good all-rounder and above average in most subjects, but not especially academic. Back at school, the nine-year-old Sophie moved to a more senior building called Coursehorn, which was mixed and took exams more seriously.

The headmaster was a middle-aged man called Robin Peverett, who Sophie and her friends, with sparkling schoolgirl wit, called 'Mister Pervert'. He was tall, with dark curly hair and would usually wear a sober grey suit and dark glasses, which the children found somewhat menacing. He would stand in front of the school at assembly and no one would know who he was watching. He was keen on school discipline; when, for instance, two pupils complained about the food, they were made to stand on a table and eat lunch there in front of 250 of their peers.

His nickname would prove to be unfortunately accurate some years later when he was revealed in a notorious court case in 2000 to be a predatory paedophile. The case became controversial because Mister Pervert escaped jail after admitting nine charges of indecently assaulting seven pupils (six girls and one boy between the ages of ten and thirteen) in the late 1960s and 1970s. Instead of a custodial sentence, he was given eighteen months suspended for two years, which caused outrage among his victims. The severity – or lack of it – was due in part to what the *Guardian* described at the time as a 'bit of nifty plea bargaining'. His victims waived their right to anonymity and gave a disturbing account of his practices to the newspaper, which confirmed that Sophie 'played no part in the police investigation' – although one of the women quoted revealed that she had been in the same class as Sophie.

The paper pointed out that the case was originally listed to last three weeks in court but suggested that 'police and witnesses realised there would be considerable media interest, mainly because the Countess of Wessex, Sophie Rhys-Jones, was a pupil at the school'. In the end, it lasted an hour and a half before Mr Peverett was allowed to go home. One can only speculate what his punishment might have been in these more enlightened times. He was subsequently stripped of his OBE.

Ironically, Mr Peverett was a great encouragement to Sophie's love of theatre and she was much in demand if he was directing the school play, sporting the bright-red crew-neck jumper he favoured if in a theatrical mood. He would usually make a special film of the school play that would be shown at the annual Parents' Day. He helped to forge an interest in drama and theatre in Sophie that would prove to be one facet of her personality that Prince Edward would find irresistible.

One of Sophie's favourite teachers was the English master James Bowler, who urged her to write her own poetry – which she enjoyed – and encouraged her fondness for Shelley, Keats and the other great Romantic poets, who all stayed with her as her preferred reading long after her schooldays. She was especially moved by Keats' 'Ode to a Nightingale':

'My heart aches, and a drowsy numbness pains

'My sense, as though of hemlock I had drunk ...'

She learned it off by heart and conquered her nerves to stand up and recite it in front of the class. She was not so keen on maths, although she did volunteer with her friends for the winter maths club that was held on Saturday mornings. This was a canny schoolgirl gambit, because it meant none of them had to spend time freezing to death on an outside activity instead.

The school chaplain was a great character, aptly named Trevor Vickery, who was known to pupils as Trev the Rev. He took Sophie's confirmation classes when she was eleven. He was a very jolly fellow who rode around his parish of Staplehurst, ten miles from Brenchley, on a penny-farthing bicycle. During the Second World War, he had been a physical training instructor on a cadet training ship, HMS *Conway*, which was anchored off Bangor, in North Wales, and it was there he learned the unlikely clerical pursuit of boxing. Every Saturday morning at the school he held boxing lessons in the gym. One term, the girls, including Sophie, decided that what was good enough for the boys was good enough for them, too. They insisted on lessons, and so Trev the Rev taught Sophie how to box, for which she proved to have a degree of flair. She wore proper boxing gloves and she and her friends were shown the rudiments of how to defend themselves. Sophie may have loved poetry but she also had a tomboyish streak and was not the least soppy when it came to sport. She would always hold her own against elder brother David if they were kicking a ball around in the back garden of Homestead Farmhouse.

When Sophie was ten, she and her best friends Tracy, Janie and Sophie D (the Famous Four) formed a witches' coven at school. Each week one of the four girls would be chief witch and have to issue dares or instructions, such as only being allowed to wear certain colours of clothing. The most difficult – and certainly the funniest – task came when Sophie decided they had to go all day without touching any metal. All went well until the coven trooped into lunch and faced the prospect of eating their soup without touching a spoon. None of the teachers could work out why four young ladies were laughing so hysterically throughout the meal.

At Coursehorn there were about ten boys to every girl, which was quite favourable odds for the deadlier of the species. Unfortunately for the four witches, they all fancied the same callow youth, one Timothy Barker. This was the first time the girls had shown a blossoming interest in 'nasty little boys'. Handsome Timothy was definitely the favourite boy in the class. He was a boarder and had a fetching suntan from visiting his parents abroad. The girls were fiercely competitive about the object of their affections and would compose little notes or snatches of poetry for him and leave them in a desk where they knew he would be sitting, so that he would find them. The notes were quite innocent – suggesting, for instance, that he should 'Meet me by the flowerbeds' – or 'Meet me in the gym hall'. The flowerbeds in question were outside the gym and were a collection of old pig troughs filled with brightly coloured flowers. The romantic pig troughs were the location for Sophie's first chaste kiss with Timothy Barker, much to the chagrin of her schoolmates. Rivalry had been intense to see who would be the first witch to pucker up with Timothy, and Sophie won. Timothy did not turn into a prince as a result of Sophie's kiss – it would be another twenty years before she kissed a real prince, but she had reached an age when her hormones were about to kick into a higher gear.

2

Crisp Sandwiches

After passing her entrance exams, Sophie moved on from Dulwich College Prep to Kent College for Girls, at Pembury, a large village close to Tunbridge Wells that was the unlikely birthplace of the late Shane MacGowan. The iconic former lead singer of the Pogues had Irish parents and would always be associated with the Emerald Isle and the working classes, but he actually won a creative writing scholarship to prestigious Westminster School in London. His Christmas classic, 'Fairytale of New York', was still a decade away when Sophie went to school in Pembury, where one of her best friends in those early teenage years was then the best-known local celebrity – not Shane, but the Olympic swimmer, Suki Brownsdon.

Sophie had soon discovered that one of the consequences of going to a new school was losing touch with the old gang. Not before, however, they had discovered the delights of raiding their fathers' drinks cupboards. Sophie and her friends would take it in turns to bring some alcoholic concoction to school. Janie Stewart recalled the hideous cocktails: 'It didn't matter what it was because you would pour it all together – a tot of whisky, some tonic water, a dash of gin, advocaat and all sorts of nasty things. We would mix it all up into one little tonic bottle and smuggle it into school. We used to hide behind the big sofa in the study and take it in turns to swig out of this bottle. We didn't get really pissed, but it was a dare. It was very exciting!'

Sophie had been a very robust little girl and always seemed fit and healthy. She was also one of the lucky ones who never had to wear braces, enjoying what used to be described as 'nice teeth' – a quality that would serve her well when she had to smile politely for the zoom lenses of the paparazzi. At Kent College, nobody could match the sporting achievements of Suki, who was just fourteen when she first represented Great Britain at the Moscow Olympics in 1980, but Sophie did come into her own as a talented all-rounder. She was soon in the athletics, swimming, netball and hockey teams. She could run like the wind, but it was on the hockey pitch that she excelled, despite now not being the tallest of teenagers; she had a reputation for being an animal with a hockey stick and she struck fear into her opponents.

Suki became a good pal in those early teenage years. She lived in Pembury with her parents, who were close friends of Christopher and Mary, and the two families socialised together. Suki was always zooming off to international competitions, but she recalled, 'We saw a lot of one another back then because our parents got on. I was very single-minded about my swimming and would spend a lot of time training or going to competitions. It wasn't a very big school and we were both very sporty. They say that your school days are the happiest, but I just wanted to leave and get on with my swimming.'

Sophie, too, was restless in her mid-teens. Pembury seemed quite an isolated backwater, even though it was an easy commuter journey to London. Although 1970s heartthrobs the Bay City Rollers had made a passing impression on Sophie and her friends in the mid-1970s – all their wardrobes contained a revolting pair of tartan trousers – they did not embrace the rapidly changing youth culture of that time. The realisation that the world of the Sex Pistols was a million miles away from Brenchley began to dawn on Sophie, especially as she became interested in boys. She had one major advantage over many of her schoolmates because she was a day girl and lived locally, which meant it was easier for her to meet the opposite sex. From being a young girl who was sociable but more of a follower than a leader, Sophie became much more boisterous.

She attended theatre workshops with Sarah Sienesi at nearby Tonbridge School and it was there, while rehearsing an Arthur Miller play, that she met her first proper boyfriend. Sophie was fifteen and not shy. David Kinder was dark-haired and very handsome, with a twinkle in his eye. He was also passionate about the theatre, a quality that Sophie would find irresistible in her men. David's parents lived in a splendid house in Chislehurst, near Bromley in Kent, and the teenagers would spend hours larking about on their tennis court. Sophie was on cloud nine that she had a real boyfriend at last – wrestling with a Bunsen burner in the school chemistry labs began to seem very juvenile; she was embarking on the great love of her life, which, as is so often the case with fifteen-year-olds, lasted all of a couple of months before they got fed up. David went on to become a professional actor but never really progressed after small roles in *Grange Hill*, *Casualty*, *Doctor Who* and an advertisement for McDonald's. He decided that the teaching profession offered greater long-term security. He has remained on excellent terms with Sophie, who he described as a 'lovely girl' after she became a celebrity thanks to her royal connection. She has also happily stayed as a guest at his parents' home. One of the recurrent themes in Sophie's life that does her great credit is her ability to remain on good terms with former boyfriends, who all stress how fortunate Prince Edward is to have found her.

Her growing interest in the opposite sex did not stop her struggling through eight O Levels, including art, history and French, the latter of which would prove invaluable when she embarked on a Swiss skiing adventure. Her strongest subject was English, and Sophie has since confessed that, if she had the chance again, she would have liked to study literature at university. She had now reached the stage when she had to decide whether to stay on at school. One factor to consider was the financial strain the school fees for Kent College and Wellington School in Somerset, which her brother attended, continued to put on her parents. Her devoted mother had persevered with secretarial work to make sure the children had the best education.

In the end, Sophie decided to leave school at sixteen and enrolled in a two-year secretarial course at West Kent College of Further Education in Tonbridge, another charming town in this part of Kent where everything seemed to be within ten miles of Sophie's home in Brenchley. Her reasons for choosing the course at West Kent – as it was then called – were familiar to thousands of girls at that time: it was something useful to do after leaving school and she would have a qualification at the end of it. Sophie made sure her chosen course did not impede her pursuit of her twin loves of English and the theatre. She started A Level classes in English at the college and was very proud when a lecturer from the University of Kent at Canterbury sat in on one of her classes and told the teacher afterwards that, even at the age of just sixteen, Sophie had the ability of a second-year university student.

Sophie went along with Sarah Sienesi to an audition for the

Cranbrook Operatic and Dramatic Society, which, although local, was quite a prestigious group. Sophie thought the audition would involve her chasing around the stage as a member of the chorus. Instead, she had to sing a solo from *My Fair Lady* that filled her with complete dread. Singing was not one of her strong points, but she battled through with just a few dubious notes and landed a part in the chorus. The best thing about it was that, because she and Sarah had been taking ballet and dance classes for more than ten years, they found learning the steps easy and ended up teaching the routines to the rest of the troupe.

On her first day at secretarial college Sophie met another local girl called Jo Last, who would become her best buddy throughout her two years at West Kent. They did not already know each other, even though Jo lived in the village of Goudhurst, just down the road from Brenchley. Jo had been at Cranbrook State School while Sophie attended Kent College. This was September 1981, when Soft Cell were at number one with 'Tainted Love' and Adam and the Ants were the most popular teen band. The two new friends would pass their days eating crisp sandwiches and moaning about boys. Jo remembered, 'We linked up on day one because we were in the same class and just hit it off. Sophie was so sweet and funny. We would talk endlessly about things, mostly what great things we were going to do with our lives and, of course, boys. Sophie would listen for hours while I would go on about my boyfriend, who was called Simon. She was so unselfish about it. She had boyfriends, too, but no one especially serious at that time. Sophie was very pretty with great skin. But best of all she always had a big smile.'

Every morning Jo would zoom down the country road between Goudhurst and Brenchley to pick up Sophie from her home; it only took about ten minutes and she would toot the horn outside Homestead and wait for Sophie, who was always punctual, to come out. Jo's father had given her an old brown Citroën as a present. She called the car Matilda and, although it was a bit battered and the sunroof stuck, it represented freedom to the two friends. At lunchtimes they would hurry down to Matilda and whizz into Tonbridge to Bentalls department store and gossip in the little café there. They then would adjourn to Matilda to eat their packed lunch before rushing back to college for afternoon classes. Their favourite lunch was salt and vinegar crisps packed into a bread roll with a Bounty bar for afters. Sophie was always one of those lucky girls who had a healthy attitude to what she ate – she never thought twice about munching a bar of chocolate if she wanted one.

These were fun-filled days, not least because the work was far from taxing. Sophie became an expert typist, due in part to her teacher's penchant for bringing tapes of Status Quo for the class to bash along to so that they could develop a good rhythm. The girls could type so fast to 'Rockin' All Over the World' that they renamed it 'Typin' All Over the World'. Sophie's growing spirit of adventure is well illustrated by the morning that the two friends set off to sit their English A Level. Jo recalled, 'We were sitting in Matilda doing some last-minute revision. Suddenly, at the same time, we looked up, grinned at each other and threw all our notes out the window. We were still giggling uncontrollably when we entered the exam room. Everyone must have thought we were mad. Sophie passed with flying colours. I flunked it.' Besides English, while at West Kent Sophie gained an A Level in law and passed her exams in shorthand and typing, so she was well equipped to find the right secretarial job.

Away from the daily routine of college, Sophie enjoyed a typical teenager's social whirl, although her adventurous streak meant she was champing at the bit to move to London, which, while not very far away as the crow flies, was a hassle to travel to and back again without a car. The last train home arrived at Paddock Wood at 12.30am, just when the night life was getting going in the capital. Even then, there was the hassle and expense of a taxi ride home, unless your parents were in a good mood and would come and pick you up.

So, like many young people stuck in the country, Sophie's social life revolved around the local pubs, where she was the life and soul of the evening. In Brenchley itself there was the Rose and Crown, while just outside the village was the Peacock, perhaps the most popular because it was very noisy and, therefore, unlikely to attract any parents. One of the regulars at the Peacock remembered Sophie as a fun-loving girl who used to wear Puffa jackets and Hunter wellies. Those wellingtons were much in evidence when everyone piled off to the point-to-point races at Charing on the other side of Maidstone; it was here that Sophie first developed a love of champagne, which always tastes delicious when served from the boot of a Range Rover.

On one memorable occasion, The Peacock 'set' decided to hold a toga party in the sailing clubhouse on nearby Bewl Water. It was a riot. Everyone turned up wearing the skimpiest sheet they could find. The best chat-up line of the night was: 'Excuse me, do you mind if I just change the sheets?' The gin and beer flowed liberally throughout the evening and everyone became very merry. Unfortunately, that also included the young man who was giving Sophie a lift back to Brenchley. He veered off the road, where the car ploughed through a hedge and ended up upside down in a ditch. They were very lucky and were rescued by other friends on their way home.

The next thing Sophie's 'chauffeur', who understandably

preferred not to be named, recalled was waking up on the floor of her living room with her father standing over him offering a restoring cup of tea and a plate of toast and marmalade. Sophie's dad was very popular with her friends, always jolly and tolerant of the 'young folk'. When Sophie, a few years later, held her twenty-first birthday party at Homestead, he made a memorable speech thanking 'the Disco Johnny for providing the music'.

Just outside Brenchley was another country pub called the Halfway House, where Sophie took her first job as a waitress to earn some extra cash while still at college. The pub was famous locally because it was said to be haunted by the ghost of a cantankerous old woman wearing a long dress and a hat and carrying a handbag. Sophie knew all about the legend but the only spirits she saw were being downed by the young men at the bar.

Her brother David held his twenty-first at the Castle Inn on the outskirts of their village. As usual, Sophie was the life and soul of the late-night party, larking about in a black trilby, flirting outrageously with the male guests, downing gin and tonics and puffing away on her favourite Benson & Hedges cigarettes. Sophie smoked for many years, although only socially, but had given up by the time she met Prince Edward. One of the party guests recalled, 'Sophie was very extrovert that night. She did a high kick for the camera while she was hugging a friend. She was laughing and giggling and thought it was a hoot. She was never worried about getting a hair out of place and could hold her own in any drinking contest. Sophie was wearing her hair short and spiky and, dressed in a man's checked shirt and skintight green jeans, her look might be described as 'smart punk'. David, with whom she continued to get on famously, was decidedly the worse for wear by the end of the evening, which Sophie found highly amusing, especially when he leaped over the bar and tried to pull his own pint.

Sophie had a valuable and attractive quality – the ability to enjoy herself and just have fun. It would remain to be seen whether she could retain that *joie de vivre* as a member of the Royal Family.

3

Happy-Go-Lucky

S ophie had a few boyfriends during her teenage years. At seventeen, she dated a local boy called Robert Scott-Mackie, the elder brother of a school friend. She also went out with the village heart-throb, Andrew Miller, who was apparently 'the sort of guy girls always go for'. While foot-loose and fancy free, she met a good-looking sporty chap called John Blackman, who would prove more significant to her. They dated only briefly but he has remained one of her dearest friends and a generous and guiding spirit. A few years after their romance, for instance, he organised some friends to club together and buy Sophie her first skiing holiday for her twenty-first birthday. She immediately loved whizzing down the slopes and would become an enthusiastic skier – so much so it proved later to be one of the great turning points of her life. Up until she met Prince Edward, Sophie would try to go skiing with John and his friends every year if she could afford it.

Her friendship with John was also helpful when she took the plunge in the summer of 1983 and moved to the capital – she was able to stay at his parents' house in south London while she looked for a job and somewhere more permanent to live. John was embarking on what would prove to be a highly

successful career in computers. Leaving college and moving
to London meant she lost touch with Jo Last, although the
two friends talked on the phone for a year or so after Sophie
moved to a flat in Kensington. Jo then went travelling to
New Zealand, met an American, fell in love and moved
6,000 miles away to live in Seattle – so she was not exactly
available for a crisp sandwich.

Sophie, meanwhile, had put together her first CV and sent
it to a host of prospective employers. She had taken advice
at college and decided – pre-empting the future – that a job
involving meeting people would be ideal. She was sociable,
confident and well-presented, so public relations seemed a
good starting point. Her luck was in almost straight away.
Just a month after leaving Brenchley she landed her first job
at the Quentin Bell PR organisation in Covent Garden as
secretary to the managing director. She stayed there for six
months before moving to a similar job with the Tim Arnold
sales promotion agency.

Sophie had found a flat to share with Sarah Sienesi and was
soon firmly established in the 'Sloane' social life in Chelsea
and Fulham, although she still took every opportunity to pop
home to Kent. For her twenty-first birthday party she had
decided on a black-tie affair, so her father hired a marquee
for the garden at Homestead. The evening was so windy
that everyone thought the marquee would blow over. The
next day, those that could remember what had happened at
the do, agreed that it had been a great evening. One of the
guests, Michael Wilkins, was found by her father the next
morning asleep under a tree still wearing his Walkman head-
phones and with his dinner jacket neatly hung on a branch.
Bodies were crashed out everywhere, but Mr Rhys-Jones
took everything in his stride, as he has always done where
his daughter is concerned.

Not long afterwards, in 1986, Sophie spotted an advertise-ment in the media section of the *Guardian*. The job was press assistant to Jan Reid, a former *Daily Mail* journalist who was then chief press officer at Capital Radio in London. Jan was impressed with Sophie at the interview and gave her the job. At first, the role was rather mundane – typing, filing and responding to letters. Mike Whitehill, who moved on to become a scriptwriter for comedian Jasper Carrott, took over from Jan and recalled, 'None of us got any glamorous trips to begin with. We went to the opening of the M25 – that's how glamorous it was. But Capital was a fun place to work then.' Surprisingly, perhaps, no Royal was drafted in to open the new motorway and it fell to then Prime Minister Margaret Thatcher to cut the ribbon.

Sophie's career reached a turning point when her respon-sibilities at Capital changed and she split her time between the press office and the promotions department run by Anita Hamilton. The two women became great friends, even though Anita was her boss, and the pair liked nothing better than to put the world to rights over an after-work drink. Anita was a firm believer in everyone mucking in together, so Sophie's actual job was not clearly defined.

She discovered another gang, another Famous Four – this time Anita, Rhona Martin, Karen Levesconte and Sophie. Most days after work they would 'go over the Square', which was the local Capital Radio pub in the West End, and social-ise with other members of staff. Sophie liked working at Capital, which was generally a happy place and gave her the chance to broaden her people skills, which would prove so useful in the future. She had the opportunity to meet some of her heroes, including Mick Jagger, who chatted with her when he came into the station. Her day-to-day work now included helping to organise launches and photocalls and writing press releases, usually about what the DJs – or Disco Johnnies as her father would have called them – were doing. Sophie was proving adept at the most important part of her PR work – being nice to people while chatting over a glass of wine. The DJs were always in the public eye and getting on with them was important for Sophie's job.

The iconic TV presenter Michael Parkinson's son Andrew became a good friend when he was at Capital producing the David Jensen show. Sophie found Andrew, who was very popular in a Mr Rugby Club sort of way, extremely good company. He had any number of great stories about his father's friends, who would come to stay at the family home in Bray, by the Thames. Andrew and Sophie dated only about four times over a period of six weeks, but he had some forthright insight into her social ambitions: 'She used to have friends at Capital, but frankly she was more interested in friends who had titles. She was always going on about places she had been to and parties in the country. That's the kind of lifestyle she always wanted.'

Sophie would need to wait a few more years to reach her social summit, but Andrew continued, 'I think beneath a very bubbly and sometimes busy character, there lurks some-body who knows their own mind and where they're going. We went out a few times and had a bit of fun. She was never serious. I would describe her as happy-go-lucky.'

Sophie's eye for social cachet is confirmed by Mike Whitehill, who observed, 'She always used to come back from weekends a bit hungover, a bit worse for wear, because she had been away for the weekend with a Giles or a Jeremy. She liked people of interesting status, the aristocracy and stuff. You would often hear her talking about these people. They sounded like complete tossers, but they obviously impressed her. She was blinded by that sort of thing. She had a very full social life. I remember she was stuck on one boyfriend for about a year – she was besotted by this chap, who I think worked in the City. She would often come in and be silent and morose. It would eventually emerge that it was something he had done. The next day it would be all sunshine and roses. I remember that being a bit of a pain in the arse, to be honest with you.'

Neil Fox, who as Dr Fox became one of Capital's best-known DJs, bumped into Sophie all the time when he joined the station in September 1987: 'As a new boy I was always out doing gigs and roadshows and she would help organise everything for me. She was always smartly dressed, not a jeans or T-shirt person. Anita Hamilton was always smart as well and I think Sophie followed that line. She wore nice skirts, blouses, scarves and trouser suits, that sort of thing. Capital was an exceedingly friendly place in which to work. Anita, Sophie, Rhona and Karen were a nice team and they remained good friends. She was just one of the girls, a good laugh and a good company person. She was not particularly flirty but I would describe her as having a good, lively past. There was nothing about her that I didn't like. She was very good-looking and the kind of girl who could go out with a group of lads and have a really good night, drinking beer and telling dirty jokes like anyone else. She was just a normal girl.'

Like many young, free and single girls who are deemed 'lively', Sophie has had to suffer the gossipmongers. One of the stories doing the rounds was that four men, who all worked for the same media company and, indeed, in the same office, discovered in the pub one night that they had all been out for a drink with Sophie at one time or another without any of the others realising. They are then supposed to have stood up on the table and toasted her in champagne. Young

women have always had to put up with this sort of story –
you have a drink with someone and everyone immediately
thinks you must be having an affair. Andrew Parkinson
described her lifestyle as 'colourful' but observed astutely, 'I
think Sophie lived life to the full. Her big weakness, if it is
one, is that she enjoys herself and that could be interpreted
incorrectly.'

The most famous 'affair' Sophie was supposed to have had
was with Chris Tarrant, one of the most famous broadcasters
in the UK and the star name at Capital Radio. Nothing was
going on: they were just two people who hit it off straight
away. Chris was very amusing company and made Sophie
laugh. At the time he was happily married to presenter
Ingrid Tarrant, although he had enjoyed a reputation as
something of a Casanova, fuelled by countless tabloid stories
and speculation. The principal source of all the rumours
about Chris and Sophie came from a notorious set of photographs taken by Chris's former co-presenter, Kara Noble,
while they were doing the show in Spain. Someone from the
publicity department would be assigned to go on the trip to
look after clients and any competition winners. In one particular photograph, Sophie is sunbathing topless on a beach
and looking gorgeous. She is fast asleep and totally unaware
that Chris Tarrant is hovering over her glistening body like
a cat eyeing a huge tub of clotted cream. The photograph,
which Andrew Parkinson described as 'the stuff of myths
and legends', took pride of place on the noticeboard of the
DJ's room at Capital HQ for many years until it was revealed
that Sophie was going out with Prince Edward. Then it was
quickly taken down.

Neil Fox, who had seen the photo literally hundreds of
times, observed, 'It's just one of those innocent pictures, but
if someone wanted to make something of it . . .' At the time

of the snap's disappearance, nobody knew what had happened to it or who had the negatives from that roll of film. Sophie would find out at arguably the worst possible time.

Foreign trips were one of the perks of Sophie's job, including a skiing trip with Dr Fox and others to the resort of Courmayeur in the Italian Alps. She was also the PR in residence in 1988 when Princess Diana's favourite DJ, Graham Dene, was the best-known broadcaster on a trip to Florida and where she acted as matchmaker between him and another guest, the artist Julie Tennant. They married four years later and are still together more than thirty years on.

Back in London, Sophie began her first serious relationship with an 'older man'. Jeremy Barkley, who she called Jez, was eleven years her senior and sold Sophie her first car, a Morris Minor, which did not sound like the start of a relationship calculated to send a mother's spirits soaring. Jeremy was one of identical twins who Sophie could never tell apart. He was her boyfriend for nearly two years, which was her longest relationship until Prince Edward came on the scene. Sophie described Jez as a 'jack of all trades', but in reality he was a successful businessman who ran his own company that sold air-conditioning units.

Jeremy may have been older than Sophie, but he never curbed her natural sense of adventure, and they never settled into being an 'old married couple'. Towards the end of what was an on-off relationship, when it was becoming more off than on, she decided to move on with her life. Some of her friends at Capital were transferring to new jobs and, even though she had enjoyed working at the station, she wanted a new challenge. She was twenty-four with a world to explore, so she started browsing through the ads to see if something appealed. Her relationship with Jeremy officially ended on amicable terms. He has said, touchingly, 'I will always have a place in my heart for her.' Sophie's mind was made up when a friend suggested trying a season skiing and working for a holiday firm. Sophie loved skiing and set about seriously applying for jobs. One of the tour companies, Bladon Lines, took her on, so she made the decision to leave her old, comfy life at Capital Radio and see what lay in store for her on the ski slopes. That future turned out to include an exciting romance.

4

Après-Ski

After completing her training course in Putney with the other new recruits, Sophie was ready to set off for the glamorous resort of Crans-Montana in the Swiss Alps. Her contract ran for the length of the 'season', the name given in the ski world to the period from the beginning of December to mid-April. She was issued with her blue Bladon Lines uniform that made her look like an air hostess, said her goodbyes and set off on her adventure. Her slight regret was that she would not be home in Brenchley at Christmas for the first time.

Sophie was soon to realise how lucky she was to have been posted to Crans-Montana in December 1989. She flew into Geneva and, as the holidaymakers would, took a three-hour coach ride through the most inspiring scenery. Crans-Montana was originally two adjoining villages in the heart of the Alps that had grown into one larger resort over the years. The twin centres are spread over the sunniest of all Alpine plateaux, dotted with lakes and larches, and Sophie was awed by the views sweeping from the forbidding slopes of the Matterhorn to the shimmering splendour of Mont Blanc. Crans was the more upmarket twin and Sophie soon discovered that the fashionable and expensive boutiques and the exclusive restaurants were well above her pay grade.

As a ski rep she made the princely sum of £50 per week, but there was no need to send for Red Cross parcels. Her skiing equipment, passes, food and board were all taken care of, so the £50 was really spending money for drinks, shampoo and Swiss chocolate, which Sophie loved. The Montana end of town was the hub of the action and the late-night bars and clubs were a magnet for the reps, the chalet girls and the ski instructors, one of whom would prove to be important in her life.

First of all, though, she had to settle in – she had no time to be homesick because Christmas was going to be very busy. Sophie was in charge of Chalet Isabella, a large three-storey chalet in the Montana district that could sleep forty-two people. Sophie, who had her own room, proved very popular with the young chalet girls, who slept in bunk beds and were really just versions of her old Sloane self. They were also the most important people in the building, because the entire operation would be reduced to chaos without them. They were also the last group you wanted to upset, either as a guest or a member of staff. One former chalet girl, who for obvious reasons wanted to remain anonymous, explained, 'If somebody gave us a hard time or was unbearably rude, we would clean the toilet with their toothbrush.'

Sophie was responsible for five girls and had to keep an eagle eye on their work. She also had to get her head around the chalet accounts and sort out any insurance problems if, for example, one of the guests broke a leg on the slopes. Some evenings she had to think of something to entertain the guests – the *après-ski* programme, as it was called. The most difficult times were when the chalet girls had the evening off: Sophie had the idea that a fondue evening might work because everyone would have to muck in together and keep the conversation flowing. They proved a great success, although the downside was having to deal with a group of chalet girls all nursing sore heads in the morning.

By far the most important aspect of life in the resort was, of course, the skiing, and Sophie had not lost her love of zipping down the runs. She discovered she had plenty of time in the afternoons to indulge her passion, after she had finished morning tasks and before the guests arrived back at the chalet in the evening. Sophie, as ever, took her sport seriously and decided she needed to take a refresher course. This proved to be a good move. Her instructor was a young Australian called Michael O'Neill, six feet tall, athletic and dark with the brooding good looks of Sean Penn.

Sophie had never met a man like Michael before. He was a breath of fresh air and there was an instant spark between the two. He was quiet and considerate but at the same time had a devil-may-care attitude that was light years away from some of the precious media types and the Fulham 'hoorays' with whom she had spent so much time over the past few years. He told her about sailing in Sydney Harbour and surfing along Queensland's Gold Coast, and Sophie was swept along on a romantic wave that never reached the shore. Sophie's friends back home in London might have been surprised at how quickly she settled into a daily routine with Michael, and to all intents and purposes she spent the 'season' as Mrs O'Neill.

In the evenings they would meet other reps and instructors at some of their favourite bars, including Bar One, Bar Two, Valentino and Absolut, where Sophie could dance the night away to Michael Jackson and Phil Collins. Sometimes, when work allowed, they would drive to the neighbouring exclusive resort of Zermatt or ski off-piste under the shadow of the Matterhorn; it was blissful.

A good friend from those chalet days noticed the telltale signs that Sophie was in love during their regular get-togethers. Three or four times a week they would meet at a little patisserie just around the corner from Bar One. Her pal recalled, 'I noticed a big difference in Sophie after she met with Michael. She seemed to enjoy her work more, even though it was very demanding. She became generally more radiant.' One final piece of evidence convinced the friend that Sophie was in love: 'I noticed she was losing weight.'

As part of her routine, Sophie would travel to Geneva Airport once a week, where all the ski reps would gather to say *bon voyage* to their charges and greet the new holidaymakers. They would sit around drinking coffee and catching up with each other's news – skiing adventures or, less welcome, the plumbing disasters of the past few days. Gareth Crump, a fellow rep, recalled that Sophie could be quiet at times – that was just because she was happy to be that way and not because she was shy. The other reps were not aware that Sophie had eyes only for Michael O'Neill. Discretion and keeping their romance a secret was not easy – privacy was at a premium in Chalet Isabella or at the ski instructor's lodge. A four-star hotel would cost a year's wages and even a basic one would set them back 50 Swiss francs and was outside their price range. The couple discovered that the only accommodation they could comfortably afford was a tent for £4 a night, which was a freezing and completely unappealing option.

The season flew by in a flurry of skiing, skating and also snowboarding – a pursuit at which Sophie discovered she was rather good. Sophie was particularly popular with the local shop and bar owners. One of them, Christian Rey, supplied Sophie with her skis and boots: 'I particularly remember Sophie of all the reps. She was very pretty but the great thing about her was that she would pop in for a chat. She didn't have to. She just made the day brighter by doing so.'

At the weekly coffee breaks at Geneva Airport, the other reps were already looking forward to next year's season. Sophie was not so sure about the future. Michael was returning to Sydney, a city he made so inviting with his descriptions of sunshine barbecues, glorious surfing and the easy-going lifestyle that came with it. Sophie had always wanted to see first-hand the Sydney Opera House and the Harbour Bridge. She would be returning to London with no job and nowhere to live but she still needed a little persuading when Michael hesitatingly suggested she might fly back with him.

He did not mention marriage, but he later explained, 'I wanted her to know this was not going to be a holiday but a serious attempt to extend our relationship. We were going to start a life together.' Disappointingly, that life in Sydney did not turn out to be sunshine and roses. Their situation wasn't helped when Michael lost his job as an insurance salesman. Struggling for money and an increasing sense of isolation were not the sort of challenges Sophie was looking for in her life. Michael observed, 'Sadly, we decided we couldn't go on.' Love, it seemed, was easier amid the splendour of the Swiss Alps.

While Sophie may have been bitterly upset about the break-up, she was not going to fly straight back to Brenchley to lick any emotional wounds. She was and is made of sterner stuff. The fact that she has never mentioned Michael in public is a strong indication of how the split affected her. In the future, she would happily admit to past boyfriends, including Jeremy Barkley, John Blackman and David Kinder, but she had not flown halfway round the world to be with them.

Fortunately for Sophie, it's a small world and she came across someone she had known in the Sloane orbit of Chelsea and Fulham. Andy Cullity, who was now happily settled in Sydney, proved to be a knight in shining armour. He had a steady girlfriend so there was no question of romance, but she happily moved into the large flat he shared with friends in the fashionable district of Paddington. He persuaded Sophie that she should give Australia a real go for a year and make the most of it. He recalled how sociable she was, fitting in well right from the start: 'She has a personality that people can relate to. She's a get-up-and-go girl who doesn't sit back in a prim and proper English manner. The great thing about Sophie is that she is a very strong person and doesn't let things get to her.'

Andy introduced Sophie, now twenty-five, to Jonathan Miller, the boss of an international shipping company, Jet Services, based in Sydney. He was immediately impressed with her dynamic attitude and hired her as his girl Friday: 'The great thing was that she didn't mind what she did – including making the coffee.' Sophie was responsible for preparing invoices, booking in couriers at the airport and chasing packages halfway around the world. The work may not have been as glamorous as life at Capital Radio, but it gave her the chance to enjoy life in Sydney.

She discovered that at night the city came alive, much more so than in the London she had left behind. The clubs and bars stayed open until dawn so there was always a place to go out and have a good time. Jonathan recalled, 'She was so bright, bubbly and vivacious. We had to socialise a lot after work and she always had loads of friends.' Sophie did not turn into a wild party animal, however, spending many evenings looking after Freddie Miller, Jonathan and his wife Karen's baby son.

At weekends Sophie would join Andy and his girlfriend on trips around New South Wales and up into the Blue Mountains. Tourists sometimes forget that there is such a beautiful landscape around the country's largest city and leave having seen nothing more than the famous opera house and harbour. That was not Sophie's way, although she loved sailing around the harbour and also joined a deep-sea diving club, which became a great passion. Everyone she met at barbecues or parties seemed to invite her on a sailing trip – this was more the life she had hoped for in Australia.

On one idyllic jaunt around the secluded bays of the south-east coast, she met a dashing graphic designer, Eon Balmain, who had changed his name from the less-exotic Ian Robertson. Eon was immediately impressed by Sophie: 'I took one look into those beautiful blue eyes and thought "Wow!".' He and Sophie were among a group of ten amateur sailors invited to spend two long lazy weekends on board a luxury 100-foot schooner called *Meridien* that may not have quite matched the Royal Yacht *Britannia* but was not far off that floating palace; the state rooms boasted crystal chandeliers while all the cabins were beautifully furnished, and there was even a hot tub for relaxation.

The host was a millionaire businessman from Queensland, John Young, who had personally invited Sophie. Eon remembered, 'When she walked on board wearing a pair of tight-fitting shorts, the whole wharf drew breath. I think she was the most attractive girl I have ever met.' While the girls had to do some chores to keep *Meridien* shipshape, this was a sojourn not far short of paradise. The days were spent sunbathing on deck with a good book for company, jumping off the boat for a swim in the bathwater-warm sea or sliding into the spa clutching a glass of champagne – the perfect way to end a day doing nothing. A net had been strung across the stern and everyone took it in turns to splash about in it, held safe by the momentum of the vessel. Sophie loved it and would giggle and splash around like a happy dolphin. She was also best at a game called 'walking the line', where you had to tiptoe as fast as possible along a line painted on the deck.

Eon had worked in radio, so he and Sophie had plenty of stories to swap. He had also told her about visiting London and watching the Trooping of the Colour and how great he thought the ceremony was. Sophie was delighted that Eon did not share the anti-Royalist feeling sweeping Australia. He may have hoped for something more than a friendship but he was impressed that Sophie was discreet about past boyfriends while remaining very easy to talk to: 'She had a very quiet and sympathetic side as well as a naturally vivacious personality. I told her my mother had died of cancer and she responded like she had known her personally. She seemed very upset.'

Some years later Sophie would be touched by a similar sadness, but for the present she decided she should see all of Australia if she possibly could. Encouraged by Andy and Jonathan, she saved her pennies and, after being in Sydney for nine months, decided it was time to move on. She joined up with a Scottish girl, Lynne Muir, who she had recently met, and they went travelling together. Their first stop was Queensland, visiting the picturesque Whitsunday Islands, diving around the magnificent Great Barrier Reef and on to Cairns, a tropical city on the north-eastern coast where Sophie went bungee jumping – a thrill she loved. She did not know it at the time, but she was incredibly lucky to have enjoyed these wonderful experiences before she met the Queen's youngest son – it would not have been considered regal to be seen bungee jumping off Tower Bridge, although the paparazzi would have loved it. Kate Middleton, for example, could not continue her competitive rowing down the Thames without the lenses watching and had to give up. If Sophie were a man, everyone would be saying how fortunate she was to have had a proper life in her twenties and be ready to settle down in her thirties. Diana, for example, never had

that chance and it does not take a psychology degree to speculate that she was far too young and naive when she married
the then-heir to the throne.

In June 1991, Sophie decided to return to the UK. She had
been away for more than a year and she missed her family.
She was keen to make it back for her father's sixtieth birthday.
She'd been hearing all about the plans for a big party, including setting up another marquee in the garden at Brenchley.
She did not want to let her mum and dad down but she also
wanted to see old friends and tell them about her adventures.
She travelled back via Thailand so that she could stop off on
the beautiful island of Ko Samui, where she spent ten days.
She arrived back in Kent on one of the wettest and windiest
June days imaginable. As she answered endless questions from
guests about her adventures abroad, the heavens opened and
the rain cascaded down – a striking contrast to her amazing
idyll of sailing and sunbathing on the other side of the world.
It was good to be home.

Sophie returned with pretty much nothing – no job, nowhere
to live and no relationship. She could easily have drifted
along for a few months in Brenchley, where her parents were
delighted to see her and reassured her that she could stay as
long as she liked. That would have been a step back, however,
and Sophie was now twenty-six; perhaps she should get cracking with her life. Her first task was to prepare a new CV, which
was looking more impressive than when she had left eighteen
months earlier – she had travelled, worked for an international company and undertaken a variety of responsibilities.
Arguably, Capital Radio was still the most attractive entry on
her job sheet, so a return to the world of promotion and public
relations seemed like a good idea. Her mum and dad agreed.

Her CV found its way to the Cancer Relief Macmillan Fund in Chelsea, who hired her to work with the national promotions manager, Jill Phillips, organising special events. Sophie impressed everyone immediately: a former colleague observed, 'She was so full of energy. She inspired everyone to do their best.' Her starting salary of just £12,000 was challenging but the work itself was very rewarding. Sophie had no idea what her future would hold at this point, but helping to raise money and the profile of good causes would represent a large part of her life both privately and later as a Royal.

Sophie also struck lucky with finding a place to live. She was introduced to an air hostess, Ulli von Herwarth, whose parents had a lovely house in Benenden, a neighbouring village to Brenchley. She was tall, blonde, very striking and related to minor German aristocracy. Sophie jumped at the chance to rent the attic room in her new friend's flat in West Kensington. The houses here were all three storeys and painted white with heavy black doors. The road itself was a busy commuter shortcut but was ideally placed for a single girl like Sophie whose social life revolved around Chelsea, Fulham and Kensington. And it would prove to be a perfect address for someone going out with a prince. To her credit, Ulli has always been the complete soul of discretion where Sophie is concerned.

The old cliché is that things always happen in threes, so after finding a job she liked and a place to live, inevitably Sophie found a new boyfriend, Tim King, who had a thriving dental practice just over Albert Bridge. Tim had an exciting hobby that Sophie found thrilling – he was a keen pilot and every weekend they would be up in the skies, often flying across the Channel to Le Touquet for a night out. Their relationship was almost brought to a shuddering halt the first time he took her for a spin – the plane's engine failed and he had to make an emergency landing, which left them both shaken but fortunately uninjured. Sophie, with typical bravado, couldn't wait to try again. On one weekend they decided to go skiing in Andorra, but the weather was dreadful and Tim had to make another emergency landing. This time he put down at Bordeaux Airport, which proved to be embarrassing as it brought the entire place to a standstill. When their romance cooled, Tim remained a good friend.

Sophie was single once more and happy to be carefree. Ulli threw a three-day weekend party at her parents' house and Sophie, naturally, went along. The invitation itself was tempting – promising 'cosmic croquet, visual vibes, mellow munchies, dizzy juggling, BBQ, dancing, tennis and swimming'. Ulli introduced Sophie to an old friend, a German law student who had driven over just for the party. They played tennis, drank cocktails and swam in the open-air swimming pool and, as he later ungallantly revealed to the *Sun* newspaper, shared the same sleeping bag.

Sophie had to dust off her CV again when her contract with Macmillan ended, but this time she found her next job easily. An old friend from Capital recommended her to Brian MacLaurin, a go-ahead Scottish PR executive whose small agency was rapidly expanding and who had many media contacts. He was immediately impressed by Sophie: 'The moment I met her, I knew she was an absolutely charming person.' Sophie joined MCM (MacLaurin Communications and Media) when it had been in business for about a year and had offices in Victoria, but after six weeks everyone moved to new premises in Hammersmith, which was very convenient for where Sophie now lived. Sophie was employed as an account manager and was one of a staff of seven. Within a year she was part of a team of eighteen. To begin with, she was mainly office-bound, but Brian liked his people to experience the real world. He explained, 'Sophie grew into the job. There is no hierarchical structure here. We are all part of a team. We don't have any promotion or anything like that. You simply earn more money as the company becomes more successful.'

Taking this job would be the serendipitous step that would change Sophie's life. For the moment, however, she needed Brian's help to build up her contacts. One of his clients was Chris Tarrant, so she was able to work well and easily with him. She also did marketing work for *Thomas the Tank Engine,* and she particularly enjoyed promoting some of the forgotten female characters in the children's favourite. She observed, 'When I was a child the stories were pretty much a boy's thing, but now I am a big fan. The Refreshment Lady character is very much a 1990s figure – she's a businesswoman.'

It's not strictly true to say that Sophie was the PR for Mr Blobby, as newspapers often do, but she was involved as part of MCM, as the agency had the account for the pink blancmange character. Once a week she would join Brian at Crinkley Bottom for the recording of *Noel's House Party,* where Mr Blobby was a bigger attraction than the host, Noel Edmonds. She did come into contact with another chart-topping artist who would provide her with her biggest success at work. She was helping with an account for Mobil Oil and managed to persuade Gene Pitney to let his number-one smash 'Twenty Four Hours from Tulsa' be used in a commercial for the petrol station. She was so pleased when his manager told her it was agreed that she squealed down the phone: 'Tell him I love him and I will have his babies.' The singer heard about this and was so amused that he mentioned Sophie numerous times on his concert tour in 1993 and repeated her offer.

The most significant PR opportunity for Sophie in those

early days was not one with a celebrity connection. The Baby Lifeline account showed her that there could be more fulfilment in her work if she embraced what were generally referred to as 'good causes'. Baby Lifeline was certainly that. The charity had been started in 1981 by Judy Ledger, a Coventry housewife who had lost three premature babies. She decided to do something to help other women who might suffer the same supremely sad fate. She set up a self-help group to raise money to buy equipment for hospitals that might help to save babies born prematurely. The cause clearly touched a public nerve because more than a million had been raised by the time MCM was on board. Judy was a great admirer of Sophie: 'She is very determined and is so genuine in her interest in the charity. I immediately liked the ideas she put forward. Sophie could create a story out of a paper bag.' Judy added, astutely, 'She's also got a very soft inside.'

Sophie already had several friends who had struggled with dreadful birth experiences and she jumped at the chance of being involved with an organisation that could help. She had no idea, of course, of the future pregnancy struggles that would affect her personally.

While her involvement with Baby Lifeline was a forerunner of her future working life, Sophie, for the moment, was determined to enjoy herself, particularly at weekends. One of her favourite jaunts was driving with friends down to Devon to watch John Blackman's cricket team in the lovely village of Stoke Fleming on the coast south of Dartmoor. First stop on Friday night was the local Green Dragon pub, where drinks and laughter flowed in equal measure. On Saturday, there was time for swimming and a great deal of sleeping and sunbathing. The team, which called itself the Fentshire Cricket Club, was made up of John's ambitious, hard-working London friends who he had recruited when he decided to reorganise the village team. They always played a match on the Sunday, and Sophie, who wasn't much bothered about cricket, dutifully helped prepare the traditional tea that seemed to be the principal point of the afternoon.

Sophie was now earning a decent wage – £20,000 a year – so life was good in the summer of 1993. She had a busy social life, many like-minded friends and a job that offered variety and presented new daily challenges. Now, where was that prince?

5

The Ardent Fellow

Edward was not exactly perceived as the royal catch of the day in the early 1990s, when Sophie first met him. The Queen's youngest son was fortunate not to have grown up in the glare of social media, but the press at the time viewed him as a bit of a waste of space. The newspapers that seemed to report the Royal Family in a dull and predictable way were not ready for one of their number to be a little different from the expected norm.

While Sophie had been revelling in her Enid Blyton schooldays in Kent, Edward was braving the austere environment of Gordonstoun, near Elgin in Morayshire. His elder brother Charles loathed his time there. Ten years later, Edward took the high road from Balmoral and would later confirm that it was not as tough as it used to be, although he still had to start the day with an eighty-yard run, then a hot shower followed by a bracing cold one to shake the final semblance of sleep from youthful bones. Edward would later tactfully tell his biographer, Ingrid Seward, 'I don't agree that schooldays are the happiest days of your life.'

He was, however, able to indulge his two great interests in life, the theatre and playing sport – passions he shared with Sophie that made their fledgling relationship much easier. He told a drama student that he would have become an actor if he had not been a prince of the realm. He persuaded the Queen and Prince Philip to travel the three hours from Balmoral to watch him in a school production of Noel Coward's *Hay Fever*. His slightly juvenile sense of humour was revealed when he put the labels 'Mum' and 'Dad' on their reserved seating. More relevant was the view of a contemporary pupil, the actor and director Jason Connery, son of Sean Connery. He directed Edward in a school play and observed: 'He listens hard and he learns fast.'

Perhaps inevitably, Edward had a tendency towards being pompous as a teenager. Any visiting bigwig to the school would call him 'Your Royal Highness'. Even the masters called him Prince Edward. He was at the top of the social step-ladder looking down. He did have one big advantage over the schooldays of Charles – Gordonstoun was now co-educational and girls would prove to be a great civilising influence on the school, and Edward, although likely to blush in their presence, was considered by them to be a charming young man.

Away from school Edward did not have to suffer the daily intrusion of paparazzi or just members of the public whose phones now are quick and easy cameras. He could move around the West End relatively unnoticed if he went to the movies to watch a James Bond film or slipped into a record store to hunt for his favourite Abba or Peter Gabriel CDs. He was also the family DJ, hosting discos in Eddie's Nightclub in a Buckingham Palace drawing room for his Royal contemporaries – as they were then known, Lady Sarah Armstrong-Jones, Viscount Linley, Lady Helen Windsor and Marina Ogilvy – who would dance the night away to Donna Summer and Boney M.

One of the wrong impressions about Edward shared by

most of the media and the general public was that he was a little weedy, an opinion seemingly endorsed by his love of all things theatrical and his later unhappy experience as a Royal Marines recruit. This is not true. He was Prince Philip's favourite child, joining his dad at the tender age of seven to shoot rabbits. He would become an accomplished marksman, and father and son would spend hours duck shooting on the Sandringham Estate, patiently crawling through reeds in search of their feathered prey. Shooting had always been an important part of the Royal Family's social agenda – something that has been enthusiastically embraced by the next generation of Prince William and Prince Harry, even though it is one not shouted about too loudly in these more enlightened times. Sophie would discover that one of the ways to a prince's heart was to act as a beater, disturbing the birds with sticks so that the men could blast them out of the skies. Even the Queen, a great supporter of country pursuits, took part in this seasonal ritual.

Despite a tendency to youthful arrogance, Edward was basically a gentle boy who grew up to be a gentle man. He never pretended to be a playboy prince or a young girl's fantasy royal. On his eighteenth birthday he did not feature on the front page of some GQ-like magazine, but on the cover of Dog World with his beloved black Labrador, Francis, who received more fan mail than he did. He was not a 'dedicated follower of fashion', to quote the famous Kinks hit of the 1960s, but a young man happiest in unfashionable cord trousers and tweed jackets. He ignored the urgings of his female cousins to wear 'groovy flares', so he got that right at least.

His one sartorial obsession was making sure his shoes were polished so that you could see your face in them. He also kept a comb in his top pocket and was constantly sweeping it through his already thinning hair – another family characteristic that William and Harry have continued.

His path in life was already well paved. He would go to Cambridge whatever his grades – he actually managed nine O Levels (a record for his family) and three low-grade A Levels that included a C in English. Although he had to suffer the press calling him 'Educated Eddie', he was an average student who would have a gap year abroad followed by a three-year university course and subsequently a career in the armed services: all neatly mapped out.

Before Jesus College, Cambridge, he was shipped out to be a junior English teacher in Whanganui, New Zealand. He was not too pleased to be tracked down there by a reporter from the *Daily Mirror*, and told him, 'What on earth gives you the right to call me? Just what the hell do you think you're doing? You've got a nerve!' The rant, of course, provided the journalist with a story. The amusing aspect of the subsequent conversation was that Edward was too polite to put the phone down, which he should have done immediately. Instead, he stayed on the line for half an hour and they eventually chatted about James Bond. Edward had not yet learned to keep his mouth firmly shut where the press was concerned.

Edward thrived at Cambridge, proving a very sociable student. Edward Windsor, as he was unstuffily known, was invited to practically every party and was very keen to accept as many chances as possible to demonstrate a common touch. He also became the life and soul of the Cambridge University Light Entertainment Society (CULES), grasping what might turn out to be his last opportunity to indulge his passion for acting. All the revenue from productions went to charity and, if Edward was appearing on stage, it would inevitably be a sell-out. In particular, Edward loved banana-skin humour and took part in many fundraising stunts, including driving

a taxi through the city streets with two fellow students dancing on the roof and being tied to a railway line in the path
of an oncoming train in the manner of a silent film heroine.
He also shared a skill with Sophie – they were both talented
mimics. Edward's party piece was a sketch of TV favourite Mike Yarwood's famous impression of Prince Charles.
Edward was right about university being his last chance at
acting, because a bout of glandular fever took him backstage
into the world of production. Fortunately, he discovered that
he enjoyed having a bright idea and putting it together step
by step just as much.

He did not desert his sporting interludes, although, perhaps wisely, he decided his rugby-playing days were over. He
loved the game but found he was spending far too much time
being crushed at the bottom of a ruck, or as it might have
been called, 'let's all jump on the prince time'. Instead, he
took up the highly skilful pursuit of real tennis – a game that
more resembled squash than the tennis played at Wimbledon
or in parks up and down the country. He fell in love with the
sport, which would indirectly be a life-changer for him – and
for Sophie.

Real tennis had always enjoyed a strong Royal connection. In this context, real did not mean genuine but is the
old French word for royal. Not many people played it – perhaps only a few hundred when Edward took it up seriously;
there were two main reasons for it languishing as a minority
sport. First, very few of the expensive and specialist enclosed
courts existed – you cannot play five-a-side football on them
and so their sole use is real tennis. The second reason is that
you need to be a rocket scientist to understand the rules – it
has a language all of its own, with a variety of French terms
including *dedans, bisque, grille* and *tambour* that sounded more
like items from a bistro menu than a sporting encounter. The

Cambridge University Real Tennis Club was like a private club – perfect as far as Edward was concerned.

He had written to his girlfriend at the time, Romy Adlington, telling her how great he thought university life was. Romy was working her way along the catwalk of modelling fame and was a beautiful catch for any young man. In years to come she would chat more than a little to the press but was never unkind about him. She observed shrewdly, 'Edward is very sensitive, which some people don't make allowances for.'

A serialisation of her account of their affair appeared in the *Sunday Mirror*. She seemed to be on good terms with his family, including the Queen, who she said was 'immediately friendly and charming'. She added, 'There was no snootiness or unpleasantness about her.' She provided some lovely images of life with the Royals, including cooking sausages on a barbecue while the Queen and Prince Philip bickered about the washing-up.

Romy was only seventeen when they started dating and was ambitious to get on in the world. She certainly wasn't ready to settle down: 'He was looking for a really committed relationship, more of a commitment than I could give him at the time.' They had parted by the time Edward was set to leave university. He was a little disappointed to manage only a 2.2 degree in English, but Cambridge had been a much-enjoyed interlude for him.

Going from intelligent discussion in his rooms at Jesus College to mud-splattered assault training at the Royal Marines camp in Lympstone, Devon, proved a leap too far. The shock was that Edward had the courage to quit, not that he wanted to. For those aware of Edward's sensitivity, there was no surprise in that. After twelve weeks of hell, he went to Sandringham for a family Christmas and decided he would not be going back to the West Country. Behind the scenes he had the support of 'Mum' and 'Dad', who would never knowingly wish him to be unhappy. An official announcement drily said, 'Prince Edward is leaving the Marines with great regret but has decided he does not wish to make the service his long-term career.'

The *New York Post* reacted to the news by calling Edward 'The Weeping Wimp of Windsor', which had the merit of being alliterative but nothing more. The royal biographer Anthony Holden sensibly observed, 'He has chosen to be his own man and thus choose his own career, not to have it chosen for him, nor to live his life purely by tradition or precedent.' A specially commissioned poll by the *Sunday Express* found that 80 per cent of the British public supported the prince.

In June 1987, while Sophie was enjoying her life at Capital Radio, Edward had the bright idea of making a royal version of the popular television series *It's a Knockout* at Alton Towers. Now that his career in the Marines was in the bin, he could devote himself to becoming a theatrical impresario, and what better way to start than roping in his family for a star-studded day of fun? The monarchy has never looked so ridiculous.

Fortunately, the future king, Prince Charles, declined to take part – as did Princess Diana. But Prince Andrew, Princess Anne and a very noisy Sarah Ferguson enthusiastically supported Edward. Presiding over proceedings like a demented jack-in-the-box was the host of the original series, Stuart Hall, who was later revealed to be a predatory paedophile and in 2013 would be jailed for multiple sex offences against young women and girls.

Edward had chosen a Tudor theme for the day's events and was a vision in yellow with a matching plumed hat and stockings that one commentator thought made him look like a minor Shakespearean court jester. Quite simply, Monday 15 June 1987 was a day without dignity. Torrential rain had turned Alton Towers into a huge mud pie. Nothing perhaps sums it up better than the sight of Hollywood great John Travolta being cheered on as he chased Cliff Richard dressed as a leek.

To make matters worse, the members of the press were treated as second-class citizens, so they were not going to ignore the chance to treat the event with scorn. Edward revealed his petulant side at the press conference when the assembled reporters and photographers were far from enthusiastic, prompting him to storm out. Andrew Morton described Edward's performance: 'He flounced out like a ballerina with a hole in his tights.' And Lynda Lee-Potter of the *Daily Mail* wrote that journalists had not hung around all day 'for the privilege of being sneered at by a rudely offensive young man'.

Years later, Edward was still defensive about that day. 'How can you call something disastrous that raised over a million pounds for charity?' The one saving grace for all those taking part was that the involvement of the disgraced Stuart Hall means it is very unlikely to be shown by the BBC again – although it is available on YouTube. Fortunately for Sophie, she had not become involved with Edward by then, although she would have much cause in the future to be as wary of the press as he was.

Despite his hot-headed dealings with the media, Edward had still not entirely learned to keep his mouth shut – although he would be very wary in the future of being pictured looking foolish in fancy dress. The negative and derisory reaction of the press to *It's a Royal Knockout* did not deter him from taking steps towards his ambition of a life and career in the theatre. The easy option would have been to start at the top. As a Royal, he had been brought up in a society where every door he wanted to open had been immediately pushed ajar by someone anxious to please. He didn't want that and was determined to learn his chosen trade.

As a result, he was the first of the Queen's children to be an 'employee' and he would have to cope with a large amount of teasing and innuendo from the media, who lost little time in referring to him as the royal tea boy at Andrew Lloyd Webber's Really Useful Group.

He started work there in February 1988 as a production assistant at the company's West End offices, and he loved it − simple day-to-day things that most people would take for granted were among his greatest pleasures. He enjoyed joining workmates for lunch in the small bistros and sandwich bars of Soho. He was one of the gang of colleagues who Andrew took out to lunch at the Last Days of the Raj, a fashionable Indian restaurant off the Strand that Edward would visit whenever he could.

With hindsight, it's easy to spot the characteristics that Edward shared with Sophie Rhys-Jones; one key area of compatibility was that they were both extremely adept at organising events and occasions − a talent in the prince that senior executives at Really Useful quickly spotted. He organised a spectacular fortieth birthday party for Prince Charles in the Picture Gallery of Buckingham Palace. Phil Collins provided the cabaret and among the mingling guests were entertainment greats Elton John, Billy Connolly, Barry Humphries and Andrew Lloyd Webber. For his boss he helped prepare *Aspects of Love* for Broadway, and was involved with the French production of *Cats*, the Vienna version of *The Phantom of the Opera* and a new London run of *Starlight Express*.

His involvement with the hit show *Cats* led directly to a long relationship with Ruthie Henshall, his most serious before Sophie. Ruthie wasn't the famous musical star she would become in those days. She was a stage school graduate, aged twenty, and just starting out in the West End. Edward was responsible for phoning her to tell her when she needed to be at the New London Theatre (now the Gillian Lynne Theatre) in Drury Lane for a rehearsal.

Edward had a trusty chat-up technique as a young man – suggesting a movie or some other low-key entertainment, followed by dinner at the Palace. Ruthie didn't even know he actually lived at the Palace! They managed to keep their relationship beneath the radar for most of its duration. The media had no idea they were an item for close to six years. Some of the credit for that must go to Ruthie's dad, who was a seasoned journalist and the editor of the *East Anglian Daily Times*. His daughter's happiness was far more important than a scoop that might become tomorrow's chip wrapping.

By the time they parted in early 1993 Ruthie was a bona-fide leading lady, playing the role of Polly in *Crazy for You* at, of all places, the Prince Edward Theatre in Old Compton Street. She and Edward remained on good terms despite realising they wanted different things. She moved on to another long relationship, this time with the actor John Gordon Sinclair, but always remained discreet about her royal connection until she was caught out during her appearance on *I'm a Celebrity . . . Get Me Out of Here!* in 2020. She thought she was off-mic but the whole world heard her tell fellow contestant Shane Richie that she had 'shagged in the Palace'.

That indiscreet aside was a long way in the future, and in the early stages of their relationship, Edward was proving to be a young master of 'putting on a show' in the best traditions of old Hollywood musicals. But throughout all this satisfying and fun work he was still a Royal who had to justify his Civil List allowance – then £20,000 a year. This involved dashing back to the Palace, smartening up ready for an official dinner and then being guest of honour at some dull function. He was only twenty-four but it was already proving difficult to hold down two jobs.

The split personality as far as Edward was concerned was that in his private, theatrical surroundings in the West End he could be relaxed and fun, but in his more formal royal world he still came across as insufferably pompous. Very occasionally, the two collided. A year after he joined Lloyd Webber's company he spent three days in Moscow as a guest of the National Youth Theatre. He loved watching the Bolshoi Ballet perform *Giselle*. A reporter from TASS, the Russian news service, asked him, 'When you go home what will you tell your mother about Russia?' Edward replied, 'I hope you're not referring to Her Majesty The Queen.'

His personal ambitions would see him leave Really Useful after a couple of years and join up with other ex-employees to form a company called Theatre Division. Edward Windsor had the title of technical director. Lloyd Webber had wished them well – in public at least – but he could have been forgiven for laughing his socks off as the company went down the toilet within a year. The debts when it collapsed in the summer of 1991 were £600,000. Edward's Civil List allowance had risen to £100,000 a year, so media sceptics were growing restless at what was perceived as an exorbitant sum for the then seventh in line to the throne. Some years before any controversy over Harry and Meghan, Edward was under a lot of pressure to demonstrate that a Royal could fulfil both private and public roles.

Edward had already shown that he had true grit where his life's course was concerned and he set about finding a new career path in television. Prince Philip was not particularly impressed with the prospect of more showbusiness razz-matazz, even if it was going to be behind the scenes – he would have preferred to have an accountant in the immediate family to keep an eye on royal finances; that was definitely not the life Edward wanted. Up until this time his great love had been theatre and that would continue to be the case, but he recognised the possibilities of TV even if the workings of that medium were foreign to him. Undaunted, he formed Ardent Productions – a venture that coincided with him losing his Civil List allowance. He was not the least strapped for cash, even if a six-figure sum was disappearing from his bank account. He put up £205,000 of his own money when he founded Ardent in 1993, became the majority shareholder and gave himself the title of joint managing director – a big step up from being the Really Useful tea boy. The other backers, who invested £750,000 between them, remained confidential, although most shrewd observers believed his principal angel to be the Sultan of Brunei, the multi-billionaire monarch and one of the richest men in the world. He liked Edward, who had become friendly with his son over a round or two of golf when Edward visited the Asian sultanate; that connection would be maintained over the years and it would be Sophie and Edward who attended his Golden Jubilee in 2017.

Playing golf was fun, setting up Ardent was ambitious, but it was a charity event that would end up bringing about by far the most important change in his life ever, just as it would for a young woman from Brenchley.

6

The Real Thing

It's not every day you have to take your top off in front of a prince – not just once but many times. Sophie is not shy but admitted that she was a 'bit nervous', even if it was all in the line of duty and she was wearing a white 'body' underneath. Edward maintained a chivalrous composure, wandered to the side of the real tennis court and pretended to practise some shots, but there was no doubt that Edward noticed that Sophie was very fit.

Fate dealt Sophie an unbeatable hand of cards that September morning; it was a royal flush. She wasn't due to meet Edward at all that day, but she proved to be an inspired choice when the popular TV presenter Sue Barker had to pull out of the photocall at the last minute. It might have been a disaster for Brian MacLaurin and the agency but, in the end, it could not have been a more resounding success.

The event had been Brian's brainchild and, like most royal engagements, was for charity. He had been asked by the Radio Authority's chairman Peter Baldwin to drum up some interest in a project called the Prince Edward Summer Challenge, which was linked to the Duke of Edinburgh's Award scheme, a cause the prince had always embraced enthusiastically. The idea was that members of the public would find sponsors for a challenge – the more daring the better. They would be supported by local radio stations who would give it all an enormous plug and the money would roll in. The problem was that Edward was not the most charismatic or exciting figurehead as far as the general public was concerned, and the idea did not take off at all.

Brian went over to Buckingham Palace for a breakfast meeting with Edward and suggested that the prince should roll up his sleeves and take on a challenge himself. He argued that there was no point in standing back and watching other people do it. Brian promised to place a copy-cleared article in a national newspaper if Edward agreed to do it. Edward was impressed with the words 'copy-cleared' because that meant he would have final approval on what was printed – an outcome unheard of as far as he was concerned. He readily said yes.

His challenge was to play his beloved real tennis for as long as possible at the prestigious Queen's Club in West Kensington – not a very exciting idea but the *Daily Mail* dutifully carried an uninspiring double-page feature on what he was going to do and which charities would benefit. Edward's 'copy-cleared' dull quote was: 'I think I'm completely mad, it's a heck of a long time but I am hoping to have some fun.'

Brian asked Sue Barker if she would join them to provide Edward with some celebrity glamour on the day. The clever touch was that she would wear a series of T-shirts each with a different commercial radio station's logo on the front – for instance, she would put on a Radio Clyde shirt and pose next to Edward so that the story would appear in the Glasgow papers. She would then change to a different station's logo so another paper could be targeted.

All was set fair until Brian received a call from an executive at Sky television saying that Sue was under contract as a presenter and would not be permitted to, in effect, advertise other commercial stations. So, with just one hour to go before the photocall at Queen's Club, Brian was faced with the arrival of Prince Edward, his private secretary and bodyguard, a photographer and a bunch of T-shirts with nobody to wear them. Brian quickly abandoned the idea of asking Edward to be the model for the day. Instead, he gazed hopefully around the office in Berghem Mews until his eye rested on Sophie working on a press release. 'Sophie,' he purred in his smoothest Glaswegian accent, 'fancy popping down to Queen's Club with me?'

Sophie's flat was just round the corner from Queen's, so she was able to quickly dash home to slip on a leotard and touch up her make-up. She also took the chance to ring Sue Barker and ask what Edward was like. Sue gave the prince a good report, which helped calm Sophie a little. After all, she wasn't going on a date – this was work, pure and simple.

When Prince Edward arrived, Brian MacLaurin explained, 'Excuse me, Sir, we have a problem. Sue Barker can no longer do the photocall, but I have brought one of my staff. Would you mind posing for pictures with her?' Edward craned his neck round the door of the office where they were chatting to sneak a look at Sophie. He liked what he saw. Her hair was blonde from the summer sun and she was smiling and chatting to a photographer in that relaxed Sophie way. 'Delighted,' said Edward. 'It's not a problem.'

And it wasn't. For the next two hours, Sophie went on the real tennis court, swapped shirts and leaned on the royal shoulder in a refreshingly natural manner. Edward was pictured grinning from ear to ear in his neatly pressed white tennis shirt and shorts. The photos proved a great success and would subsequently be seen all over the world when it became apparent they were in a 'real' relationship. One of the reasons the photographs worked so well is that it's very rare for any royal couple to be pictured so close together – the closer they are in private, the further apart they appear to be in public.

Articles written many years later would suggest that she had already met Edward during her spell at Capital Radio. That is 'categorically untrue', according to someone who was at the real tennis. Both the prince and his private secretary were asked confidentially and they both confirmed this was the occasion when they met for the first time.

Back at the office, Sophie was bubbling over with the excitement of it all. Brian, shrewdly realising she had been a hit, decided there and then that she should be his assistant on the prestigious account. Sophie was delighted, although she never gave any indication even at this early stage that she fancied Edward. Nobody at the photocall noticed any electricity between them and there was no question of the prince phoning up to suggest a trip to the movies. At this stage their relationship was strictly business, although she did confide in friends that Edward seemed like a 'nice guy'. Sophie joined her boss for meetings at Buckingham Palace and helped Brian generate the publicity everyone wanted for the challenge.

On the actual day of the Prince Edward Summer Challenge, 13 September 1993, several photographers turned up hoping to take a shot of Edward with Ruthie Henshall, who they still thought was his girlfriend. They had no idea that they had already split and that although the musical favourite had turned up, it was just to add a touch of star quality and support. They should have been taking pictures of Sophie! One of the press photographers, Andrew Murray, who had liked Sophie since meeting her in the Capital Radio days, recalled, 'I was speaking to Sophie and she was talking about Edward this and Edward that and that the prince had been talking a lot about this game. I thought "that's a bit friendly" but I didn't click. I should have put two and two together.' One of Edward's opponents was another face from Sophie's Capital days, Neil Fox, who was impressed with Edward and thought him an 'exceedingly nice bloke'. He observed, 'My impression was that he was as down to earth as a prince of the realm could be.'

By this time, Sophie had known Edward for a couple of months but they hadn't yet been on a proper date. He may have been paying the attractive PR lady a lot of attention but he did not appear to want to take things any further. He was clearly waiting for the serious business of the real tennis challenge to be completed satisfactorily, however – his day on court raising a handsome £29,000 for charity, which would be worth more than £60,000 thirty years later. Sophie had given him her private phone number in case there were any problems with the challenge and Brian MacLaurin could not be reached, but he had no need to call. And then one evening, out of the blue, the phone rang. You can imagine Sophie's surprise and excitement at hearing Prince Edward's voice on the end of the line. They chatted a little about the challenge before Edward suggested she might like to join him for a game of real tennis and perhaps a bite of supper afterwards at the Palace – not a bad chat-up line.

The evening itself sped by, as first dates often do. For her outfit, she settled on a smart woollen jacket and trousers and strolled the short distance to Queen's Club. Although she had watched from the sidelines as the challenge unfolded, she did not really know much about real tennis, but Edward was happy to knock a few balls about to explain some aspects of the game to a novice; it was definitely more of an ice-breaker than a serious coaching lesson. That was perfect for Sophie, who did not want to spend their first date running breathlessly around the court.

They were able to relax immediately in each other's company, which was a very promising start. The prince suggested Sophie might call him Edward rather than 'Sir'. Sophie had always had the precious gift of making men feel totally at ease and Edward was no exception. She may be chatty and good fun but, just as importantly, she is a good listener. She also played a trump card at this very early stage of their relationship by suggesting she should take some proper lessons so that she could give the prince a 'real' game. Edward beamed – his natural shyness melting in Sophie's smile. Subsequently, one of the first presents he gave her was her own real tennis racket.

They could have talked for hours by the courtside, but supper beckoned and Sophie was soon speeding through the gates of Buckingham Palace. On the occasions when Edward invited a young woman to his private second-floor suite, supper invariably followed the same routine. The meal was prepared by his valet, Brian Tougher, and laid out as a buffet on a small card table covered with a linen cloth so that they could help themselves. A bottle of Edward's favourite German Riesling would be chilling in a wine cooler and there was a supply of Malvern water in the fridge. Best of all, the couple were left alone – both the valet and the detective were given the night off, so it was very cosy and intimate.

Common ground was easily found through their mutual love of theatre and they laughed naturally at each other's favourite stories, particularly about their stumbling attempts at acting at school. Edward told Sophie that his first role was playing Mole in a production of *Toad of Toad Hall*. His opening line was, 'Scrape and scratch and scrabble and scrooge', which he recited while lurking beneath a trap door with a completely empty stage above: 'Then, suddenly out I popped right there in the middle of the stage!' The Queen – 'Mum' – was in the audience and loved it.

For her part, Sophie recalled her first role in amateur dramatics in Brenchley. She played a cockerel and treated Edward to her impression of a rooster awakening. They swapped stories about celebrities. Edward laughed uproariously at her Gene Pitney anecdote, his familiar laugh ringing out around the Palace corridors. When Edward's friend, the producer Peter Brown, subsequently had dinner with them he was very struck by the way they shared a similar sense of humour. At the end of their first evening, if they had made a list about the things they discovered they both enjoyed it would have included movies, skiing, sailing, swimming and walking in wellington boots. Edward may not have been too sure about drinking but perhaps he could learn to like it as much as Sophie.

The evening drew to a close when the antique carriage clock in his sitting room chimed midnight. Edward preferred to rise early in the morning so he did not stay up too late during the week. His valet would bring him a cup of tea and a biscuit at 6am precisely. Edward insisted that his chauffeur take Sophie home, and he escorted her down to the waiting green Rover, which would become a regular sight from then on purring along the streets of West Kensington. They agreed that Edward would call her for a second date, perhaps a trip to the theatre. He kissed Sophie softly on the cheek before waving her off into the night.

It had been wonderful.

7

Soph and Gus

Sophie was being swept along in the delight of a blossoming romance. Edward was obviously very keen, too, so it wasn't at all one-sided. He was on the phone to her all the time, two or three times a day at the office and then again at night. On one occasion at work, publicity manager Neil Crispin answered the phone and asked who was calling. 'Edward' came the reply. 'Hello, Sir,' said Neil, instantly recognising the distinctive royal voice. 'Oh, so you spotted the *nom de plume*,' responded a disappointed prince. 'Well, it was easy,' confided Neil, 'It *is* your name.' From then on, Edward would always leave the name Richard or Gus when he rang. He had not been fond of nicknames since he was called 'Jaws' at school because of the heavy braces he wore on his teeth for a while. He was happy to call his new girlfriend simply 'Soph'; it was easy and comfortable.

Obviously, Sophie confided her new romance to her close friends, who readily agreed to keep it a secret. They were happy to be discreet as long as they remained part of her close circle. One observed, 'Sophie is good fun, a laugh, attractive and the sort of girl that most men would enjoy chatting with into the night. Edward is serious, quiet and, as is probably the case with most Royals, somewhat arrogant and overbearing.

You wouldn't have thought they were at all suited. But when Edward is with Sophie, he becomes good fun, too.'

For the most part Edward and Sophie were like any young couple relishing the thrill of a new relationship – with one or two glaring differences. In the early days, the thing Sophie found most difficult was that when they went on dates there were always three of them – herself, Edward and his detective, Steve. For the prince, having a member of the Royalty Protection Group along was like putting on a tie in the morning. He was so used to it. If Edward was driving, Steve was obliged to sit in the front passenger seat, with Sophie leaning forward to chat to her boyfriend.

Edward would drive them down to enjoy some real tennis at Hampton Court Palace, where many of his friends played. Sophie was still very much a novice, so it was a relief when Ingrid Tarrant and Babs Powell, the wife of actor Robert Powell, invited her to join them for their weekly girls' game. Edward and Sophie also did normal date things, including going to the theatre and cinema, although these were a little nerve-racking because Edward was paranoid about being photographed with an attractive blonde on his arm – and he certainly did not want to hear the click of camera shutters when they left the building. As a result, poor Sophie had to become accustomed to stumbling to her seat in the dark after the lights had gone down. Edward was still on good terms with the Really Useful Group and could be guaranteed discretion if they wanted to slip into one of Andrew Lloyd Webber's shows. They loved their night out at the aptly named Her Majesty's Theatre to watch *The Phantom of the Opera*, even though they had both already seen it more than once.

Edward also took an early opportunity to sneak Sophie into one of his favourite restaurants, the Last Days of the Raj, in Drury Lane. His love of curry was unusual in the Royal

Family, where pheasant pie was more likely to be served at dinner. In the restaurant, Edward and Sophie helped themselves to each other's meals, as many couples do – a small, everyday sign of intimacy. More frequently than eating out, they shared cosy suppers in his apartment at Buckingham Palace. The rooms had originally been the nursery area for Prince Andrew and Edward and he had yet to shake off some of the trappings of a pampered childhood. His housekeeper, for instance, still turned down his linen sheets and drew back his silk curtains in the morning.

Edward's valet would usually prepare supper, but they both enjoyed giving him the night off and cooking something themselves. Sophie was particularly adept at rice and pasta dishes, the sort of quick and easy meals that were perfect after a day at the office and before one slumped in front of the television. The Palace apartment was like a second home for Sophie. Edward was happy to pick her up from the flat in West Kensington but he did not want to be spotted spending an evening there or, worse, photographed when he left.

Early in November 1993, about six weeks after they started dating, Edward flew to Swaziland in southern Africa on behalf of the Duke of Edinburgh's Award scheme. The old chestnut 'absence makes the heart grow fonder' had never been truer than when the young couple had thousands of miles between them. Edward was lonely and miserable in his hotel and the international phone lines were red hot with 'Gus' calling his sweetheart at all hours of the day. Just before he left to fly home, he called her to arrange when they would meet. Sophie suggested he would be tired when he got back and that they should meet up the day after, when he had rested with a good night's sleep. Edward was unimpressed by her concern for his wellbeing. He told her, 'I get in at six o'clock. I'll pick you up at five past.'

One of their shared pursuits that Sophie most enjoyed in these early days of courtship was swimming together in the private Buckingham Palace pool. Sophie was an accomplished swimmer, much more at home in the water than on the real tennis court. One day, while relaxing after some lengths, she wondered what would happen if the Queen came in while she was splashing around. 'If the Queen walks in, do I have to curtsy underwater?' she asked her prince. Edward thought this was hilarious, although he was sensitive enough to realise that Sophie, quite naturally, was more than a little intimidated at the prospect of meeting his mother.

The question of when she would be introduced to Her Majesty did not occupy her thoughts every minute. But it didn't help that her friends were just as curious as she was about when it might happen. Was it too soon to start practising her curtsy, just in case? Men have it much easier where royal protocol is concerned. A cursory incline of the head counts as a bow. For women it's much more involved even if it becomes second nature; Princess Anne, for instance, was always obliged to curtsy to the Queen in private, and in recent times the Meghan Markle curtsy demonstration generated many column inches and media comment, as everything connected with the Duchess of Sussex tends to do.

Sophie never had a problem with boyfriends' mothers. They seemed to like her 'girl next door' personality. The only potential hiccough was that Edward's mother was HM The Queen. Sophie was well used to meeting the public in her job, as well as socialising easily on the Fulham social circuit, but tea with the sovereign would be a giant step up in class. Fortunately, her flatmate Ulli was practised in the use of solid silver cutlery. In any case, Edward appeared to be in no rush to make the introduction to his mother – or so Sophie thought.

Shortly after he returned from Africa, Edward suggested they should spend the weekend together at Windsor Castle, where Edward had private apartments in the Queen's Tower with a superb position overlooking the Long Walk. The view, however, was not uppermost in Sophie's mind, but Edward calmly reassured her that the Queen would be leaving as they arrived so there was no need to worry about meeting her. This was a small white lie that members of the Royal Family habitually employed to spare guests days of nervous agony wondering what to do and say when they met the monarch. Eventually he told her that his mother might still be there for lunch.

Edward's valet Brian, who was well used to guests making fools of themselves, kindly gave an anxious Sophie some advice on the finer points of sharing a meal with the Royal Family – it was clearly a different world, although Edward strongly maintained that there was not a rigid class structure about proceedings. He even gave Sophie a warning of a particular faux pas that many guests made that caused much merriment in the family. Towards the end of the meal, each diner receives a crystal bowl of water with a knife on top of a napkin placed on a separate plate. Brian told Sophie that the bowl was strictly for cleansing her hands; she should put the napkin on her lap and use the knife for peeling and chopping the various pieces of fruit on offer. Those guests not in the know would spend a number of agonising minutes, red-faced, chasing around bits of peaches and kiwi fruit that they had mistakenly placed in the water meant for washing their hands.

The big day arrived. Sophie had driven herself to Windsor in her old Fiat Panda and, as per Edward's instructions, parked in the courtyard near his apartment. She was obviously preoccupied so she didn't fully appreciate that his rooms there were far more homely than those at Buckingham Palace. Malcolm Cockren, the chairman of Ardent, told Ingrid Seward, 'If you see Prince Edward's rooms at Windsor you know Edward. All the things he likes are there.' And, on this occasion, the things he liked included one Miss Sophie Rhys-Jones.

The apartment was on the top floor of the Queen's Tower and had a private entrance. Sophie had her own bedroom and bathroom and was allocated a maid for her stay. Her name was Isabel, a reminder of Chalet Isabella in Crans-Montana. As many young women would have done, Sophie brought most of her wardrobe with her so that she was prepared for any eventuality. She did not have to wait long to realise that was a good move, because Edward bounced in to announce they were going riding. This would be the first of many wonderful rides around the estate. She also discovered that one of the many advantages of going riding with the Royals was that the more boring tasks of saddling, brushing and mucking out are all done for you.

Finally, it was lunchtime. Once more Brian had done his best to ease any nerves by assuring her that lunch would be served in a particularly large dining room and the Queen probably would not speak to her. She had chosen a blouse, skirt and jacket for the informal meal. When she walked in, she realised Brian had told another little white lie, because the room was tiny and the Queen was certainly not a speck at the other end of the table.

The big moment arrived. Edward introduced Sophie to the Queen and the brief handshake and curtsy were over in the blink of an eye: all that practising at home had been worth it. The lunch itself was a blur. Sophie was seated between Prince Philip and Princess Anne's husband, Tim Laurence, but took no part in a conversation that centred mainly on the morning's service and politics in general. She was smart enough to know that the way to make a good impression in this company was to keep her mouth firmly shut. The most important task of the entire lunch was making sure there were no disasters while serving herself from the dishes offered by the squad of butlers.

Sophie could be forgiven for letting out a big sigh of relief after coming through her first meal in the presence of the Queen. The experience had been a little like a visit to the dentist – never as bad as you think it's going to be and something you feel pleased with yourself for having done. The only thing she later recalled about the entire encounter was the Queen, then aged sixty-seven, dashing over to the window to watch Concorde fly over, dutifully followed by the rest of the family as if they had never seen the iconic plane's silhouette before.

When lunch was over and Her Majesty had left the room, Edward suggested a walk in the grounds, taking care not to stray onto the Queen's favoured route for an afternoon stroll so that he and Sophie could enjoy some relaxing time together. They did, however, bump into Prince Andrew and Sarah Ferguson bringing the Queen's two granddaughters, five-year-old Beatrice and Eugenie, three, for tea. The notorious toe-sucking pictures that ruined Fergie's relationship with the Royal Family – and, for the most part, the British public – had been published in the *Daily Mirror* in August 1992. The couple were formally separated at this time but did not divorce until May 1996.

Sophie was invited to join them for tea and found that the Queen as grandma was a far less daunting prospect. For the first time she chatted politely, if a little stiffly, with Edward's mother. The ice was broken. The Queen was later heard to say of meeting Sophie, 'You wouldn't notice her in a crowd', a view that was nothing like as unflattering as it sounded. Fergie and Princess Diana were the tabloid gift that kept on giving, so it was greatly to Sophie's advantage to maintain a low profile. She would have to face intense media scrutiny herself in the future, but for the moment she could quietly establish herself as a dependable presence.

The Royal Family, it seemed, liked her, and both the Queen and Prince Philip were delighted that their youngest child had found someone genuinely nice. Throughout their courtship, weekends away, usually at Windsor, were very much a welcome routine. Edward would drive them down in the Rover on Friday evening in time for drinks in the Green Drawing Room followed by dinner in the Oak Drawing Room. The ladies would wear simple dresses, although the Queen would finish off her outfit with a very expensive string of pearls. The men wore lounge suits. Royal men seemed to spend 80 per cent of their waking lives in suits.

Invariably the main course at dinner would be something the Royals had either shot or hooked on the end of a line and Sophie had been warned early on to watch out for any stray buckshot. Romy Adlington once observed, 'You wouldn't believe how often they eat pheasant, roast duck, casserole of grouse or salmon.' At least Sophie did not have to plough through leftovers for breakfast. She and the other female guests could enjoy croissants and some fruit brought on a silver tray to their room by a maid or a footman in a Royal livery of black with scarlet lapels and cuffs and shiny silver buttons. She could have started the day with a 'full English', but it seemed that everyone was forever eating so she gave bacon and eggs a miss. Now that she had lost her initial nerves, Sophie loved the pomp and splendour of these royal days. She felt like a princess.

Fortunately, she did not make any social faux pas that would become the stuff of legend upstairs and downstairs. One young woman was so worried about leaving mascara on a royal pillow that she brought her own. Another cut her finger while opening the make-up she had brought especially and had hysterics when she dripped blood on a monogrammed towel. One famous tale concerned an old girlfriend of Prince Charles who came across his father, Prince Philip, in a corridor wearing a short dressing gown. She gave one of her best curtsies only to look up and see a pair of very hairy knees.

Sophie embraced the traditional pursuits of a Windsor weekend, such as the Queen serving tea on Sunday with her favourite chocolate cake or helping Her Majesty pick up the birds after a Sunday shoot. She did, however, manage to include a little of her own thing, like putting on a tracksuit and going for a jog in the grounds or enjoying a refreshing swim in the Castle's solar-heated pool. She wasn't yet an expert horsewoman, so joining the Queen out riding would be something to work on for the future.

More immediately, she understood the importance of the Sunday morning church service – this could not be missed. She had been introduced to the Queen Mum on her second visit to Windsor and was invited to join the Queen and her mother in the Royal Family's private pews at St George's Chapel. Perhaps these two grand ladies saw something in Sophie even at this early stage – she might be a keeper. Sophie greatly enjoyed the first of many visits to the chapel – it would make a lovely venue for a wedding.

PART TWO
THE ROYAL APPRENTICE

8

Public Relations

Just as everything was winding down for Christmas in 1993, Sophie's life took another momentous turn on what seemed like an ordinary Friday at the office in Hammersmith. She was busy at her desk working on a press release when the imposing figure of royal biographer Andrew Morton strode purposefully up and announced loudly, 'May I be the first to call you Your Royal Highness?' Everyone in the office was stunned and Sophie was shaking down to her boots. She knew immediately who it was. Andrew had achieved worldwide fame the previous year with the publication of his book *Diana: Her True Story*, which had revealed the truth about the unhappy marriage of the Prince and Princess of Wales.

Andrew has never revealed his source about this new revelation but he was cautious about the tip-off that Edward had met someone and it was already a serious relationship. He was concerned that it might be a set-up to discredit him as a writer. He kept an eye on things for a couple of weeks and, as he would later write, on consecutive nights he counted Sophie out of her flat in West Kensington but did not count her in until the next morning. Happy that this was the real deal, he decided to meet her in person.

Fortunately for Sophie, Brian MacLaurin was in the office

and he was able to deal with the situation in a calm and professional manner: 'I quickly realised I couldn't put Morton's arm up his back and put him through the door. Besides the fact that he's a foot taller than me, I'm a PR man and this was a PR company. So I did the most sensible thing I could think of and separated them. I took Sophie, shaking, into the boardroom to calm down while I went out to talk to Morton.'

'Andrew, what is it you are here to do?' asked Brian. Andrew proceeded to give Sophie's boss chapter and verse on the relationship, including their visits to the theatre and photographs of them together. Brian had a vague idea about the private friendship that had grown up between Sophie and Edward, but the details were news to him. He was agog and was dying to hear more but, instead, all he said in response was 'fine' and went back to Sophie. He told her that Andrew had pictures of her and Edward together just the previous night. He ran through what Andrew had told him, so Sophie could not deny it, and then proceeded to write her a statement. He invited Andrew to join them and Sophie read it out: 'Prince Edward and I are good friends and we work together. He is a private person and so am I. I have nothing more to add.'

The quote, although rather lame, was enough for Andrew to place the scoop in a Sunday newspaper so that everyone could take a breath, relax a little and have a coffee. He assured Sophie that he was not going to stitch her up in any way and even gave some hints on how to deal with the inevitable onslaught of public interest and, in particular, what to do when confronted with the paparazzi – something she would have to face for the rest of her life if she and Edward stayed together. He also assured Sophie that he would not reveal where her parents lived – a promise that he kept, although Sophie must have realised that it would take the rest of the media two minutes to find the address. All Sophie could think of saying to Andrew as he put on his coat was, 'Please don't say my hair is ginger.' Brian MacLaurin observed simply, 'Andrew Morton was very decent.'

Sophie's first task was to ring Edward and tell him what had happened. They were already due to spend the weekend at Windsor Castle and she had taken her weekend bag to the office, so it was a case of working out how best to get there. They decided that Brian would drive her to Hampton Court where Edward's car would be waiting to meet her. Brian and Sophie sped off over Hammersmith Bridge in his silver Mazda sports car, hotly pursued by three leather-clad men on motorbikes. They were obviously being tailed. The ensuing chase through the streets of West London was like something out of the classic 1970s TV series, *The Sweeney*, with Brian roaring down Castelnau, through Roehampton, before cutting left into Dover House Road. A breathless Sophie spent the drive on the phone to Edward in his car telling him exactly what was happening and that they had lost their pursuers by doubling back by Roehampton Church. They later discovered that the three bikers were photographers from the *News of the World*. While the chase was undeniably exciting, it would be less than four years later that a paparazzi pursuit through the streets of Paris ended in the death of Princess Diana.

Edward's green Rover was waiting for them and the couple drove off to Windsor. Saturday was a day spent on tenterhooks at what might appear in the Sunday papers. The Queen was informed of developments and primed to expect some revelations the next day. The monarch was well used to them and actually apologised to Sophie, telling her that this was the downside of being associated with her family – it was another small sign of how much the Queen liked her.

At breakfast the following day, the papers were laid out as usual next to the Queen's place setting. The *News of the World* would usually have been on top but a servant had tactfully put it underneath a copy of the *Sunday Express* so that a sensational headline would not ruin the first royal meal of the day. The story was actually quite sweet: EDWARD IN LOVE it shouted on the front page. 'A Christmas Romance to touch your heart' and 'Sophie set to be royal bride next summer' were the secondary headlines.

Some of the details of the 'Royal Scoop of the Year' were true and some were not – at least not yet. The first paragraph read: 'Prince Edward is in love and ready to marry the girl of his dreams next year.' Edward *was* deeply in love with Sophie, but a quickstep up the aisle was not in his immediate plans. The Queen had already soothed Sophie's worries that she would be sidelined by the revelations. Messages of support from Prince Philip and Prince Charles were welcome. She also spoke to her parents and discussed how they should deal with the inevitable media interest.

The most eye-catching revelation was that Sophie and Edward had spent the night together. The implication that theirs was already a sexual relationship was quite clear and, if nothing else, it countered the general view that Edward was a closet gay.

Sophie could not hide away in Windsor Castle. After the initial shock, she was determined to be the rock on whom her hot-headed boyfriend could rely. She even cheerily suggested that no one would be particularly interested in the news that Edward had a girlfriend. After all, the daily diet of Diana and Fergie was surely a big enough royal meal for anyone. That view was soon proven to be wide of the mark. She would discover that the one thing far worse than a newspaper scoop, normally undertaken in secret by one or two journalists, was the follow-ups. They were a free-for-all as the other newspapers and media tried to catch up with the breaking story. She would witness this bedlam the very next day.

She stayed overnight on Sunday at Brian MacLaurin's Surrey home so that he could drive them both bright and early into the office on Monday morning before the press was up and running. They arrived at the office at 6.45am expecting to slip in unnoticed. Three television crews and fifty or sixty photographers and journalists were waiting – so much for a lack of interest. Fortunately for Sophie, she was no longer wearing her hair in the style depicted in the photograph in the *News of the World*. The newspaper had used one from that first meeting at Queen's Club. In October she had her hair restyled into a smart blonde bob, was also slimmer and was not immediately recognisable to the snappers and reporters huddled around in the pouring rain. Kenny Lennox, one of the best-known photographers, put his head through the car window and asked cheerily, 'Where have you put her, Brian, in the boot?'

As the gates to the underground car park opened, Brian looked across and said 'Kenny!' and pointed at Sophie. 'You should have seen the look on his face,' recalled Brian, chuckling. He drove Sophie in and not one flash bulb had gone off. While there was an element of fun involved in all of this, there was the decision to make on what to actually do next. Brian realised he had to think of something – after all, this was a PR agency that needed good media relations, and a bad move now could sour attitudes towards Sophie for years to come. He called Edward, who unhelpfully suggested he tell the press to go away. Brian explained the need to keep the media onside and Edward grudgingly agreed he could tell them he had spoken to him and to please leave Sophie and him alone. Brian went outside, asked for hush and told everyone that he had spoken to both Edward and Sophie and they had asked 'could you give us a break'.

Two hours later the first edition of that day's *Evening Standard* hit the news stands in London with the front-page splash proclaiming EDWARD: GIVE US A BREAK. Brian had also given a few interviews in which he praised Sophie as being a fantastic person, which kept the journalists happy while they were all getting soaked in the driving rain. He also took out a tray or two of teas and coffees to keep things ticking along. Sophie was aware that at some point she would have to face the clicking cameras. She had always been happy to pose for photographs but there was a world of difference between happy holiday snaps and having a Nikon shoved up your nose. Brian was trying to keep the situation calm so that the rest of the staff could leave for the office Christmas party – the disruption of this annual event was to become the norm for MacLaurin Communication and Media Limited. At this stage the police arrived to erect some riot barriers so that casual observers might have thought the Queen herself was expected, not Sophie Rhys-Jones from Brenchley.

Eventually, Sophie came out of the office next to Brian. As they reached the bank of photographers, Brian dropped back to enable everyone to have a clear view of Sophie. She stopped just before she settled into the car, looked straight at the photographers, counted to three and then got in. She made it. Sophie is still counting to three more than twenty-five years later, but everyone agreed she did brilliantly on this first of many days in the public eye. Her lifelong love of acting had helped to see her through, as it would on many red-carpet occasions in the future.

Edward, meanwhile, was back at the Palace preparing a

letter to the press with the help of his long-standing friend and PR advisor, Abel Hadden. His first draft was littered with heavy-handed sarcasm aimed at the media, which fortunately ended up in the bin after some tactful discussion with his private secretary, Sean O'Dwyer. As other members of the Royal Family would discover, the press never forgets. Instead, Edward's final version was much more conciliatory: 'I am conscious that other members of my family have been subjected to similar attention and it has not been at all beneficial to their relationships.'

Understandably, Edward was very keen to know the source of the leak to Andrew Morton. The chief suspect was Sarah Ferguson, but she strongly denied she was the culprit. Instead, police or Palace staff were thought to be to blame, but it was just as likely to be a friend of Sophie's. Edward hadn't finished yet and his office circulated a memo marked 'Top Secret' that began, 'The story now running in the press plus the Andrew Morton involvement means things will not quieten down for a while.' Unsurprisingly, the 'top secret' document readily found its way into Andrew's hands.

Edward's prediction would prove to be correct, although you did not have to be a rocket scientist to realise that would be the case. The memo went out to Sophie and her parents, warning them not to use mobile phones or put their rubbish out the night before it was due to be collected. The prospect of unnamed Sunday newspaper hacks rifling through their rubbish bags outside in the street to see what sort of breakfast cereal they ate or the brand of shampoo they favoured reduced Sophie and her flatmate Ulli to tears of laughter. The memo also suggested the best way of dealing with the paparazzi: 'If they turn up at your home, send them out a cup of tea. If it's Christmas, send them a cracker.' Sophie may have enjoyed a chuckle in private but she also knew that she had to treat Edward with care and seriousness when he was in pompous mode.

Sophie's parents handled the attention gracefully, particularly her father, who decided there was nothing to be gained by being unfriendly. He told his local paper: 'Sophie was upset in the beginning by all the media attention because she just wants a quiet life. She is a normal girl who has had a normal life. She grew up around here and did all the things that little girls do. She loves the theatre and loved learning ballet as a child. After doing a typing course near here she left to make her fortune in London as girls often do and has been having a great time ever since.' And that is basically all he has ever had to say on the subject, having been well advised by Sophie that the best comment you can ever make is no comment.

As planned, Sophie was home in Brenchley for Christmas and was able to see how everything was going for her parents and to have as normal a time as possible amid all the excitement. You would not have guessed anything had happened to disturb the sleepy middle-class comfort of the village, where it would have been considered the height of bad manners to appear too curious. She may have been the chief topic of conversation behind closed doors but when she and her parents popped to the pub for some seasonal cheer nobody asked, 'How's Eddie?' Instead, all the talk was of the usual trivial gossip. By now the Rhys-Jones family had lived locally for nearly thirty years and were liked and well respected.

Christopher and Mary were also sensible enough to realise they were unlikely to be consulted much going forward. The late Mrs Anne Phillips, the mother of Mark Phillips, lamented after her son became engaged to Princess Anne, 'The Palace never tells us what is going on. We feel like complete outsiders.' Sophie's father was his usual affable self in company, joking merrily to friends about Edward's 'prospects' and having to hock the family silver to pay for the wedding at Westminster Abbey.

At least they could be happy that their daughter was no longer obliged to keep her relationship with Edward a secret, especially when she was dying to tell all her friends, not just the very few with whom she was in daily contact. Just two days before 'all hell let loose' when Andrew Morton dropped by, she had bumped into another Andrew, former boyfriend Andrew Parkinson, and had managed to keep it to herself when he asked if she was seeing anyone. As he noted, 'The secrecy, subterfuge and little white lies told to those she held dear were taking their toll.' After all, she was Prince Edward's girlfriend and she was proud of that. He undoubtedly had prospects, but as New Year 1994 approached, what exactly were hers?

9

It's Unofficial!

Sophie had passed the Windsor Castle Sunday lunch test with flying colours. She wasn't exactly regarded as part of the royal furniture yet but the Queen had clearly warmed to her, a quintessentially nice, unassuming English girl. She was already au fait with most of the regal rules and discovered that they became second nature once properly absorbed. 'It's just like being at school,' she told a close friend. 'If you think of the Queen as the headmistress you can't go far wrong.'

Just a fortnight after her relationship with Edward had been revealed to the public, she drove herself from Brenchley, around the M25 and up the A10, to Sandringham, the official residence in north Norfolk where the Royal Family traditionally gather for Christmas, to see in the New Year and enjoy a January filled with pheasant shooting and lavish entertaining.

The arrangements for Sophie to be one of the guests had already been made before the Andrew Morton revelations, and her subsequent handling of everything in the right way had greatly advanced her standing with the Queen. Sandringham House is a mock-Tudor mansion that Edward, Prince of Wales (later King Edward VII), acquired in 1862 when his mother Victoria was on the throne. The atmosphere was very relaxed compared to the stuffiness of Buckingham Palace or even Windsor Castle. Sophie was let in through the front door that opened into a large hall that could have been an old-style hotel foyer, with many comfortable chairs scattered around, perfect for snoozing.

Just inside the front door, which had screens around it to keep out the bitterly cold North Sea winds, were a pair of sitting scales that looked rather like buckets. They had been installed at the request of Edward VII, who liked to weigh all his guests as they arrived and again when they left after feasting at his table. Sophie had to take her turn in the bucket, which was just the sort of silly thing she always found fun. The hall also boasted a piano which Princess Margaret liked to play and lead everyone in an evening sing-song, as well as a card table and another that had some magazines on it for cosy reading – although the Queen apparently was not too keen on copies of *Hello!* that featured her soon-to-be-ex daughter-in-law, Sarah Ferguson. The hall opened up to the height of two floors, and from a well-chosen vantage point the Queen could sit and watch guests arrive in their cars, which in Sophie's case was her white, clapped-out Fiat Panda crammed full of clothes for her stay.

Sophie was now accustomed to the informal dress code for her royal visits; she needed about five outfits a day – riding, shooting, lunch, tea and dinner. The only time she did not have to dress up was for breakfast in her room, which she could enjoy in her pyjamas. New Year's Eve was a black-tie occasion so she had to find a new ball gown for that night – once again the men in the usual dinner jackets had it easy, especially if a valet was on hand to expertly fix a bow tie.

Edward collected his girlfriend from her room to proudly escort her for pre-dinner drinks in the drawing room. Sophie was handed a large dry martini specially mixed by an equerry.

The measures were always generous but the trick was to make your first drink last as long as possible and to ignore the staff hovering at your shoulder keen to offer you a refill. The problem with being nervous is that you tend to gulp down your drinks. Fortunately, Sophie was past that stage and was well aware that it would be considered very bad form to have one too many. If that happened, then the Queen would pretend not to notice. Her sister Margaret and the Queen Mum always enjoyed a tipple or two, but the Queen never overdid it. She might, on New Year's Eve, become a little 'giggly'. Edward, who did not have much practice at helping himself, was hopeless at pouring drinks and always mixed far too strong a measure – something Sophie quickly became adept at avoiding. The night itself was an old-fashioned celebration with laughing, drinking, dancing and a rousing rendition of 'Auld Lang Syne'. The couple had a delightful time and came to an 'understanding' that night that they were unofficially engaged. Edward wanted to show Sophie the strength of his feelings and to reassure her that they were a team and they could stand firm against any public scrutiny – something Sophie in particular would face in the future.

During her first Sandringham New Year Sophie learned that there were two annual traditions. The first was the Queen's jigsaw puzzle and the second was the screening of Prince Philip's favourite film. The giant jigsaw was laid out over two card tables so that guests and family could amuse themselves if it was raining or they were first back from the daily ride. The unwritten law was that if a guest should deprive the Queen of the thrill of finishing the holiday jigsaw, they could expect a bed to be made up for them in the Tower of London. One traumatic year, the Queen was excitedly finishing off a particularly difficult landscape when she triumphantly prepared to insert the final piece; only there was no sign of it. Servants were summoned and the room turned upside down until the fuming monarch stormed off. A message of strong complaint was dispatched via her private secretary's office to the manufacturers. To save their necks, they sent a replacement straight away, having first completed it themselves to make sure it was satisfactory and all the pieces were included.

Saturday night at Sandringham was movie night in the ballroom. After dinner, all the house guests were expected to attend, and the rule was that they had to find a comfortable armchair or sofa on which to sit before the Queen arrived. She had the best seat next to Prince Philip in the 'centre stalls'. All the staff and their families were invited to attend as well, although they were expected to sit at the back on collapsible, director-style canvas chairs. One of the servants was the projectionist while an equerry would be positioned close to the Queen so that she could easily signal if she thought the sound too loud or too low. Usually there was a selection of two or three soon-to-be-released films to choose from and then, finally, the lights would go down and the movie would start – without any pesky 'coming soon' trailers.

At New Year, the film was invariably the 1939 black-and-white classic *The Hound of the Baskervilles,* in which Basil Rathbone portrayed Sherlock Holmes. Prince Philip loved it and talked the whole way through it as if he was part of the action, while the rest of the audience gently dozed. Sophie quickly realised that for family members who had seen it many times, the screening ranked second only to the *Royal Variety Performance* on the snoozometer. Right on cue, as Sherlock closed in on the villain, Edward's father would spring from his seat and shout, 'For God's sake, man, get on with it.' It was the same every year.

Edward and Sophie were happy to be back in the

reassuring cocoon of friends and family after the glare of
the media spotlight had taken away some of the magic from
their love affair. Edward was determined that Sophie should
not be cast in the role of a passing flight of fancy. That was
the patronising view of royal girlfriends that Meghan Markle
would have to face in the future when she was first revealed
as Prince Harry's 'girl' at the age of thirty-five. Edward was
very serious about Sophie and wanted the relationship to
last, but he was obstinate where the press was concerned and
did not want to appear in any way influenced by what was
written about them as a couple.

They were not going to be steamrollered. Sophie was
content not to rush things – although she might not have
realised she would have to wait more than five years to be a
bride. At least from a very early stage she had the support of
the Queen and Prince Philip. The Queen in particular was
sympathetic because she had also faced the uncertainty of an
unofficial engagement when she was Princess Elizabeth. That
was in 1946, when she fell madly in love with the dashing
naval officer Philip Mountbatten. She had to overcome the
resistance of her father, King George VI, and of the Palace
establishment. The King did not want to lose the eldest
daughter he adored and the courtiers considered the future
Prince Philip unsuitable, despite his Greek and Danish royal
blood. The King's private secretary, Sir Alan Lascelles, confided to his friend, the royal biographer Harold Nicholson,
that they feared Philip was 'rough, uneducated and probably
would not be faithful'. The need for outsiders to overcome
negative opinion seems never to have changed. In the end
it took Elizabeth and Philip a year to persuade the King to
allow their marriage. They were married for seventy-four
years.

The Queen was sympathetic when Edward told her in

confidence about his desire to control his destiny and choose the right time to be married and not be rushed into things by the media or the Palace machine. She supported any arrangement Edward and Sophie might make, provided that it was understood that they would eventually marry. As a result, Sophie benefited from the full weight of the Queen's approval. Significantly, she was allowed to travel to church in the same car as the Queen. This may not seem much, but it was, in fact, a huge privilege. Serena Stanhope, for instance, was not allowed to do this until she and the then Viscount Linley had formally declared their intentions. They married in October 1993, shortly after Edward met Sophie, but divorced 'amicably' in 2020. Linley's former girlfriend, the fashion presenter and journalist Susannah Constantine, a fixture by his side throughout the 1980s, was discreet and popular with the other Royals but was never given this honour. Nor was Diana Spencer.

Churchgoing was an essential part of the Queen's life. She made sure she never missed church on Sunday, and Sandringham was no exception, however informal the annual visit might be. Guests were quietly informed that Sunday church was not compulsory, although the Queen 'preferred' it if they attended with her. Princess Margaret usually stayed in bed.

The unspoken support of the Queen made life much easier for Sophie behind Palace doors – and would be an enormous benefit during choppier times ahead – but the more immediate problem was that she was firmly the focus of the paparazzi. Her daily routine was now completely different, as photographers hung around outside her office hoping to snap the new royal girlfriend on the block scurrying into work. One thing changed straight away. Up until the Andrew Morton revelations, Sophie had parked in the street, but now that would entail walking past the clicking cameras. Brian MacLaurin arranged a pass for the underground car park so that she could avoid that daily ordeal. That worked well, except for one occasion when she popped the car on a yellow line and dashed into the office for a minute. That was all the time it took for her to receive a parking ticket, much to the amusement of the waiting paparazzi. One of the photographers, Andrew Murray, recalled, 'We moved the ticket so that when she got in she couldn't see out of the windscreen so she had to get out to take the ticket off, and then we all got the picture. It was one of the funniest pictures we ever did.'

Colleague Leanne Tritton-Jones observed that Sophie coped with the attention by trying to behave normally: 'If I was going to get a sandwich from the local deli for lunch she would come too and walk there with me. A few people would look up as we strolled down the street because everyone now knew who she was, but she didn't or *wouldn't* notice.' Sophie was lucky in that she and Edward were courting before social media gripped the public consciousness – imagine if this had been Kate Middleton or Meghan Markle grabbing a bacon sarnie.

Edward had the chance to give Sophie a token of his love away from the prying family eyes that devour every present at Christmas time, when she turned twenty-nine at the end of January 1994. He could have slipped into Garrard's, the Royal jewellers, to select a discreet diamond in appreciation of how deftly his unofficial intended was handling the public interest in their romance. Instead, he chose a suitcase. Admittedly, it was a very smart suitcase, with her initials engraved on the top, but hardly designed to sweep a girl off her feet. Sophie was faced with having to answer the inevitable question from friends, 'What did Edward give you?' with the far from impressive words, 'A jolly nice suitcase.'

The problem with giving jewellery as a present when you are a Royal is that the media will draw attention to it and make the gift very public. The following autumn, for instance, the press noticed she was wearing a teddy-bear brooch. The papers were quickly on the case and declared it to be diamond-encrusted and to have cost Edward an eye-watering £12,000. The sweet ornament was actually a little prezzie that had been given to Sophie by a child at one of the charity events her firm had helped to organise.

The suitcase may have been more practical than romantic but it did not do justice to Edward's true nature. A friend who had seen letters he wrote to Sophie confided that he called her 'Darling' and signed off 'with masses of love, Edward', with four kisses and two hearts at the end. He would also happily bombard Sophie with phone calls declaring his love and he would surprise her with an enormous bouquet of red roses delivered to her flat.

On the evening of her birthday Edward and Sophie planned a quiet supper at his place – or so she thought. He phoned to say he would be late as he was meeting a television producer. Sophie could be forgiven for being a touch grumpy when she arrived at his Palace apartment. A forlorn-looking bunch of balloons was tied half-heartedly to a chair but she could see no sign of supper – it was very disappointing. Suddenly, the door was flung open and a bunch of her best friends rushed in followed by an exuberant Edward: 'Surprise!' they shouted in unison. Sophie had had absolutely no idea of Edward's plans and she was absolutely thrilled. Her prince had turned up trumps with the most wonderful treat – a birthday party at Buckingham Palace.

At the end of the evening, after the guests had left and they were alone together, Edward sheepishly produced a second present – an antique silver frame containing a photograph of him from his days as a Marine. A delighted Sophie promised to keep it by her bed at the flat in West Kensington. She could store the suitcase under the bed. A friend of Sophie's summed it up: 'Edward *is* romantic but he is also Royal. But you should see the glint in her eye when she speaks of him.'

Soon it was time to take the suitcase out from the under the bed for their first proper holiday together. Edward was well aware of Sophie's ability as a skier. She was certainly a better skier than him and would be near the top of any royal skiing league – perhaps behind only Sarah Ferguson and Charles. Unsurprisingly, therefore, they decided on a winter break in St Anton, the Austrian resort Edward had always enjoyed visiting as a boy. Just before they were about to leave, Edward cancelled the entire trip when he discovered that Princess Diana would be taking her sons, William and Harry, to the neighbouring village of Lech. Edward thought so many Royals in close proximity would lure a host of paparazzi; that was true, but they would probably have had their lenses firmly focused on Diana.

Sophie was heartbroken that their first holiday together was finished before it had begun. Fortunately, there was a romantic substitute. Rather than sit at home feeling miserable, Edward suggested they fly up to Scotland and stay at Craigowan Lodge, a five-minute walk among towering pine trees from Balmoral. The six-bedroomed 'country cottage' was originally built for Queen Victoria's private secretaries but had since become a sort of royal honeymoon hotel. Princess Anne and her first husband Mark Phillips announced their engagement there and she then went one better with Tim Laurence by spending her wedding night at the house. The Duke and Duchess of Kent also enjoyed their honeymoon among the tartan rugs and simple pine furniture. Charles took Diana there before they were married and when they were still talking to one another.

Sophie instantly adored it. She was always far happier breathing country air than she was among the traffic fumes of Hammersmith Broadway. Country weekends with Edward away from London were blissful and this first holiday together was even better. Craigowan was not exactly spartan, of course, boasting a sauna and satellite television, but they had the 50,000-acre Balmoral Estate almost to themselves.

The only cloud was another occasion when Edward could not control his enormous mistrust and general hatred of the press – this time over the infamous kite-flying pictures. They were not particularly interesting – a series of long-lens pictures of Edward and Sophie larking about with a large yellow kite. In one of them Sophie had fallen over and landed on her bottom. In another they were sharing an innocent kiss. They are completely harmless and showed them to be happy, relaxed and pretty normal. Edward, however, went ballistic when they appeared in the national newspapers and promptly made a formal complaint to the Press Complaints Commission, in another example of questionable judgement.

The Commission upheld his complaint and the newspapers apologised half-heartedly, except the *Sun*, which took the opportunity to call Edward a 'pompous, petulant and precious prig'. Even though he would soon turn thirty, Edward had yet to learn the art of not turning a light breeze into a hurricane as far as the media were concerned. He withdrew the complaint and, instead, invited all the Fleet Street editors to Buckingham Palace to discuss privacy issues going forward. In the end, only two attended the informal discussion because of the sad death the same day of the much-admired

Labour leader, John Smith. Edward's agenda fizzled out but it remained surprising, considering what Sophie did for a living, that the couple would lurch from one media disaster to another.

For Edward's thirtieth birthday at the end of March, Sophie decided she would repay the favour of her own surprise party by organising one for her prince. From modest beginnings, the 'surprise' soon escalated into one of the social events of the year. Sophie was lumbered with organising it all. Once again, the Queen paid her a huge compliment by putting in an appearance at the Savoy Hotel in the Strand, the venue Sophie had chosen after long and careful consideration. She had decided that somewhere in the West End would best suit Edward's many friends from the world of the theatre. For the menu, she chose smoked salmon filled with smoked trout and avocado followed by mussel soup. The main course was fillets of lamb with dauphinoise potatoes and spinach. The yummy pudding was a chocolate cup filled with pecan ice cream. Everyone congratulated Sophie on a marvellous party – fit for a prince. And then came the bill for £2,000. The prospect of having to nip into the kitchens of the Savoy and tackle £2,000-worth of washing up was not one that greatly appealed. Fortunately, Malcolm Cockren, the chairman of Ardent, had already discreetly spared her financial blushes and all was well. Edward was not ungenerous but, as a royal, it would never have occurred to him that money might be a problem for anyone he knew. He had, however, already noted approvingly that Sophie was prudent with her cash, not realising that she had to be.

10

Sophie v Diana

Sophie's 'prospects' were far from bright if a story that appeared in a national newspaper the following summer was to be believed. IT'S OFF, proclaimed the front page of the *Daily Mirror* on 27 June 1994. Sophie was mortified. The first she heard about it was on the car radio as she drove to meet Brian MacLaurin for a morning press call. He recalled, 'She was genuinely very upset.' She had been taken completely by surprise; was this how members of Edward's family ditched their girlfriends, leaking a Dear John letter to the press – in this case the cheerful and chubby James Whitaker, one of the best-known royal journalists in the country? This was much worse than the Andrew Morton surprise.

The Whitaker exclusive was just the sort of rubbish that would soon be forgotten, but not before Sophie again had to face a pack of reporters and photographers all wanting a bite of the story. The reality of such exclusives is that a denial just allows the opportunity to generate another day of headlines – that's why the Royal Family have finally worked out that the best policy is to make no comment – sensible advice that Prince Andrew would have been well advised to follow in the wake of the Epstein allegations instead of the now-infamous 2019 TV interview with Emily Maitlis that ruined his Royal standing.

By the time Sophie arrived at what was expected to be a very lightly attended charity event at Wycombe Air Park in Buckinghamshire, the place was heaving; it was the last thing she needed on this particular morning but she was able to turn it to her advantage, again with a little help from Brian. He wrote her a short speech on the spot. Sophie was calm, collected and smiling broadly when she told the press, 'One of the reasons I actually enjoy working with you guys is that I don't know what I'm going to read next.' Her response was pitch-perfect and went down very well with Edward, who decided to laugh off the story and not compose another pompous 'top-secret' memorandum – perhaps he was grow- ing up a little too, which helped.

Having impressed with her response, Sophie proceeded to be happy and vivacious as she accompanied the star guest, Mr Blobby, around the event, which was in aid of 4,000 children with disabilities and a cause rather more important than the update on her love life. The next day, however, she was again the headline when the papers carried her cheerful denial: DON'T MAKE ME LAUGH shouted the *Sun*, happy to promote the idea that the *Mirror* exclusive was nonsense.

Sophie was not the only one shocked by Whitaker's orig- inal story. Her mother, Mary, stuck well away from it all in Brenchley, was aghast and worried for her daughter. A family friend in the village recalled, 'I know she was deeply upset when the newspapers said the relationship was off. She imme- diately telephoned Sophie but didn't want to interfere and ask her directly about the story. Mary took it that if Sophie didn't refer to it then it probably wasn't true. Mary then told the rest of the village not to believe everything they read. As she said, 'I spoke to Sophie and she mentioned nothing to me. She was her normal self.' Imagine if Twitter, or X, had existed in 1994 – the story would have been all around the word and believed by a million and more before anyone could have denied it.

In James Whitaker's defence, rumours about Edward and Sophie had been floating around since she'd failed to show for Royal Ascot earlier in the month. They may have been experiencing a rocky patch as Sophie, understandably, struggled to come to terms with the constant media attention generated by the Andrew Morton revelations. And she had the additional frustration of not being able to tell the world that they had come to an 'understanding' and would eventually marry.

Behind the scenes at the Palace, it was decided that there should be an informal campaign to show Edward and Sophie as a happy couple and very much together – and that they had the Queen's full approval. First of all, it was reported that Sophie's mother and father would be guests at Balmoral in August – indicating that the relationship continued to have the full support of Her Majesty. Then they attended the July wedding of Princess Margaret's popular daughter Sarah Armstrong-Jones to artist and actor Daniel Chatto. Their presence led to some good-humoured 'Will they be next?' speculation in the newspapers.

The low-key royal occasion was held on a fine July day at the Christopher Wren-designed St Stephen Walbrook church in the City of London. The Queen was there, but perhaps most interestingly it was the first indication that there might be some friction between Princess Diana and Sophie. Diana had arrived by herself in a super-elegant, navy-blue skirt suit, a pearl necklace with matching earrings and a wide-brimmed navy wedding hat. Perhaps she wanted to be pictured next to Sophie so that commentators could find in her favour, or perhaps she wasn't used to not being the sole focus of the photographers' attention. Sophie was wise to what was going on and made sure that she was never standing right next to the much taller Princess of Wales. Edward and other members of the Royal Family were pleased, and even the Queen noticed Diana's intention. Sophie might also have mused on the fact that Sarah and Daniel were dating for eight years before they married – in comparison, she and Edward were only just starting out. Sarah and Daniel celebrated their thirtieth wedding anniversary last year, although Lady Sarah Chatto, as she is now, undertakes very few royal engagements.

Sophie was only just about to set foot on that particular path: a couple of weeks later it was time for her first royal engagement alongside Edward. The Royal Tournament at the Earls Court Exhibition Centre might not have been most young women's first choice for a great night out but, on this occasion, the annual event offered just the right blend of solid respectability and photo opportunity.

Edward was patron of this now-defunct jamboree and so arrived first for some official duties. Sophie and a few friends joined him later with a police escort – another subtle sign of her acceptance into the royal fold. She had chosen to wear a striking, shiny, gold designer jacket that one might have expected Princess Diana or Liz Hurley to wear if they knew photographs would be taken. Her outfit guaranteed a prominent picture or two. Sophie sat behind Edward, and he made a point of turning around frequently and whispering some amusing asides to her. While it was relatively low key, Sophie could have been forgiven for thinking she was quite important on the night.

A relatively quiet summer month had turned into something very significant for Sophie. These four things by themselves – her parents' invitation to Balmoral, the wedding of Princess Margaret's daughter, the Royal Tournament and the police escort might not seem much in the great maelstrom of the Royal Family but together they represented a breakthrough. Up until the James Whitaker story, Sophie had been perceived as merely Edward's pretty girlfriend; now in the all-important eyes of the public as well as the press, they were a royal couple – it was a huge step.

They needed to furnish the public, forever thirsty for royal news, with just one more ingredient – they had to show themselves to be a genuinely loving couple. Charles and Diana had fooled no one when they declared everything was OK and yet appeared like strangers when they both attended a royal function. The perfect opportunity for Edward and Sophie presented itself a few days later during the annual Cowes sailing regatta on the Isle of Wight. They enjoyed a very public four-day break on the Royal Yacht *Britannia*.

Sophie was looking forward to enjoying some holiday sports, namely windsurfing and water skiing, which promised to provide plenty of photo opportunities of her skipping gracefully over the sun-kissed water in her black and red wetsuit. She certainly created a splash on more than one outing, but not exactly the sort she was expecting. She treated the assembled press to a series of daily embarrassments. First, she was waterskiing when her tow rope became entangled in the propeller of a speed boat and she ended up stranded in the water. Princess Anne's teenage son, Peter Phillips, gallantly dived in to try to free the rope but, in the end, Sophie had to be rescued by a passing dinghy typically full of chortling photographers. Sophie was a bright shade of crimson as they ferried her good-naturedly to shore.

Next up, she tried her hand at windsurfing. She started well but then resumed her acquaintance with the Solent. Pictures of her humiliation were 'splashed' all over the newspapers. When one reporter harmlessly asked if she was enjoying herself, she snapped his head off by declaring she was not. Sophie was revealing herself to be refreshingly normal and not perfect. Coincidentally, she and Edward danced at the Royal Yacht Squadron Ball to strains of 'I Will Survive', the classic Gloria Gaynor hit that would prove to be a perfect signature tune for Sophie Rhys-Jones.

She had to survive a totally false story in Australia that seemed designed to undermine Sophie and Edward's relationship – perhaps contrived within royal circles jealous of her new status. Australian test all-rounder Greg Matthews said he was one of several Aussie stars who had been targeted over a six-month period to reveal that he was the mystery cricketer with whom Sophie was alleged to have had a fling; it was another nonsense rumour but one that was extremely upsetting to Greg and his wife Jill. He explained, 'I must admit you get extremely paranoid even though you're totally innocent. I found the whole thing very sinister – there must have been some people out there trying to create problems.'

Greg discovered that the affair was supposed to have happened during the 1993 Ashes tour, a trip he was not even on. Apparently, Sophie had joined the Australian cricketers at a pub quiz night called the Aussie Brain Strain, sponsored by Castlemaine XXXX beer. Greg was not the only one targeted by Fleet Street. When a reporter from the *Sun* went to the home of the future Australian captain, Steve Waugh, he was told by the cricketer's wife to 'XXXX off!' In the end nothing ever appeared in the newspapers.

The Queen did not need to be involved with this sort of baloney story, but she lent a sympathetic ear to a big dilemma for Sophie that proved to be the last hurrah for her job in frontline PR. Surprisingly, the cause of her anguish was a proposal for a glossy spread about her and Edward in *Hello!* magazine – not generally expected to be controversial regarding the Royal Family. An independent company put together a package for *Hello!* to produce an issue centred around a charity launch for Baby Lifeline, a cause that at the time Sophie was devoted to helping, and not just in her capacity as a PR executive. The idea was that *Hello!* would produce £25,000 worth of sponsorship for the charity, a sum of money that would have been extremely helpful back in 1995. The carrot was that the magazine would sponsor a dinner that would give it access to Sophie and Edward. Sophie felt that she was being railroaded into giving what amounted to a personal interview, but, if she pulled out, Baby Lifeline would not receive the £25,000 and she would be letting down a lot of people. She went and saw the Queen for a private conversation to assure her she was not trying to capitalise on her new position as a semi-official member of the Royal Family. She did not want to be seen as a controversial figure or liability like Sarah Ferguson. Reassuringly, the Queen was not too bothered. If Sophie had announced she was pregnant, the sovereign's eyebrow might have been raised a notch, but the Queen pragmatically regarded dealing with the press as part of growing up.

In the end, the event could scarcely have gone any better. Sophie had smoothed things in advance by contacting the magazine's chief international fixer, the Marquesa de Varela, and insisting on final copy and picture approval. Sophie wanted the main focus of the coverage to be Baby Lifeline and not Sophie Rhys-Jones. As part of that deal, she was interviewed alongside the charity's founder Judy Ledger at the office in Hammersmith, where they both answered very safe questions about the charity, avoiding any indiscreet banana skins concerning Edward or the Queen. Judy commented, 'Sophie's support and encouragement have been astounding.'

The charity evening was held at Weston Park, the stately home in Staffordshire owned by the Earl of Bradford. Sophie clearly was growing into her semi-royal status, showing greater poise and self-assurance, reflected in her more glamorous and grown-up choice of dress for the occasion – she wore a bottle-green velvet gown that swept elegantly to the floor, accompanied by four strands of pearls around her neck. Fortunately, it was not a cool evening, as her frock plunged both front and back, which might have meant an outbreak of goosebumps had the temperature fallen.

Sophie's smile lit up the room as she chatted happily with guests – many of them, including Chris Tarrant and Paul Daniels, were clients of Brian MacLaurin, who turned up in a kilt. Robert and Babs Powell were there to help Sophie feel more at ease and among friends, even though she was quite clearly the guest everyone wanted to see. Even Edward was able to relax and enjoy the evening, secure in the knowledge that he was not the centre of attention and that there were no paparazzi pretending to be waiters.

Two weeks later Sophie's smile dazzled the front page of the next *Hello!* edition. The banner headline read, THEY DANCED ALONG WITH 200 GUESTS – PRINCE EDWARD AND SOPHIE RHYS-JONES AT THE AUTUMN BALL HELD IN WESTON PARK IN AID OF BABY LIFELINE. The magazine also slipped in the reader-grabbing: PORTRAIT OF THE WOMAN WHO HAS CAPTURED THE PRINCE'S HEART. Thank goodness, Sophie, now thirty, was not described as the 'girl' who had bewitched Edward.

Inside, eleven pages were basically devoted to Sophie. She was pictured chatting to Edward, dancing with him to the sounds of the Pasadena Roof Orchestra, chatting to Chris Tarrant and enjoying the company of actor Ben Kingsley, a patron of Baby Lifeline. This was a glimpse of the old Sophie, the Brenchley Belle, and the new Sophie, a princess in all but name. She would face far tougher challenges in the years ahead, but for now this was quite a triumph. She came across as beautiful and fun, so it was a job well done.

On this occasion, Sophie did not have to compete with Diana. She would not have had to wait so long for her royal wedding if it had not been for the almost daily controversy that surrounded Diana, Princess of Wales. The two women did not like each other. The polite description of their relationship, as preferred by the more diplomatic of Sophie's friends, was to say that there was 'no love lost' between them. Without Diana's all-consuming presence, Sophie would quite possibly have already been a princess, an HRH, mistress of a royal household and been taking the Queen's latest grandchild for tea with the monarch.

Nothing summed up the situation better than what began as an innocuous afternoon tea with the Queen at Windsor Castle, attended by both Sophie and Diana, who came with her children, William and Harry. Every time an animated Sophie started to say something, Diana would begin speaking herself, which meant that Sophie had to keep quiet – it is a ridiculous tradition that if a more senior Royal starts talking, the junior Royal has to shut up and keep quiet. In other words, if you are giving a brief analysis of Einstein's theory of relativity and a more senior Royal starts up about this week's special offers in Tesco, you have to button your lip. After what seemed like an age of being silenced by Diana, Sophie could stand no more and, having obtained the Queen's permission to leave, strode back to Edward's apartment seething with rage. On another occasion she ran back to the apartment in floods of tears after a dinner at which Diana spent the whole time blatantly and intently staring at her.

Sophie would do her utmost to avoid Diana if she possibly could. The Princess of Wales had a strongly held view that no commoner could possibly survive within the cold steel embrace of the Royal Family. Sophie was determined to refute that opinion. Diana, who had no glamorous competition within those ranks, was not happy that Sophie, a middle-class girl from Kent, might succeed where she, an authentic aristocrat, had so abjectly failed. As a mutual acquaintance put it, 'Diana came into the Royal Family as a teenage lamb and she has left it as a lion. The young Diana had never been in the real world. Sophie met Edward when she was a mature, well-travelled woman with a career. She's been around a bit. She was always going to deal with things better than Diana Spencer.'

Diana and Sophie were both outsiders but they were light years apart – even though they were of the same generation. When Sophie met Edward at the real tennis press call, she was twenty-eight and Diana was thirty-one. The most telling and obvious difference was money. Diana, a multi-millionairess, had it in sack loads and Sophie did not. She had to do her best in the fashion stakes on £25,000 a year – her salary at MCM. Diana would spend six times that per annum on clothes alone – it was not cheap being a global superstar and icon. One television programme estimated that she spent £7,000 alone on lingerie. That figure may have been eye-watering but it was nothing to the woman who would secure £15 million in her divorce settlement.

Sophie was not stupid enough to become involved in some sort of fashion contest with Diana because she knew she would trail in a poor second. At this stage of her life, she did not have the time, the inclination or the money to transform herself into the royal equivalent of a movie star. Quite simply, if Diana saw something she liked, she bought it. Sophie was only just beginning to take her first tentative steps on the public catwalk, on which all royal women have to parade when they face the harsh lenses of professional photographers. One of the inane comments that royal ladies have to read is the one declaring that they had worn a particular outfit before. Sophie was smart, however, and hitched her star to a particular designer in the knowledge that they could be good for each other. She established an informal partnership with Tomasz Starzewski of Sloane Street, in which she advised him on public relations at a time when the acclaimed designer was expanding into foreign markets. Starzewski had a flamboyant style but also was very down to earth about his job as a fashion designer: 'I have to make a woman look the best she can. I must highlight the good points and hide the bad.'

In Sophie's case there were far more good points than bad but that did not mean she could escape criticism in the press. *Tatler* magazine, for instance, declared that she dressed like dowdy Saffy, the character portrayed by Julia Sawalha in the much-loved television comedy *Absolutely Fabulous*. Sophie was happiest wrapping up warm in some sensible clothes for a walk in the countryside. Diana would pop on a designer dress for the walk from her car to the entrance of her favourite restaurant, San Lorenzo, in Knightsbridge. And always the paparazzi would be waiting.

Sophie was minor competition for Diana as regards the paps. In reality, nobody could match the worldwide thirst for photographs that the princess commanded just by stepping outside the front door of her Kensington Palace apartment. You could literally sell any old Diana picture. She was the front-page splash – Sophie was an inside-page feature.

In the 1990s Diana was definitely more Hollywood than Holyrood. She had transformed herself from the gauche and slightly podgy teenager into an international force for good as well as one of the most beautiful women in the world. Sophie could do a very passable imitation of her nemesis – the clipped vowels and the Bambi look to camera that were so much in evidence in the notorious 1995 *Panorama* interview. One of the reasons Sophie's impression of Diana was so good is that they bore more than a passing resemblance to one another – a comparison neither woman enjoyed.

When she saw Sophie approaching at some function Diana would be heard to mutter, 'Oh look, here comes my double.' Or, less politely, 'Here comes Miss Goody Two Shoes.' Leading royal commentator Judy Wade noted that Diana would often say that Sophie should 'get her own look'. Judy observed, 'She chose red dresses that were almost identical to things that Diana wore. She seemed to be copying Diana, and Diana was sort of partly amused and partly irritated by it.'

In retrospect, Sophie having her hair clipped short in a Diana-style blonde bob was probably a mistake. Diana had the height and physical presence to carry it off. Fashion expert Alison Jane Reid observed, 'Sophie looked more appealing when her hair was shoulder length and blunt cut. You could not beat Diana's hair. It was superb.'

Sophie's nine-to-five job – plus all the extra hours that being a PR entailed – meant that she could not devote herself to working out to the same degree as Diana, who had transformed her physique through a regime of sustained machine work in the gym, running and swimming. Her shoulder blades would have done credit to an Olympic swimmer, although she had always been an accomplished sportswoman, winning cups at school and even hitting tennis balls with the legendary Wimbledon champion Steffi Graf.

Sophie was perhaps the better all-round sportswoman but both women shared a love of ballet. Diana had wanted to be a ballet dancer but, as she once lamented, 'I grew too tall.' Instead, she enjoyed devising her own routines to jazz, tap and traditional ballet. She was accomplished enough to dance easily with John Travolta at the White House and Wayne Sleep at the Royal Opera House. Sophie could probably have handled these spins well, too, but has had to make do with clutching the hand of Prince Edward when they take to the floor at an official ball.

Over the years Diana had very few serious relationships, but it seemed the hand of doom had rested on the shoulder of all of them. Her marriage to Charles was a well-documented saga of betrayal and despair. Then, equally well-documented love affairs with, among others, James Hewitt, Oliver Hoare and Hasnat Khan ended disappointingly. She was involved with the last named at the time of the *Panorama* interview.

The general public only seemed to see Diana looking gorgeous and having fun, but *Panorama* revealed an inner torment that highlighted a crucial difference between the lives of the Princess of Wales and Sophie. Diana had dealt with a great deal of unhappiness, whereas Sophie, for the most part, had enjoyed more fun. Sophie had a clear academic edge – but both women had become smart through having to deal with a wide variety of people every day – Sophie in her job and Diana as the most famous person in the country (and arguably the world). Diana came from what used to be described as a 'broken home', while Sophie had always enjoyed a very happy and stable family life.

Sophie was blessed with far more grit and determination than was realised at the time. She kept her eye firmly on the prize. When her Australian friend Eon Balmain called her to see how things were going, she told him, 'I haven't gone through all this for nothing.'

11

R-JH

Edward had stood by Sophie during one of the biggest evenings of her life to date. He was not the story on that occasion and his quiet support in public had set a welcome precedent. The only worry the two of them had was whether they would be the latest victims of the curse of *Hello!*, as the press gleefully called it. This was the alarming coincidence of how often happy couples who had been featured in the magazine subsequently split up.

After the excitement of the Autumn Ball had died down, Edward, prompted by the Palace machine, suggested that Sophie should give up being a frontline PR executive. Sophie knew it made sense; she could not be put in that position again, especially if at some point in the future she was a countess or a duchess. She also needed more money. She was finding it very hard to survive on less than £400 a week.

She handed in her notice to Brian MacLaurin on 22 November 1995, two days after Princess Diana's shocking *Panorama* interview with Martin Bashir. Diana spoke frankly about her emotional and physical problems, including her battle with bulimia, as well as uttering the immortal observation about her husband's affair with Camilla Parker

Bowles: 'There were three of us in this marriage, so it was a bit crowded.' Sophie's willingness to distance herself from bumping into the press on a daily basis was a great plus in her favour at this point. A girlfriend of Sophie's explained, 'She reflects the company line at all times. If the company hated the *Panorama* programme then Sophie hated it. She is very smart like that. She is very controlled about press stories and never comments on one about herself.'

Sophie had genuinely enjoyed working at MCM and Brian can take a great deal of credit for helping to guide her through the minefield of being a royal girlfriend. A former colleague, Nick Skeens, observed, 'Brian MacLaurin was brilliant for Sophie.' She had loved the fast pace and the buzz of mixing with celebrity clients that included Jimmy Nail, Noel Edmonds and Paul Daniels – not forgetting Mr Blobby; but it was time, however, to settle her future, especially with the expectation of an engagement announcement sooner rather than later.

With Brian's agreement, it was decided she should carry on for the moment with Baby Lifeline, a cause so close to her heart, as well as continue to consult for Searcys, the thriving high-society caterers. She would also work two days a week for the Duke of Edinburgh's Award scheme – a perfect introduction for more official roles in the future. The remainder of her working week would be spent as a PR consultant for a company called Hollander, which had offices in unfashionable South Acton on a slow road out of West London. In essence, she would now be guiding and advising clients instead of being on the frontline of their PR.

Her leaving do was disrupted, as was the norm with the media in those days. She joined Brian and sixteen members of staff at Deals restaurant in Hammersmith only for them to spot journalists from the *Sun* and the *Daily Mirror* at nearby tables. The entire evening was ruined when the paparazzi burst in to rattle off some pictures of Sophie. After that intrusion, nobody dared to move; it was all the proof she needed that she was making the right decision.

On the day Sophie left the Hammersmith office for the last time, Brian walked her to her car just as he had done on that fateful day when Andrew Morton had revealed her romance to the world. Again, the usual group of reporters volleyed questions at her about Christmas plans and the possibility of an engagement – it was a long-playing record that never left the turntable. Sophie had not been coached in how to deal with the media but she was a professional PR who knew – or so it seemed – the right balance between private and public life. Work colleagues were impressed by how she dealt with phone calls from reporters. She would chat happily about Mr Blobby but everyone knew that at the end of the conversation she would be asked if she was seeing Edward later and if there was any marriage news. The barriers would then go up. Leanne Tritton-Jones admitted, 'I would have lost my rag and that would have been a disaster.'

Sophie had undoubtedly changed since she first joined MCM. One of her close friends confided that her greatest fear for Sophie was that she was becoming bland: 'She has to be on her guard so much about what she says and does, that it's now become natural for her.' Nick Skeens agreed, 'When I first met Sophie, she was very open and jolly. She has definitely become more introspective.' She had arrived back from Australia carefree, tousled-haired and casually dressed. She left MCM with all the rough edges ironed out – there was literally not a hair out of place as she clutched a bouquet of flowers and declared, 'I am just changing jobs', before driving away in her new Rover company car, having finally retired the old Fiat Panda. Brian waved her off. He paid her a lovely compliment: 'From the moment I met Sophie I knew she was a girl who could charm the birds out of the trees.'

Both Edward and the Palace courtiers were delighted that Sophie would no longer be so close to journalists on a daily basis. The expected engagement announcement was still proving problematic, however. Edward had raised anticipation by popping into Garrard's, the Crown jewellers in Mayfair and casting an eye over suitable rings. He had planned to go down on bended knee straight away but the volcanic *Panorama* programme had made him think again. He was never going to be used by the Palace machine to calm stormy waters. He decided to wait until the fuss about the interview had calmed down. Once more, Sophie had to tell her parents that it would happen . . . eventually.

The next plan was for a New Year announcement accompanied by an engagement party at Buckingham Palace for their closest friends. Edward and Sophie decided on 11 January 1996, a date that would allow everyone time to return to London after the festive holiday. They chose to keep the occasion small and intimate – no more than twelve people around the large table in Edward's private dining room. They had been unofficially engaged for what seemed an age and he still hadn't actually formally popped the question, but he wanted to let their inner circle know their plans before the rest of the world – and the media – found out. He did, however, confide to a friend that he could picture himself walking with Sophie across the frost-covered lawns of the Palace displaying their love to the world. Once again, he was far more romantic than anyone realised.

The party went ahead and was a great success. Sophie was vivacious and happy. She already knew that Diana had once more put a dampener on things. This time it was just seven words that she had spoken at the annual Christmas party at the Lanesborough Hotel in Knightsbridge at which both she and still – just – her husband Charles thanked their seventy servants and other staff. Diana sidled up to her children's nanny, the very popular Tiggy Legge-Bourke, and said, 'So sorry to hear about the baby.' Apparently Diana had believed the completely unfounded story that not only was her estranged husband having an affair with the nanny but that she had gone abroad for an abortion. The false allegation was some years later revealed to be partly the fault of her *Panorama* interviewer, Martin Bashir. The BBC made a public apology to Tiggy in July 2022 and agreed to pay her a substantial six-figure sum in damages. It had been a long time coming.

At the time of the poisonous remark, Tiggy's family issued a legal rebuttal through the well-known libel lawyer Peter Carter-Ruck. The Queen was furious when she heard about it all and was not the least laid-back and philosophical about things. She wrote Diana and Charles a stern letter that was in effect a sovereign command that they should be divorced as soon as possible. The letter was conveniently leaked, so its contents needed to be acted upon. From that day on, Diana's days as a member of the Royal Family were numbered, and the divorce deal was thrashed out behind closed doors.

While Diana would soon lose her title of Her Royal Highness, perhaps Sophie was now an HRH in waiting. She would have to be patient once more as Edward put his foot firmly down, determined that any good publicity concerning their upcoming marriage was not going to be used to counter the bad news of the divorce. Instead, the strategy at the Palace was to leak the divorce details in dribs and drabs so that it appeared old headlines by the time it was all officially sorted. Secretly, everyone was hoping to announce to coincide with a peace settlement in Northern Ireland, but when that did not happen, the Palace settled on 12 July 1996, the day that Tony Blair revealed the Labour Party manifesto, 'New Labour: New Life for Britain'. Royal author Margaret Holder was impressed that Edward had refused to be a pawn of the 'Queen Machine'. She observed, 'It was a private victory for Edward. He had refused to be used. He had stood his ground and won.'

Sophie, however, still had to deal with some attention from the media. On the very day that the divorce was legally finalised there were two royal stories. The front page of the *Sun* was devoted to DIVORCE TODAY, concerning Charles and Diana. But inside the newspaper you could read about Sophie's night spent in a potting shed with a German law student. It was the story of their encounter at flatmate Ulli's party in Benenden and was a slice of old-fashioned slap and tickle that seems very dated now. One can only speculate whether the Sophie tale – before she met Edward – was an attempt by the Palace to deflect attention from what was a momentous event in royal history.

Edward was not a prude about such coverage in the media – having been a target himself for many years. The story quickly went away, much to Sophie's relief. She realised, though, that she would become the centre of more fevered speculation about their engagement announcement. Ever since the world realised they were a couple, scarcely a week had gone by without the announcement confidently being predicted by some royal 'expert'. It would be at Christmas, then New Year, then her birthday, his birthday, Valentine's Day, and so on – not forgetting when they attended the weddings of friends and were the subject of stories that they would be next. Sophie had to admit to friends that she did not have a clue, but she would be ready when he was ready.

Having agreed to be unofficially engaged for three years, she could hardly turn around and throw a wobbly now.

A Rhys-Jones did get married in 1996, but it wasn't Sophie. Her elder brother David married Zara Freeland at a church in Northiam, East Sussex, although Sophie and Edward were the centre of media attention when they attended. The day was a happy family event but that did not stop press circulating that it was a dry run for the groom's sister. Even *Hello!* was finding the recurring marriage questions tiresome, declaring that trying to push them into a wedding was an 'unfair and totally ridiculous attitude'. The magazine's royal commentator, Judy Wade, observed, 'The scrutiny she has undergone so far will be nothing compared to life as a royal wife, with her wardrobe, her weight and every word she utters subjected to minute examination.'

Sophie decided to throw herself into her work. The press and public were still obsessed with all things Diana and Charles, and the divorce had not dampened that enthusiasm. Speculation about when Sophie and Edward might marry was matched by more stories about them splitting up. Keeping a deliberately low profile meant it was open season for such inaccurate scoops. It was the *Sunday Mirror* this time that told the world Edward was going to part from her. The day before publication they had gone riding in Windsor Great Park and then driven to Twickenham to watch the Barbarians rugby team play Australia. All Sophie could do was ignore the following day's headlines – yet again.

She had been impressed with how the fortunes of Edward's Ardent Productions were improving, with the signing of a £2 million American TV deal. She may have been earning more than she had been at MCM, but even doubling her salary meant that in royal terms she was still very much on the breadline. She discovered that one of her workmates at Hollander, Murray Harkin, who was the same age as her and equally ambitious, was thinking of setting up his own agency. Murray was originally from London but grew up in Dorset, where he had sat his O Levels at Seldown secondary school in Poole, and his A Levels at Bournemouth College before abandoning teacher training in favour of media studies at Goldsmiths, University of London. There he obtained a BA in sociology and communications and subsequently was briefly a DJ, enjoying the celebrity world of Soho and the West End before moving into the world of PR and promotion, which is where he met Sophie. The BBC would later describe Murray as a bachelor who had enjoyed a colourful career, which was basically saying he was gay without actually saying that. He decided to join forces with Sophie to form an upmarket PR consultancy, R-JH (Rhys-Jones Harkin), which would be less Mr Blobby and more Monsieur Blobby.

For the first time, Sophie became a fixture at blue-chip fashion events where it was Gucci and Hermès one week, followed by Dior and Estée Lauder the next. The world suddenly realised that Sophie was naturally very pretty and photogenic: there was a world of difference between a snatched photo as she dived into a car and a considered picture of her wearing a fabulous, scarlet, off-the-shoulder evening dress for a party at Asprey's, the jewellers in Bond Street. Back in 1997 that dress would have cost £1,500 – which Edward might have paid for – but it was a shrewd investment in that it gave Sophie confidence to be seen in public.

In the following months Sophie's networking began to pay off: in the publicity business one good client would often lead to another. First to sign up to R-JH was her hairdresser,

Andrew Collinge, who was based in Manchester but was a frequent visitor to London and had become well known nationally thanks to his appearances on *This Morning*, hosted by Richard Madeley and Judy Finnigan. He had been responsible for giving Sophie a short, layered bob, which was very much a style of the time.

Sophie and Murray found upmarket premises for their fledgling company in South Audley Street, Mayfair, in the same building as the famous photographer, Terry O'Neill. The new HQ helped in acquiring a prestigious client list for R-JH. Sophie met Rumi Verjee, a successful businessman and, at the time, co-owner of Watford Football Club with Elton John. He also owned the upmarket china and glassware store Thomas Goode, conveniently just a couple of doors down from her office. Now Baron Verjee, he would subsequently become one of the UK's leading philanthropists. He astutely thought Sophie had the right credentials to organise parties and events for him – a contract worth £80,000 a year. Sophie was extremely capable but it would be naive to suggest that her royal connections were not helpful to her business. She did not, however, ignore good causes – she took on the Haven Trust breast cancer charity for a reported fee of £60,000 a year.

Sophie was thriving on the hard work, but she and Edward found time to slip away for a June break in St Tropez. There's really no such thing as a private royal holiday on the French Riviera and, unsurprisingly, they were quickly discovered by the paparazzi, and pictures appeared in the papers of them apparently looking glum. They were nothing of the kind, of course, but as they never smiled and waved for the exclusive benefit of the cameras it was interpreted simplistically as them being miserable.

The break gave the couple the chance to draw breath

in what was proving to be a very busy time. Edward had decided that this was the year to start putting everything in place for their marriage. Sophie was giving her life a spring clean. As well as the exciting work developments, she decided to find a new place to live. She didn't move far – just a mile away to Coleherne Court, a mansion block in Earl's Court that had already enjoyed a moment of fame as the home of the then Lady Diana Spencer when she became engaged to Prince Charles. Sophie had been happy and settled at her old flat but the new rental gave her greater security, privacy and luxury. The press had wrongly assumed that she was already living with Edward in Buckingham Palace as his common-law wife, but that was not the case – it would have been a step too far for the Queen, who had already given her official approval to Sophie by granting her security clearance to come and go as she pleased. Sophie was careful not to abuse that privilege: there were two bedrooms in his apartment – one for each of them. When she stayed over, Edward still made sure he was back in his own room by 5.30am, ready for his valet to bring his early morning tea and biscuits half an hour later; it was a routine Edward was anxious not to upset, and Sophie was happy to respect that.

Weekends out of London were easier, although not without unexpected events. One of Sophie's favourite anecdotes concerns the time at Windsor Castle when Edward was sneaking into her bedroom for a cuddle. On the way, he had to tiptoe past the Queen's own boudoir, but in his haste he accidentally trod on one of his mother's beloved corgis asleep outside her door. The poor little dog started howling and barking, forcing Edward to forsake all thought of passion and retreat rapidly to his room.

The Hilarious Incident of the Dog in the Night-Time did not feature in her first full-scale interview. She cannily realised that she could follow the lead of the Baby Lifeline ball by promoting the Haven Trust – and her business – in the pages of *Hello!* This time Sophie – just Sophie – was the cover story and the focus of the magazine's attention. She looked beautiful. She wasn't posing for engagement photos or for bridal pictures. Her ultra-fashionable blonde bob, her gold earrings, her make-up and pearly white teeth were immaculate. The headline said it all: SOPHIE RHYS-JONES SPEAKS CANDIDLY ABOUT HER LIFE AND HOW SHE SEES HER FUTURE.

Inside there were a dozen glorious colour pictures of Sophie, and in most of them she was wearing Edward's signet ring – a personal symbol of their unofficial engagement. This was the first time that Sophie had been the centre of exclusive attention. The exercise, from her point of view, had two benefits. First, she was able to publicise the Haven Trust, one of her agency's first clients. The second reason for granting such personal access was to plug R-JH and invite the magazine to their impressive new offices in Mayfair – conveniently close to Buckingham Palace – which already boasted a staff of six. *Hello!* was suitably complimentary: 'Sophie Rhys-Jones is the epitome of a late twentieth-century woman, independent, strong and with an inner knowledge of her direction in life.'

She chatted harmlessly with the interviewer, Sarah Cartledge, about her windsurfing disaster and the fact that she had what was known in equestrian circles as an 'electric bottom', which meant that whenever she sat on a horse it charged off whether she wanted it to or not – something that always made the Queen and Prince Philip chuckle.

Best of all, Sophie came across as a normal, relatable woman of thirty-two, admitting candidly, 'I don't have much willpower when it comes to chocolate – I can eat it until I feel sick. I can't just eat one square. I have to have the whole lot.'

Sophie also stressed that she did not try to emulate the way Diana looked or dressed, but pointed out that friends had noticed a similarity when she was still a teenager in Brenchley, from the moment the Princess of Wales had stepped into the public spotlight: the media back then had not heard of Sophie Rhys-Jones.

For once Diana was not the big story. While Sophie was the magazine's 'splash', Diana was making a smaller ripple with a new relationship. Tucked away at the bottom of the front page was the taster: DIANA SAILS INTO A STORM OF SPECULATION ABOUT DODI AL FAYED ON THE EVE OF HER TRIP TO BOSNIA.

Publication day on 16 August 1997 coincided with the completion of the Queen's last journey on the Royal Yacht *Britannia*. She wanted her close family with her for the ten-day voyage that very much had a sentimental feel to it, evoking memories of happy cruises around the Western Isles. Charles was there with his sons William and Harry, Anne was present with her husband Tim Laurence and her children Peter and Zara. Edward was on board with Sophie – another very clear indication of how close she now was to the inner sanctum. After they docked in Aberdeen, everyone adjourned for the annual summer idyll in Balmoral.

Diana, obviously, was not there. She was cruising the Mediterranean with her new boyfriend, the film producer Dodi Fayed, in his family's luxury yacht, *Jonikal*. It was very early days in the relationship because Diana was still recovering from the break-up of what appeared to be a much more important relationship with heart surgeon Hasnat Khan.

Diana may or may not have thought that her Mediterranean sojourn would provide a timely contrast with the Royal

Family cruise. Her sons had been with her for the first part of the trip to St Tropez but were home in time to set sail on *Britannia* and were enjoying the usual vacation in Balmoral. Diana had flown back to the Riviera pursued by the perpetual paparazzi gang. On 24 August she was famously photographed sitting at the end of the yacht's diving board. Six days later they were in Paris, still being relentlessly dogged by the photographers.

And then came the news that shocked the world: they were both dead, killed when their car crashed in the Pont de l'Alma tunnel. Dodi died instantly and Diana was declared dead in hospital during the night. In his memoir, *Spare*, Prince Harry movingly tells of his father giving him the news: 'Darling Boy, Mummy's been in a car crash.' Her death affected the world like an atomic bomb of grief, and the Royal Family took most of the fallout. Edward and Sophie had already left Scotland to go back to work in London and were enjoying their usual weekend at Windsor Castle when the awful news broke. Charles travelled to Paris to bring her body home while the Queen and most of the family stayed in Balmoral. That did not impress the papers; the *Sun* ran the headline: SHOW US YOU CARE.

A statement from Prime Minister Tony Blair, who had only been in Downing Street for four months, captured the public need for collective sadness and appreciation: 'She was the People's Princess, and that is how she will stay, how she will remain in our hearts and our memories for ever.' His words were a little more statesmanlike than those uttered by Prince Philip to the hordes of media assembled outside Balmoral. He announced over the tannoy: 'Fuck off' – a sentiment reportedly appreciated by the Queen herself.

Tony Blair politely advised the Queen that the public needed to see the human side of her family, and described the reluctance to speak publicly of Diana's death as 'bizarre'. Eventually, nearly a week later, the Queen finally spoke of her family's grief and acknowledged the public despair.

The funeral itself was suitably ceremonial and regal, if not officially a state occasion. More than two *billion* people watched on television as the princess's two young sons – William, aged fifteen and Harry, twelve – walked behind the coffin as it made its way down The Mall from Kensington Palace to Westminster Abbey. In the Abbey itself, Elton John sang 'Candle in the Wind 1997' as a dedicated goodbye to 'England's rose'. The place was full of the most famous celebrities in the world: Tom Cruise, Tom Hanks, George Michael, Hillary Clinton, Luciano Pavarotti, Donatella Versace and Richard Branson were just some of the head-liners. The Royal Family turned out in force: Edward was pictured standing next to Sarah Ferguson; even the Queen Mum was there, having just turned ninety-seven.

Sophie Rhys-Jones was nowhere to be seen. She did not attend. She had an obvious and reasonable excuse: a friend at the Palace explained, 'Sophie decided it would be too upsetting for the crowd if she went. She's well aware that she looks like Princess Diana from a distance and made her decision in a caring and thoughtful way. The Royal Family fully supported that.'

12

It's Official!

Sophie was thirty-two and had grown up a lot in the past few years. She very quickly realised that there could be no marriage for a considerable length of time while the nation recovered from mourning Diana; it would not be fitting. All the Royal Family could do was keep their heads down. At least Edward and Sophie could plunge themselves back into work, pausing only to consider possible houses that might become their first marital home. They were impressed with the handsome Newtown Park, set in four hundred acres on the edge of the New Forest in Hampshire. The Palladian mansion was on the market for £2 million but did boast six bedrooms, five reception rooms and an outdoor swimming pool, which caught Sophie's eye. Another promising candidate was Anmer Hall, a large Georgian mansion owned by the Sandringham Estate that had been leased by the Duke and Duchess of Kent for nearly twenty years. One possible drawback was the presence of a ghost from Tudor times that was supposed to walk the corridors.

Neither of these two houses passed the most important test for Edward and Sophie: their future marital home needed to be within one hour's drive of Buckingham Palace and the R-JH offices in Mayfair. Eventually, while thumbing through Crown Estate properties one evening, they discovered the magnificent Victorian gothic mansion Bagshot Park, in Surrey, just a few miles from Windsor Castle and close to the M25. Depending on traffic, from there it takes almost exactly an hour to drive to the Palace. The easiest journey was the quick commute by train to Knightsbridge, but that crowded rush-hour joy was not something Sophie planned to embrace.

Edward drove Sophie out one weekend to take a look and she fell in love with the house immediately. She told friends that it had so much character. As anyone with experience of properties with 'character' will tell you, this description usually means they need a lot of work, and Bagshot Park was no exception. Edward was impressed by how 'incredibly private' the house was and he was determined to restore the mansion to its former glory. The main house had been built in 1877 on Queen Victoria's instructions as a wedding present for her third and favourite son, Prince Arthur, Duke of Connaught, and his new wife, Princess Louise Marguerite. They had married at St George's Chapel, Windsor, a portent perhaps of a welcome future event in the life of Sophie and Edward. Coincidentally, the Queen gifted Anmer Hall to William and Kate when they became engaged and it has proved a happy home for their family.

Initially, Edward took a fifty-year lease on the property from the Crown Estate – effectively making his mother his landlady – that would cost about £50,000 a year. He subsequently extended the lease to 150 years at an estimated cost of £5 million. The renovations he had in mind would restore some of its original character while making it a home for a modern family. Sophie was happy to go along with his plans, realising that it might be well over a year before they were choosing curtain material. She also understood that Edward was a perfectionist and that everything would need to be just right. As he himself observed, 'It will require imagination and that little bit of extra effort. There is no point in just diving in and giving it an extra lick of paint.'

Bagshot Park had the potential to be their little paradise. For starters, it was set in more than fifty acres and surrounded by trees. Among the many wonderful features were its eye-catching wrought-iron gates, and Portland stone and red-brick Gothic façade. Inside, there was a chimney piece designed by the renowned Sir Edwin Lutyens and an Indian room that was a wedding present to the Duke of Connaught from an Indian princess. The Duke died aged ninety-two in 1942 and the house was requisitioned by the army. After the war, it was briefly considered as a country home for the young Princess Elizabeth before she became Queen. Instead, it was made available to the Ministry of Defence as a training centre for army chaplains until 1996, when spending cuts forced its closure – perfect timing for Edward and Sophie.

Their plan for the house was to make it smaller rather than bigger. The usual figure given for the number of rooms is 120, but nobody has been around with a calculator; whatever the exact figure is immaterial – it is a massive country pile and unmanageable for a couple, even a royal one. To begin with, they planned on having just three members of staff living with them – a chef, a secretary and Edward's trusted valet, Brian – who would occupy the three staff flats. When everything was finished there would be nine en-suite bedrooms and five reception rooms. Both Highgrove, the country home of Charles, and Gatcombe Park, where Anne has lived since 1976, boasted the exact same number of bedrooms.

Edward planned to demolish one complete wing but retain a private chapel. Close to the house was a lake, which quickly became a haven for Sophie on her visits down to inspect the progress of the building work. Edward, displaying his old sense of humour, put up a sign that read, 'Please don't walk on the water.' Sophie was particularly pleased that a new, large and bright conservatory would be the perfect place to entertain and enjoy a view of the gardens if it was too chilly to sit outside.

Edward and Sophie's intention to marry had not wavered despite everything that had occurred the previous year. Work on the house would take at least two years to complete. Edward told Colin Randall of the *Daily Telegraph* that his plans for Bagshot Park and his relationship to Sophie were unconnected. 'Please do not read too much into this in terms of any changes in my private life. They are totally separate issues. This is not some circuitous route of changing my private life.' He added, only slightly pompously, 'These things will be announced when the time comes, not before.'

One of the things not announced was who paid for the renovations, rumoured to cost £1.8 million. Coincidentally, that was the exact amount the Ministry of Defence was reported to have handed over to the Crown Estate when it vacated the rundown property. Edward's first priority was to move Ardent Productions into the large stable block, which would help to make the redevelopment more cost-effective. The tide was tentatively turning for the better for Edward's company after it had lost £1.5 million in its first four years. Some of the optimism for the future was due, to a large extent, to Edward's status in the US, wooing TV bosses on the understanding that he would be the 'star' of documentaries, mainly royal but not exclusively so, in which he had the attractive standing of being an insider – although some thought he was rather stiff and dull in front of the camera. Edward didn't do 'gravitas' that well.

He travelled to Pasadena, in California, to be the guest speaker at a conference of the Television Critics Association, where delegates were served English tea in china cups and ate cucumber finger sandwiches. He was promoting two Ardent series: *Crown and Country* and *Tales from the Tower*. Trailers for the former on the History Channel announced, 'Prince Edward is a man whose intimate familiarity with the monarchy enables him to reveal the kind of royal stories few others can.' The schmoozing 'paid' off when CBS gave Ardent a contract worth reportedly £2.5 million for proposed documentaries on leading American families, including the Kennedys and the Gettys.

Edward was unarguably cashing in on his royal credentials and 1998 was a good year. Ardent posted a small profit on a turnover of more than £3 million. Productions included the TV feature film *The Cater Street Hangman*, the first of the Inspector Pitt Victorian crime novels written by Anne Perry. A stellar cast included Keeley Hawes and Eoin McCarthy, but only one book was adapted by Ardent.

Arguably, Sophie was doing even better. By May 1998 the annual income of R-JH was being estimated as close to £1 million and Sophie's shareholding was a very healthy 54 per cent. Her list of clients was the envy of the bitchy PR world, especially as the firm had only been open for business for a year or so. She had produced a glossy seventeen-page prospectus listing a number of blue-chip clients that included the Lanesborough Hotel, society jewellers Boodle and Dunthorne (now Boodles) and Lady Apsley Training School for Butlers. A trendy new gym, The Club at County Hall, had snapped her up for £70,000. She also landed the Comité Colbert account, which was the association promoting the French luxury goods trade that included such household names as Moët & Chandon, Chanel, Dior and Wonderbra.

When Sophie met Edward she was just about breaking the £20,000 per annum barrier. Now she was earning ten times that and was well on her way to making her first million.

In many ways Edward and Sophie were like an old married couple. They worked hard during the week running their companies, and at weekends they would either be at Windsor or visiting friends in the country, including Lord Ivar Mountbatten, whose wedding to Penny Thompson was one of the first they attended as a couple in 1994. Sophie used her PR expertise to help organise a star-studded fiftieth birthday party for the Prince of Wales at Highgrove. Some of his favourite performers, including Stephen Fry and Rowan Atkinson, assembled for the do. The event received a lot of positive coverage, which all went to help his rehabilitation in the eyes of the public and the acceptance of his new life with Camilla Parker Bowles. On the afternoon of the party Sophie was spotted in nearby Tetbury doing some last-minute shopping. She was now so adept at slipping about unnoticed that you would have been forgiven for not knowing she was even at the party.

Edward had mellowed considerably under Sophie's influence and they enjoyed a pleasant upper-class life sharing pursuits including shooting and riding with their close and loyal friends. Sophie even took shooting lessons at Sandringham so that she could upgrade from being a beater and join in. The only slight cloud on the horizon was the thought that she would be celebrating her thirty-fourth birthday in January 1999 and her biological clock was ticking. Sophie had answered invasive questions about it by cheerfully declaring that she would like children at some stage but would 'cross that bridge when she came to it'. There was no question of that bridge being crossed unmarried.

If you are going to choose the perfect place to propose then a holiday in the Bahamas is not a bad choice. Sophie had absolutely no idea that Edward was going to be decisive at last. Just before Christmas in 1998, he had impulsively – or so it seemed – whisked Sophie away for a short break in paradise. They stayed at the blissfully private Hamilton House, a beachside four-bedroom villa on the island of Eleuthera. The property was owned by the Duke of Abercorn, a long-standing friend and courtier who had acted as a judge on the infamous *It's a Royal Knockout*.

After two sun-kissed days they were enjoying a candle-lit dinner when Edward dropped to one knee and asked, 'Darling, will you marry me?' Sophie was stunned and could scarcely speak the word 'yes' before finding her voice and replying, 'Yes please!' Even though they had talked of marriage and a proper engagement many times, Edward had managed to take Sophie completely by surprise. They hadn't spoken of it seriously for three years. Edward's gallant proposal was a dream come true.

They flew back to England on 23 December and parted for Christmas at home with their respective parents. Sophie went to Brenchley while Edward travelled up to Sandringham. They promised to keep their news secret for a few days more so that Edward could formally ask Sophie's father for her hand. Sophie understandably wanted to shout it to the world, but they agreed that they would share their news on 6 January 1999. Sophie knew the design of the engagement ring she wanted, and royal jewellers Asprey & Garrard, with whom she enjoyed close informal links, were happy to oblige, and so was the groom-to-be. She did not want some prehistoric piece that an ancient ancestor had once worn. She also spoke to Tomasz Starzewski about a suitable dress design for the announcement. For his part, Edward, who loved a surprise, was looking forward to springing this one on the media.

Unfortunately, his idea of high drama was slightly spoiled by the *Sun,* which broke the news with a front-page story on the very morning of the big announcement: EDWARD TO WED SOPHIE, the paper boldly declared on its front page. The news rocketed around the world, not least to the royal rat pack of reporters and photographers who were enjoying their annual jaunt to Klosters in Switzerland, where Charles and his son Harry were skiing. They were taken completely by surprise and needed to check return flights to London.

At 10am, Buckingham Palace made it official with a quaintly old-fashioned statement: 'The Queen and the Duke of Edinburgh are delighted to announce the engagement of their youngest son, Prince Edward, to Miss Sophie Rhys-Jones. The couple sought the permission of their respective parents between Christmas and the New Year. Both families are thrilled at the news. No decision has been taken yet regarding the venue and date for the wedding. However, Prince Edward and Miss Rhys-Jones hope that it might be possible to use St George's Chapel, Windsor, in the late spring or summer.'

The whole world seemed to be thrilled – at last, some royal good news. Certainly, the villagers of Brenchley were happy to send the couple their best wishes. Sophie's father Christopher, a little more nervously than usual, greeted the press who had gathered outside his front door: 'We like Edward immensely and, of course, we have known him for some time. He is a very, very nice chap. I think Sophie will do very well. She has not exactly been catapulted in – it's been a fairly long apprenticeship.' Sophie's mother Mary was overjoyed and simply said, 'I'm very happy,' her face a picture of smiles.

Shortly after the official announcement, Sophie and Edward strolled out into the January sunshine to pose for photographs in front of St James's Palace. Sophie wore a Starzewski-designed, hourglass tailored suit with beaded lapels and elongated silver buttons. She was moving in more fashion-conscious circles these days, and fittingly it was in the season's favourite colour, grey. Renowned fashion commentator and magazine editor Alison Jane Reid observed, 'The suit works because it is beautifully tailored. The devil is in that twinkling detail. Tomasz is a maestro of power dressing and tailoring. His signature is elegant simplicity, married to a wonderful dash of detail, in this case the luxurious beading.'

For once there was no need to feel exasperated at the clicking of cameras. They were holding hands and smiling happily. Sophie's smile dazzled almost as much as the fabulous diamond engagement ring she was proudly showing off – an exceptionally pretty design of a two-carat, central oval diamond flanked by two heart-shaped diamonds in a white gold setting. The ring echoed the style of his mother's engagement ring and oozed classic class – not surprising considering it cost Edward an estimated £105,000. He warned the photographers, 'If it catches the sun, you'll be blinded.' He added, a little cornily, 'Diamonds are a girl's best friend, so I'm told.' Quick as a flash Sophie chipped in, 'No, you're my best friend.' That loving banter was their common bond.

They contentedly answered the usual flurry of questions. Asked why they made such a good couple, Edward replied a little lamely, 'I don't know. We just do really.' Sophie, who had let Edward answer first, was more helpful, recognising the need for a good quote: 'We share a lot of interests, we laugh a lot and we have a great friendship.' Asked how he proposed, the prince replied, 'Well, I spoke it.' He was more forthcoming about the wedding plans: 'There is no such thing as a private wedding, but I hope it will be predominantly a family wedding. We chose St George's Chapel because it is a wonderful setting, it is a glorious piece of architecture and it is somewhere slightly different.' He could have added that Sophie had dreamed of her wedding there since the first time she had been to Sunday church with the Queen more than five years ago.

Thankfully, there was no repeat of the toe-curling awkwardness of the Charles and Diana engagement interview. When asked innocently if the couple were in love, Diana, nineteen, replied shyly, 'Of course', while her fiancé said, infamously, 'Whatever in love means', as he looked uncomfortably to the floor that should have opened up and swallowed him. Edward did much better, neatly deflecting a question about the failed marriages of his sister and brothers by observing, 'I think if anyone is going to get married I hope they think they will get it right. We are the best of friends and we happen to love each other very much, and long may that continue.'

For her part, Sophie had handled the occasion in the manner of an accomplished mature woman – she was fifteen years older than Diana had been. Asked how she felt about joining the Royal Family, she answered, 'It is slightly nerve-racking in many ways but I am ready for it now. I'm fully aware of the responsibilities and commitments and I think now I am ready.'

The British public was also ready for some good royal news and Sophie was providing it. Edward placed a gentle kiss on Sophie's cheek and the cameras clicked and whirred happily. So, now, it was all systems go for organising the summer wedding. What could possibly go wrong?

13

Premeditated Cruelty

The immediate speculation when everyone had absorbed the happy news was who Sophie would choose to design her wedding dress. Big names were apparently in the frame, including Tomasz Starzewski, unsurprisingly, as well as Amanda Wakeley, David Fielden and Neil Cunningham. In the end Sophie chose Samantha Shaw, a lesser-known name in this exclusive circle but a well-connected young woman who understood Sophie's world of wealthy friends and clients, although they hadn't met before she received the commission.

Samantha, who is four years younger than Sophie, had been one of a number of designers invited to send in some ideas in sketch form to the R-JH office. Sophie was impressed and asked Samantha to come in for a chat, quickly deciding that she was right person. Samantha had just four months to design and finish, making sure she revealed absolutely nothing to the outside world. Fittings had to be secret and arranged around Sophie's hectic work schedule. Samantha soon discovered that being newsworthy brought its own drawbacks. A friend recommended a security guard to keep an eye on her studio at night, which proved a sound idea when someone – perhaps a journalist – was discovered loitering around and going through the bins.

One might have thought the press would give Sophie an easy time in the run-up to the big day. That proved not to be the case ... Murray Harkin picked up the phone that was ringing in the wee small hours of the morning. It was Sophie on the line. She was, he recalled, in floods of tears. 'She was so upset because she felt that she was "letting the side down" before her wedding.' The reason for her anguish soon became very clear. Under the banner headline SOPHIE TOPLESS, the *Sun* had reproduced the photo of Sophie with Chris Tarrant taken in Spain when she was with Capital Radio. The picture itself was reproduced on Page Three, of course.

Sophie wasn't prone to tearful outbursts – although it was reported that Princess Diana had once made her cry. But her immediate fear was that this would tarnish the build-up to her wedding, now little more than three weeks away. She was acutely aware that the Royal Family needed some good news. The engagement announcement had been greeted warmly but a royal wedding, even if fairly low-key one at St George's Chapel and not St Paul's or Westminster Abbey, was destined to be the British pick-me-up of the year.

This totally unexpected, old-style titillation threatened to torpedo her innocent excitement and the support of the public. Or so she thought. Unexpectedly, the backlash was all against the tabloid newspaper and the perceived villain of the piece, her former Capital Radio colleague, Kara Noble. Much of the positive reaction towards Sophie was due to the unwavering support from the Queen. In all her dealings with the press and media over the years, Sophie has always had the strongest backing from the Queen and this would prove to be no exception.

Buckingham Palace moved very swiftly, issuing a withering criticism of the story stating that it was 'premeditated cruelty' and making a formal complaint to the Press Complaints Commission.

The *Sun*'s editor, David Yelland, quickly reassessed the situation and issued a somewhat patronising statement: 'An editorial expressing our regret will appear in tomorrow's *Sun*. We clearly upset Miss Rhys-Jones. It's clear to me that we have caused her great distress. I have therefore decided to apologise to her and to the Palace. I believe that is the right thing to do. No more topless pictures of Miss Rhys-Jones will appear in the *Sun*. I wish her and Prince Edward the very best, although I don't expect to be invited to the wedding.'

The jokey phrasing did not actually admit any wrongdoing. It was Sophie's reaction and 'distress' that seemed to prompt the apology, not an admission of poor judgement. In Yelland's defence, the *Sun* had reportedly won a bidding war for the pictures when everyone realised they existed. His apology did deflect attention away from the paper and onto Kara Noble, who was promptly sacked by Heart, the London-based radio station she had joined as a DJ on leaving Capital.

Chris Tarrant had to deny that he had ever been in any improper relationship with Sophie. He broadcast a statement on his breakfast show: 'To the person who has sold these pictures, you know who you are. Kara, how will you ever be able to look Sophie in the face again? I don't feel angry. I don't feel disgust – I feel deeply saddened.'

Richard Huntingford, the boss of the Chrysalis Group, the parent company of Heart, was robust: 'We are shocked and disappointed that Kara Noble has betrayed the trust of Sophie Rhys-Jones and everyone here at Heart 106.2.' Her co-host on the breakfast show, Jono Coleman, was 'disappointed and shocked', although he had pointed out that the snaps were 'not exactly hard porn'.

Even Downing Street, where former tabloid journalist

Alastair Campbell was in charge of Tony Blair's press, had something to say: 'Freedom of the press is very important, but with freedom comes responsibility and it's important that when the media exercise that freedom, you show judgement.'

The photograph used by the *Sun* was one taken in the back of a car, with Tarrant mischievously lifting up Sophie's bikini top. While it was generally agreed that the photo itself was not the least bit shocking, the timing of its publication certainly was. The newspaper backed up its editor's thoughts the following day with a full-page apology and the headline SORRY SOPHIE. The statement said, 'We thought we were publishing a saucy but harmless picture of Sophie Rhys-Jones. We thought it showed the fun-loving side of a woman who is bringing a breath of fresh air to the Royals. We were wrong.' It promised that there would be no more revelations that might cause Sophie offence, and confirmed that all profits from syndication of the pictures would go to two charities that Sophie could nominate. She chose the Haven Trust and the Tuberous Sclerosis Association, an important organisation that offered support and ongoing research into the genetic condition.

The *Sun* did not reveal if the paper had sold more copies the day before. An apology, though, however well meant, is never as eye-catching as the original scoop. Attention swiftly turned to how much Kara had made from selling her camera roll of film. First guess was that it must have been £100k. After all, why jeopardise your comfortable life and career for anything less than six figures? In the end, the estimated sum was £40k, which appeared ridiculously low. Everyone at Capital and among the press seemed to know these pictures existed, but it was the timing that seemed heartless and ill-judged.

Kara Noble, and not Sophie Rhys-Jones, had become the

story. The *Guardian* newspaper suggested in a lengthy profile that she may have been prompted by her antipathy towards Chris Tarrant, who she had apparently labelled as being 'very selfish, rude and insensitive'. The article adjudged, 'Betrayal is not a question of degree, but rather of intent. And Noble's intention, however it was prompted, was cruel.'

Unsurprisingly, David Yelland was not sacked by the *Sun*. He quit the job in 2003 for, ironically, a career in PR and consultancy. Kara Noble's career, however, was in tatters and she left the UK to quietly start a new life in Los Angeles. One of the more damning revelations was that she had actually recently reassured Sophie that the pictures would not find their way into the public domain. A year later, when Sophie was established as the Countess of Wessex, Noble finally apologised, telling the *Mail on Sunday*, 'I realise I made the biggest mistake and the most public mistake one could ever make. I'll always be known for selling that photo and it's something I've got to live with. I just want to say sorry to everyone involved.'

Sophie and Edward realised that the best policy was to move on as quickly as possible and refocus everyone's attention on the wedding. Old friends rallied round. In Australia, Michael O'Neill gave a rare interview: 'Sophie is a lovely girl and I have very fond memories of her. She is a genuine person. I know from my own time with Sophie that Prince Edward is a very lucky man.' Student friend Jo Last also lent her full support: 'People have said to me, "Isn't she lucky to be marrying a handsome prince? My reaction is that Edward is the lucky one for getting her. She is a normal, wonderfully down-to-earth and decent girl. She'll be the best thing to happen to the Royal Family.' Brian MacLaurin also stepped in to help soothe things. Just a few days after the publication, he said that the royal couple thought 'it was time to forget this'. He added, 'Kara was stupid, silly and misguided, but she is not a traitor.

Sophie has spoken to Chris Tarrant and they are all aware that Kara is being followed by the media. They think she has suffered enough and she should not be hassled. Sophie is well aware of what it is like to be followed by the media.'

The last sentence said it all.

Sophie still had three weeks to be nervous in the immediate run-up to the wedding. Ironically, she and Samantha had another important wedding to attend before the big day – Samantha's own. She married David Keswick, the son of Sir Chips and Lady Sarah Keswick, long-standing friends of Prince Charles, at Chelsea Old Church, only a mile and a half from the flat in Coleherne Court that Sophie had given up so that she could start her own married life at Bagshot Park. She seemed her usual composed self as she turned to photographers calling her name as she walked towards the church steps. The photo opportunity was very brief but it was enough. After all, this wasn't her day.

Sophie was again the centre of attention one week before her wedding, but this time photographers did not have to shout at her for a picture. She was one of the Royal Family attending the annual Trooping of the Colour ceremony held on the second Saturday of June to mark the Queen's official birthday. This was a very public demonstration of support for Sophie from the Queen and the Queen Mother, which ensured that the topless photo saga was completely dismissed in time for the big day the following weekend. Sophie looked enchanting in a very big, broad-brimmed summer hat, in the same horse-drawn carriage as Edward; she was seated next to the Queen Mother as they acknowledged the crowds gathered alongside Horse Guards Parade. Her husband-to-be smiled reassuringly as she took her place next to him on the balcony of Buckingham Palace alongside Princess Anne, Tim Laurence, Prince Philip and, of course, the Queen, in a striking lemon-yellow outfit; it was a very big occasion for Sophie.

Nearer the actual wedding day Edward and Sophie decided to give a candid interview at Bagshot Park to the BBC, and who better to conduct proceedings than Sue Barker, who inadvertently had been the catalyst for it all. In conversation, Edward revealed that he had waited so long to officially pop the question because the media interest in their relationship had put him off.

The interview was relaxed and cheerful, with many home truths dressed up in a cocoon of politeness. Edward declared that the tragic death of Diana in a car crash was the only way it was going to end for her: 'It was the era when there was a huge market in photographs and people would do the most ridiculous things to get them. It was only a matter of time before something really nasty happened.' Sophie revealed that she had jumped traffic lights to try to avoid the pursuing paparazzi, a course of action that endangered others: 'I didn't want to be responsible for someone else being hurt,' she said.

For what seemed like the millionth time, Sophie deflected questions about the similarity between herself and Diana. She answered diplomatically, 'I don't think anybody can be unhappy about being compared to someone like her. But it's two very different people. She had her personality and I have mine.'

Asked about the already notorious publication of the topless photo, Sophie admitted that it had been 'completely devastating' but that she had found comfort in the reaction from the public. She had received hundreds of letters and countless phone calls offering sympathy for what had happened. That general reaction boded very well for 19 June 1999.

14

Tying the Windsor Knot

Technically, Sophie would become Princess Edward upon her marriage to the Queen's youngest son, but she did not fancy that at all. She did not want to be a princess – it would only tempt more unwelcome comparisons between herself and the much-missed Diana, the 'People's Princess'. Anne was still soldiering on as Princess Royal, but she had been given that title many years before. The initial expectation was that Edward and Sophie would become the Duke and Duchess of Cambridge – after all, he did study there – but that title would be destined for another royal couple not yet on the public radar.

Sophie would automatically become an HRH – Her Royal Highness – upon marriage, but that seemed a rather cumbersome mouthful, so it was a case of wait and see what the Queen decided to do. The one title that would definitely be Edward's at some point was Duke of Edinburgh, when his father died; that title had been given to him on his own wedding day. Prince Philip had sat down next to them at Windsor Castle and, to their great surprise, had asked if they would take on the dukedom. Sophie recalled, 'We sat there slightly stunned. He literally came straight in and said, "Right. I'd like it very much if you would consider that."'

They hoped that would be some years in the future. For now, a few hours before everyone gathered at St George's Chapel, the Queen made Edward Earl of Wessex, so Sophie would officially become HRH, The Countess of Wessex or, as she preferred, Sophie Wessex. Amusingly, Earl had been one of Edward's nicknames at Gordonstoun because it represented his initials – Edward Anthony Richard Louis. Edward had fancied being Lord Wessex ever since the previous year when he and Sophie had enjoyed the film *Shakespeare in Love*, in which Colin Firth had played a character with that name. As a royal title it had not been used for close to a thousand years, back when the Anglo-Saxons had ruled England. The well-known television historian Dr David Starkey was unimpressed: 'The title itself is a total fiction. There is nowhere called Wessex. It belongs to the novels of Thomas Hardy.'

The speculation about possible titles had been the last thing on Sophie's mind as she prepared for her walk down the aisle. The actual *walk* was far more important. Sophie took the precaution of having private lessons at Buckingham Palace to ensure she could walk elegantly in what would be perilously sky-high heels underneath her flowing wedding outfit. She was far more comfortable wearing trainers. She did not want the story of the day to be her falling flat on her face while Edward looked on from the altar and 200 million people watched on television. The silk crepe shoes were nearly the fashion story of the day when it was discovered at one of the final fittings that they were the wrong colour – too pink. They were redone very speedily.

The Queen, at 5ft 3ins, and the Queen Mother, 5ft 2ins, were even more petite than Sophie, so they could have passed on a lifetime of experience of tottering with confidence. The Royal grandes dames could also have told her that the whole world would be fixated on her dress. Before the great reveal, however, there was the chance to see what everyone else was wearing. Sophie and Edward were keen to have a less formal occasion than the weddings of his elder siblings, so they opted for an early evening ceremony that meant no hats – although it seemed the Queen Mother did not get that memo. The ladies were allowed to wear a small, feathered headpiece in their hair and the Queen chose a lilac decoration that matched her understated yet very elegant gown. As well as dispensing with hats, the less formal occasion meant there was no need for anyone to be weighed down by full military dress and a chest full of medals. They had done that the week before at the Trooping of the Colour. Instead, the men wore tails without the top hats. Although it was widely described as a smaller, family occasion, there were still 550 guests – that was a dramatic reduction on the 3,500 who filled Westminster Abbey when Charles and Diana married in 1981. Other than the Queen, Prince Philip, Princess Margaret and the Queen Mum, the guests all arrived at the church in an imposing fleet of white minibuses.

Edward walked the short distance from Windsor Castle to the chapel with his older brothers on either side of him as if they were on their way to the finest society ball of the year – which in a way they were. Charles and Andrew were his 'supporters', the term the Royal Family always use instead of best man. The stroll only took five minutes but the trio were greeted by much cheering along the way. The bride and groom had specifically asked for an occasion without rows of politicians looking important or foreign princes and princesses who they hadn't met. One of the handful of guests from abroad was Edward's business backer, the Sultan of Brunei, who turned up with two of his wives. One glaring omission from the guest list was Fergie, although her young daughters, Beatrice and Eugenie, were invited. William and Harry were there too, on one of the rare occasions when they were not the centre of attention.

And then Sophie arrived in a Rolls-Royce. Her father Christopher looked distinguished and calm beside her. He was actually celebrating his sixty-eighth birthday. At the chapel steps everyone had a chance to see the dress properly as he sorted out his daughter's train with the help of her four small attendants who, for the first time at a royal wedding, were all 'commoners' and the children of close friends. The two pages were Felix Sowerbutts and Harry Warburton, while the two bridesmaids were Olivia Taylor and Edward's goddaughter, Camilla Hadden. Inside, Sophie's arrival was marked by the band of the Royal Marines striking up 'A Fanfare for Sophie', which had been composed for the occasion by David Cole, the former music director on the Royal Yacht *Britannia*, who achieved nationwide recognition when he took on that role for the Festival of Remembrance. She walked confidently up the aisle to the organ playing 'Marche Héroïque', which was written during the First World War by Herbert Brewer.

For the bride, Samantha Shaw had designed two garments in one – allowing Sophie to slip off the outer fitted coat dress to reveal a stunning ivory evening gown for the subsequent private evening reception. It was a triumph. Alison Jane Reid observed, 'The ensemble could not have been more different from Diana's controversial, over-the-top, *Gone with the Wind* meringue of a gown designed by David and Elizabeth Emanuel.' The coat for the aisle featured a striking V shape and was made from a flowing, hand-dyed, silk crepe with medieval-style fluted sleeves. The gown beneath consisted of a structured, ivory silk organza dress, hand-dyed to match the colour of the stone in the chapel. Samantha had made a secret trip to Windsor to study first-hand the exact shade of that stone.

The wedding gown and coat dress sparkled with 325,000 hand-stitched, cut-glass beads and pearls, which Samantha had used to embellish the neckline, back, sleeves and train. Alison Jane was impressed: 'It worked because it was regal, refined, contemporary and elegant, with exquisite detailing and tailoring – just right for a royal wedding gown.' The accessories were also well chosen, with a full-length veil and a pearl cross necklace that had been the wedding gift from Edward. Her now-famous and much-admired diamond, anthemion-motif tiara featured petal shapes that radiated as if they were delicate flowers. The diamonds were from antique pieces among the Queen's private collection, but the tiara was redesigned for Sophie, although the bride herself has always maintained a little mystery about its exact origins. It would become one of her most treasured possessions, which Sophie would wear many times in the future when she and Edward represented the monarch at royal weddings abroad. She was even reported to have had the piece remodelled for the state visit of Donald Trump to the Palace in 2019.

Edward gave a barely noticeable wink to his bride when she arrived at the altar, just to calm any nerves, but Sophie didn't show any – not outwardly at least. The forty-five-minute traditional religious service was conducted by the Right Reverend Peter Nott, who was soon to retire as Bishop of Norwich and whose diocese included Sandringham. Sophie's brother David read the lesson from the Gospel of St John. Neither Edward nor Sophie fluffed their lines. Unlike Diana at her wedding to Charles, Sophie decided she would promise to 'obey' Edward – a decision that pleased the Queen. The *Guardian* was unimpressed by her declaration, labelling it 'palpable misogyny'. Sophie had already dismissed the idea that the word meant a life of servitude, explaining, 'I am saying I trust him to take those decisions that will be good for us. It doesn't mean I am going to walk in his shadow or kow-tow.'

Edward had a small struggle slipping the gold wedding ring onto Sophie's finger. The gold for the ring had originally come from the aptly named Prince Edward mine in Trawsfynydd, in the Snowdonia National Park. After the service the couple slipped away quietly to sign the register in private before bowing and curtsying to the Queen on their way out – all done with great care. With the strains of Walton's 'Crown Imperial' coronation march resonating around the chapel, they posed for photographers on the steps. They declined to do the obvious and share a corny kiss which would have been reproduced the day after, and the year after and the year after that, for the rest of time. They were both in their mid-thirties but youthful smiles never seemed to leave their faces.

They left the church in an open horse-drawn carriage from which they waved to the crowd of 20,000 well-wishers who could glimpse Sophie's dress for the first time. The cheers for the couple were evidence that the enthusiasm for all things Royal Family still existed in a country beaten down by the bad news of a decade of 'annus horribilis'; there had been squidgygate, tampongate, Panoramagate, the Windsor Castle fire and, worst of all by far, Diana's tragic death. But here was the belle of Brenchley putting a smile back on everyone's faces – even the Queen radiated happiness.

In the state rooms at Windsor Castle, the couple posed with their close and wider family for the official wedding pictures taken by the society photographer and friend of the Queen, Sir Geoffrey Shakerley. He had taken the advice of his brother-in-law, Patrick Lichfield, and arrived with a

Life changed for ever when her romance with Edward became public. There always seemed to be a photographer. Nothing to smile about when she was pictured windsurfing in Cowes in July 1994.

At last – it's official! A truly happy smile when they pose for pictures at St James's Palace after announcing their engagement in January 1999.

The day after, still smiling – just – as police and paparazzi surround her on her way in to work.

Sophie looked beautiful on her wedding day, 19 June 1999.

The Queen was a stickler for formality but not so much where her favourite daughter-in-law was concerned. She even affectionately adjusts Sophie's hat before the Christmas Day Service at Sandringham Church in 2002.

After Sophie had a difficult time giving birth, the christening of Lady Louise at Windsor Castle in April 2004 was a chance to celebrate with the family. Sophie's beaming mother and father, Mary and Christopher, had a front-row seat on one side while the Queen and Prince Philip posed contentedly on the other.

Making a difference: at home – Sophie is cheered as she completes her marathon bike ride from Edinburgh to Buckingham Palace in September 2016. She raised more than £180,000 for the Duke of Edinburgh Diamond Jubilee Appeal

As the royal patron of Mencap, Sophie joined the charity's learning disability running team to run the first 1.5 miles of its Virtual London Marathon in Windsor Great Park, October 2020.

Getting an affectionate welcome from a puppy when she visited the National Guide Dog Centre in Leamington Spa, soon after becoming the charity's patron in 2021.

Sophie cuddles a very cute rabbit at the Countryside Education Trust in Beaulieu, Hampshire, in March 2023.

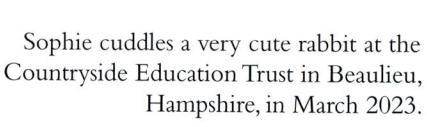

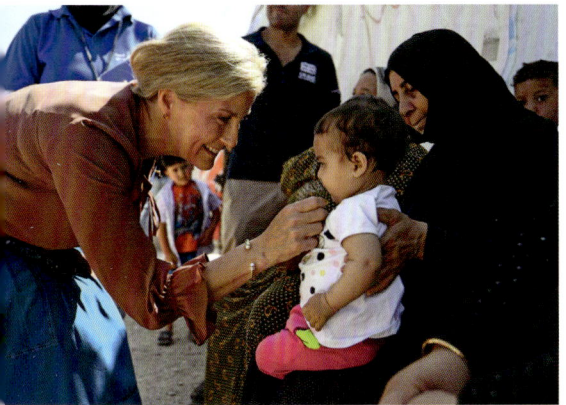

Making a difference: abroad – in 2019, Sophie was the first British Royal to visit Lebanon, where she met Syrian women and children refugees displaced by the conflict in their home country. She shared a tender moment with a baby at a settlement in Beqaa Valley.

Sophie travelled to Sierra Leone in 2020 to focus attention on sexual and gender based violence in war zones. She visited a health clinic that provided much-needed family planning and maternal care in a country where an estimated 20 per cent of all girls aged 15 to 19 are either pregnant or already have a child.

PA Images/Alamy Stock Photo

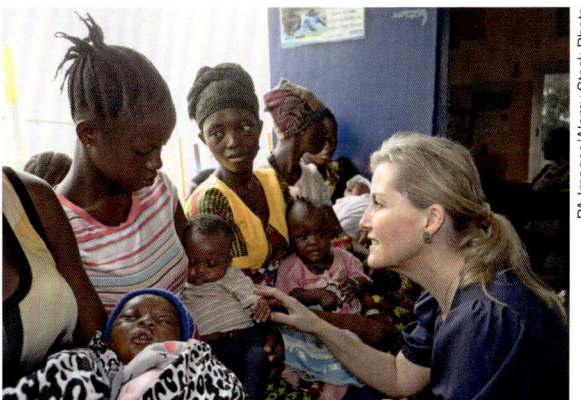

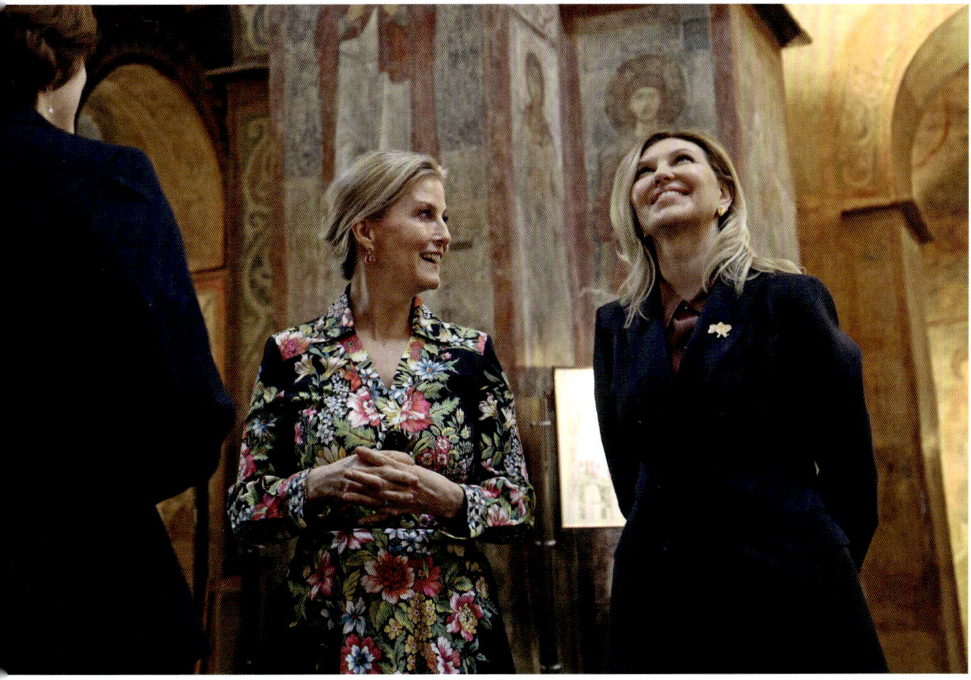

Continuing her vocal support for victims of conflict rape and sexual violence, she became the first Royal to visit Ukraine following the Russian invasion, in April 2024. She joined her friend First Lady Olena Zelenska to admire the aptly named Saint Sophia Cathedral in Kyiv.

Just like the late Queen, Sophie loves the annual visit to Royal Ascot and the carriage parade. She almost fell on her pal Kate in 2017, and the two Royal ladies dissolved into fits of laughter.

A year later, she was happy to keep Meghan company on her first trip down the course when everyone is checking out the royal hats.

Charles, Camilla and Sophie kept up the tradition in 2023 – although it looks as if none of them backed the winner.

The making of a Royal family: gradually, we've seen a little more of Edward and Sophie's children. Here, Louise and James join everyone for the traditional Trooping of the Colour fly-past on the Buckingham Palace balcony in June 2016.

Obeying the 'Rule of Six' during the Covid lockdown of September 2020, they take part in the Great British Beach Clean in Southsea.

Coronation Day, 6 May 2023 – with all the pomp and circumstance, you might think it was Edward and Sophie about to be crowned. Louise and James follow them down the aisle of Westminster Abbey.

Something in the way Sophie moves – having fun on the zebra crossing in Abbey Road made famous by the Beatles for the front cover of their iconic album of the same name.

bundle of phone books for the more diminutive guests to stand on so that they appeared taller and could clearly be seen if they were at the back: 'Patrick said, whatever you do, take telephone books. We didn't take enough. We took ten huge Yellow Pages that caused a certain amount of merriment – everybody standing on Yellow Pages.'

The telephone directories were not a problem, but Prince William was. He looked so miserable stood on the end of things. Edward mentioned this to Geoffrey, who found a happier snap from the day, in which William was smiling happily, and digitally imposed a new face on the glum one. Harry was standing immediately behind Princess Margaret, who had braved the day in a wheelchair having badly scalded her feet in a hot bath while holidaying three months before on her favourite Caribbean island of Mustique. One of the best smiles radiated from the face of Sophie's mother who was, quite simply, overjoyed.

Sophie took everything in her stride – after all, she had already negotiated the nerve-racking part of the day and this was no more than a very busy photocall, and she had organised many of those throughout her working life. Geoffrey recalled, 'She was incredibly relaxed and very natural, very easy, needed very, very little encouragement or direction from me.'

After the pictures, it was time to greet the guests for the receptions. Celebrities who had kept a very low profile continued to do so. They included Tom Jones, Robert Powell, Billy Connolly, Stephen Fry and John Travolta – a reward for being a good sport on *It's a Royal Knockout*. Andrew Lloyd Webber, who was now Lord Lloyd Webber, was there with his wife Madeleine, and Edward's former girlfriend Ruthie Henshall ensured that the West End theatre world he so loved was represented. At this stage she had not been indiscreet about their past relationship. The occasions may have been lower-key than usual for a royal wedding reception, but there were still 9,000 canapés to be served and enough beef stroganoff to feed a small army.

Edward made everyone chuckle – including his mum – when he thanked his 'host' at the start of his speech. He also described the Queen, touchingly, as 'perhaps the most wonderful mother in the world'. The ten-foot-tall chocolate wedding cake had seven tiers and, in an amusing, very Edward touch, was decorated with a pair of real tennis rackets. Unsurprisingly, Prince Philip, who loved a party, was one of the first to take to the dance floor. As if to prove that this really was as near to a normal wedding as the Royal Family could manage, the highlight of the dancing was everyone joining in for a chorus or two of 'YMCA'. After speaking to as many of the guests as they could manage, the newlyweds changed into their going-away clothes – Sophie in a cream suit and Edward in a dinner jacket and black tie. They sped off in a limo with heart-shaped balloons tied to the rear bumper.

Going away was not far. They were spending their first night as man and wife at Bagshot Park. The following day, Sophie's mother and father hosted a lunch party there, for which the Queen and Prince Philip popped over from the Castle. Mid-afternoon, Sophie and Edward watched a helicopter land in the garden to whisk them away on honeymoon. They had chosen the traditional royal destination of the Balmoral estate – recalling their lovely first holiday together when they were by themselves in the beautiful Highlands of Scotland. This time they spent an idyllic ten days at Birkhall, the summer home of the Queen Mother. They had planned to be away for only a week, but the weather was surprisingly sunny and the walks so wonderful they decided to stay a little longer before flying home. As Sophie had said, there was much work to be done on the house and garden – and she had a living to earn.

Sophie had been at pains to point out in pre-wedding interviews that she and Edward had never actually lived together, although they had spent many nights next to one another. One aspect of their lives that did not change when they moved into Bagshot Park was that they kept separate bedrooms. At least there were no corgis for Edward to avoid on his way back to his own room to enjoy his early morning cup of tea and biscuits brought at daybreak by his valet, Brian.

Hello! magazine, which had always stood firmly behind Sophie, produced a special edition with many lovely pictures of her wedding day. The headline on the front cover: PRINCE EDWARD MARRIES HIS SOPHIE. She may have promised to 'obey' Edward, but Sophie, HRH, The Countess of Wessex, was definitely not his possession.

15

Fake News

An epithalamium, for those not familiar with that tongue-twister, is a poem or song specially written to celebrate a marriage. Sophie and Edward had one provided for them by the new Poet Laureate, Andrew Motion. He had only been in the prestigious position since 1 May 1999, following the death the year before of the previous incumbent, Ted Hughes. Andrew wrote a lyrical twelve lines that critics immediately recognised as a coded message to the newspapers to leave the couple alone. He wrote that the vows included hope 'for privacy and what its secrets show'.

After the upset of the topless picture, perhaps the newly-weds hoped they would be spared negative attention from the tabloid press. That would prove not to be the case. An apology in the paper does not mean that you are going to be ignored in the future; it took less than three months for the knives to come out again – this time over the suggestion that Sophie was using her royal position to secure profitable business for R-JH. The catalyst for the new flurry of stories was when she posed next to a gleaming new maroon Rover 75 at the Frankfurt Motor Show, having reportedly secured a £250,000 contract to publicise it.

That storm was easily weathered, but it was an early

indication of the difficulty Sophie faced in business: her new position inevitably would open doors and possibilities. For the next year or so, however, R-JH progressed rapidly. Turnover in 2000 was estimated at about £650,000, which was expected to reach £1 million in 2001. Both Sophie and Murray were paid a salary of close to £100,000, according to published accounts: the business could hardly have been doing better – and then along came the Fake Sheikh and everything Sophie had worked for was ruined in a trice.

The Fake Sheikh was the jolly media nickname for the investigative reporter Mazher Mahmood, the Birmingham-born son of two journalists from Pakistan who had arrived in England three years before his birth in 1963. He was a first-generation British Asian of Punjabi heritage and not remotely Arab, but his mainly white targets could not tell the difference, it seemed.

He had worked for both the *Sunday People* newspaper and the *Sunday Times* before joining the *News of the World* at the start of the 1990s. By the end of that decade he was one of the best-known journalists in the country, but nobody knew what he looked like as he carefully avoided his picture being revealed in any publication. He even had a clause written into his contract that his picture could not be used, and was rarely seen at the newspaper's offices in Wapping. He was named Reporter of the Year at the British Press Awards in 1999 for his exposé of two Newcastle United FC bosses, but had never taken aim at a member of the Royal Family.

The original target of the sting was reportedly Murray Harkin, but it soon escalated into the story of the year when Sophie became involved. She was apparently lured into the web of deceit by the carrot of a £20,000-a-month contract for two years with the bogus sheikh referred to in that persona as His Highness. His work colleagues called him Maz.

The first contact, set up by the notorious Max Clifford (jailed 2014, sex offences), was between a disgruntled R-JH account manager and the *News of the World*, at which point Mahmood became part of the story. He very much liked to set things up, working alone with his own squad of people coordinated by the paper's news editor Greg Miskiw (jailed 2014, phone hacking).

Posing as a sheikh who wanted to open an international sports facility in Dubai – a suggestion almost guaranteed to interest a firm run by Sophie, who was so adept at promoting sport – he set up a couple of meetings with Murray at expensive hotels in Park Lane. Apparently, they met in a suite that had cost Mahmood £1,295 to hire for the day. That was one of the canniest things about his sting operations – the appearance of wealth encourages confidence and indiscretion; traditional Arab dress would be accessorised by an expensive Rolex watch.

Transcripts that later appeared in the press reveal that Murray was unguarded in his conversation as he 'schmoozed' the potential new client. He mentioned fashionable gay clubs in London, ecstasy and cocaine, although it wasn't anything wild enough to make a self-respecting rock band jealous. His most indiscreet remark, however, came when the Fake Sheikh asked him about the rumours of Edward's sexuality. He responded, 'There have been rumours for years about Edward. I'm a great believer that there's no smoke without fire. He's not what you expect!'

Another meeting was arranged, at the Dorchester Hotel; imagine His Highness's surprise and delight when Sophie walked through the door. This time the quietly spoken Fake Sheikh was wearing a smart suit. He and Sophie proceeded to chat as if they were sitting next to each other at a cosy dinner party in Chelsea. She had no idea that the conversation was being recorded, and had something to say about literally everything. In retrospect her comments about Tony and Cheri Blair, William Hague (although she did a terrific impersonation of his flat delivery of speech) and John Major are less interesting than her insight into Charles and Camilla. She defended Charles as a fun and relaxed father: 'He's a man who has always been ahead of his years. He was damned as a complete quack. People laughed at him for his views on architecture but now they are starting to take notice.' She also hinted that Charles and Camilla might marry after the death of the Queen Mother. She observed, 'It's a very difficult situation. On the one hand there's no reason why she shouldn't be accepted because he's divorced and she's divorced, but then again you've got issues of the monarch being the head of the Church.'

She also returned to the subject of Diana and how the public wanted to make her 'the new Diana' but realised that would never work: 'They thought "this isn't going to be much good because she's not going to be turning up every day in different outfits, opening children's hospitals." I do some of that but not as much of that as they'd like.'

Everything was very friendly and informal, and Sophie was happy that a deal had been sealed by the time she returned to the R-JH office in Mayfair. By mid-afternoon her smile had vanished. A concerned member of staff at the *News of the World* had called up to tell her what had happened.

Desperate attempts to remedy the catastrophe were set in motion. They included lawyers for R-JH rushing to the High Court to secure an injunction against the company's now ex-employee to prevent him from revealing or publishing anything further. The Palace machine went into overdrive to try to soothe the *News of the World* and the paper's editor, Rebekah Wade, as Rebekah Brooks was known professionally then. As a result, Sophie was made available for an exclusive interview with a feature writer on the paper, Carole Aye Maung, in return for handing over the 'Sophie tapes', as they were now being called.

Much to everyone's surprise, Sophie was actually more interesting and forthcoming than she had been to the Fake Sheikh. She spoke of not having children yet at the age of thirty-six: 'I certainly do not think that I have left it too late. I would explore all avenues and I certainly wouldn't rule out IVF.'

She addressed the rumours about Edward's sexuality: 'I had heard something before we met, but I put it down to the fact that he was working in theatre and people had presumed he was gay. I never believed it – so it wasn't something that crossed my mind when I met him. How I'd love to be able to go out and sing from the rooftops: it is not true! I want to prove it to people but it's impossible to do that.'

The interview spawned the unforgettable headline in the *News of the World*, MY EDWARD IS NOT GAY! The agreement with the paper, however, was not a quiet end to the matter because the original Fake Sheikh transcript was leaked to the *Mail on Sunday*. The story, it seemed, was going to run and run. Sophie did not help matters by writing a personal letter of apology to the Blairs, William Hague, Charles and the Queen. The thought was well-meaning but could be interpreted as Sophie admitting she had been in the wrong. She suggested to the Queen that she might leave R-JH immediately. The Queen had readily agreed that it was a good idea. Murray Harkin resigned, too. They had both unintentionally flouted the first rule of PR – never become the story yourself.

Before she set off for the Dorchester that sunny May morning, her company was valued at £3.5 million. Sophie would have soon been a millionaire. Now you would be hard pressed to give it away. The *Observer* summed up the sheikh storm memorably: 'It apparently involves The Queen, her children, the Prime Minister's wife, cocaine, prostitutes, hundreds of thousands of pounds and a man posing as a sheikh who puts on a funny accent. As tabloid journalists say, you couldn't make it up.'

Murray Harkin was a little-publicised casualty of what happened. While Sophie could retreat behind the formidable gates of Bagshot Park, he had to contend with the clicking of cameras every time he opened the door of his south London home. He left the country and spent a year in Sydney, Australia, before coming back to the UK and starting over. He told *PR Week*, five years later: 'I chose a strategy which was really stupid, which was not to say anything and hope it would go away. But it didn't.' He added with disarming honesty: 'It took me many years to stop shaking every time I picked up a newspaper or to stop looking over my shoulder.'

With hindsight, Sophie did not do much wrong. Helping to seal one of the biggest contracts R-JH had won was looking after the interests of her company. She could not possibly have known she was being set up by a consummate professional, even if it all seems a bit Alan Partridge from a distance. She did not divulge any state secrets, offer the Fake Sheikh any drugs, talk about 'shagging' in the Palace or offer to match-fix a game of real tennis. She was just having a pretty innocuous gossip that the whole world seemed to think was far more important than it actually was. Murray Harkin had even referred to her in a sweet way during his own conversation with Mahmood. The thirty-something Sophie was very different from the twenty-something version: 'Sophie is just the most purest thing you've ever seen. She hardly ever drinks, bless her. The odd occasion she goes out with a star at Christmas she used to let her hair down and drink. She used to get hammered on three glasses of champagne.'

The most memorable words of the whole conversation

between Sophie and the Fake Sheikh were when she referred to the Queen, pretty harmlessly, as the 'old dear'. The throwaway line could have been so much worse if she had called her the 'old dragon' or the 'old battleaxe'. In reality, it was just a sweet way of describing her mother-in-law, who she called 'Mama' in private – just as Edward did. Mazher Mahmood had not finished with the Royal Family. He found Princess Michael of Kent an easy target in 2005. Apparently, she was far less delicate than Sophie had been, describing Diana as a 'bitter' and 'nasty' woman. She also predicted correctly that Camilla would one day be Queen. The Fake Sheikh wrote that her 'deeply offensive remarks' constituted an 'appalling act of betrayal' to the Royal Family.

Without fuss, Sophie did not completely desert R-JH after falling victim to the sting. While Murray was never seen again in the Mayfair HQ and lost all contact with his former business partner, the R-J half did not want to leave the staff shipwrecked. The company was her 'baby' and she continued to attend board meetings even though she was no longer on the payroll. One report suggested she was on the phone to the office two or three times a week; it never recovered from the trauma of the Fake Sheikh sting, however, and within five years a tortuous winding-up process began that was completed by liquidators in 2009. The *Daily Mail* said its debts amounted to £1.7 million.

By then Edward had also stepped down at Ardent Productions after a saga that would prove almost as embarrassing as the Sophie tapes. His nephew, Prince William, had gone up to the University of St Andrews as an undergraduate in September 2001. For the first week or so, he was very wary of any media that might be lurking, even though the university's Lord Rector, Andrew Neil, the former editor of the *Sunday Times*, had brokered a deal that he could be left alone to enjoy university life. The agreement was not just for

William's benefit but also for that of the other students around him, both on his art history course and in his residential block, St Salvator's Hall, more commonly referred to as Sallies. They included Kate Middleton, 'Beautiful Kate' as she was nicknamed, whose room was two floors below William's. They had yet to meet, but at least she would benefit from not having a member of the press nonchalantly trying to buy her a drink in one of the town's bars.

Hilariously, the agreement was broken not by one of the tabloid newspapers but by his own uncle, Prince Edward. William was understandably much aggrieved to discover that a television crew was trying to film him and his fellow undergraduates after all the other media had, as agreed, left the town. When his security intervened, it was discovered that they worked for Ardent. Apparently, they were shooting a television show for America called *The A–Z of Royalty*, which would be a welcome financial boost for Edward's company. Edward was forced to apologise after his elder brother, Charles, phoned him and, according to one report, shouted at the top of his voice that he was a 'fucking idiot'.

Mark Bolland, who was responsible for William's press at that time, observed with masterly understatement: 'Nobody expected it to be a family member who would breach the embargo.' Andrew Neil added, 'You just couldn't make it up. It set a terrible example for the rest of the media.'

As a result of this embarrassment, both Edward and Sophie took stock of their lives and made the decision – with more than a little encouragement and financial help from Mama – that they would give up their efforts to make a commercial success away from the umbrella of the Royal Family. What a disastrous year it had been! They did not know that before the end of 2001 they would face a crisis that made everything else seem totally unimportant.

16

Air Ambulance

Having a child was a priority for Sophie, even before she was married. In the run-up to her wedding, and without fuss, she would slip into Central London to visit the clinic of the woman known as the 'baby whisperer'. Zita West believed in a non-white-coat approach and concentrated on wellbeing to enhance the prospects of a client becoming pregnant. She was also completely discreet. The two women forged a strong bond, helped by Zita declaring that their friendship was 'very private'.

Sophie could stroll the half mile between the R-JH offices in Mayfair to Zeta's clinic in Marylebone, where she had advised Kate Winslet, Cate Blanchett, Ulrika Jonsson and Princess Diana. The 'natural therapies' included Pilates, yoga, general birth counselling and acupuncture, which particularly interested Sophie. Zita, a midwife by profession, believed that a mindset approach was just as important as a medical one and would tailor suggested treatments individually. Sophie was so impressed that she quietly became a director of Zita West Products Ltd when it started up in the autumn of 2000. The company was the mail-order arm of the clinic, supplying pregnancy therapies and vitamin supplements.

A year later, Sophie and Edward did not rush to tell anyone

that she was expecting their first child. She was just six weeks pregnant so there was plenty of time to let everybody know the good news. At the start of 2001 she had spoken of their desire to start a family: 'One of each would be nice,' she said, adding, 'It's amazing how many friends have had problems, either conceiving or losing children.'

It was December, a month before her thirty-seventh birthday; this was the Christmas present the couple had longed for and one that would cast the horrible times of the Fake Sheikh and the St Andrews debacle into the dustbin of memories, but then, on a dull Wednesday night, Sophie started to suffer serious stomach pains. By the early hours of the morning, she was literally doubled up in agony and, in a frantic state, woke her husband.

Edward acted decisively. He called Dr Richard Thompson, head of the Queen's medical staff, who immediately suspected she might be experiencing an ectopic pregnancy – a condition where the fertilised egg implants itself outside the womb, usually in a fallopian tube. Sometimes this can be corrected naturally, but not in cases where the woman is in sudden and absolute pain. Dr Thompson called the Thames Valley and Chiltern Air Ambulance and the distinctive red helicopter was despatched from Maidenhead and landed on the lawn of Bagshot Park.

Sophie was whisked off for immediate surgery at the King Edward VII's Hospital, just 500 yards from Zita's clinic in Marylebone. She was in theatre for three hours and required five pints of blood. The full paramedic team in the helicopter meant there was no room for Edward, so he drove himself to London, stopping off at Buckingham Palace to tell the Queen and Prince Philip what had happened before continuing on to the private hospital. For once, dramatic reports that Sophie's condition was life-threatening were not over the top. If left untreated, it would have been very serious.

As it was, a statement from Buckingham Palace saying that she was 'comfortable' was medically true, but the reality was that Sophie was distraught. One of her close friends said, 'It has been a year of hell for them both and it has ended in a dreadfully personal and tragic way. The Countess is terribly, terribly upset.' The BBC's renowned royal correspondent Jennie Bond revealed that Sophie had been very tearful after her operation.

Edward did his best to support his wife, clutching a beautiful bouquet of cream and lilac lilies for her and spending an hour and a half by her bedside, sharing her sadness. Afterwards, outside the hospital he bravely, yet haltingly, addressed the media: 'It's obviously a very traumatic time and my wife has . . . It's quite the most painful thing anyone can undergo. It's a pretty traumatic experience. As the pain reduces, so the relief will increase.'

The press sped off to doorstep Sophie's parents in Kent, only to discover they had moved. They had sold Homestead Farmhouse earlier in the year for £600,000 and bought a four-bedroom detached property ten miles away in the equally picturesque village of Benenden. Both Christopher and Mary had reached retirement age and downsizing to the new house would free up some capital as well as being easier to manage and maintain while being close enough to keep in touch with their long-standing friends. The house was still big enough to entertain friends and enjoy weekend visits from their children, but it was more practical because of some early concerns over the health of Sophie's mother.

Sophie's father politely answered enquiries: 'You can imagine our worry,' he said before setting off with Mary to visit their daughter in hospital. Afterwards he was as courteous as ever, telling journalists, 'She is fine but a bit tired. Thanks very much for your concern.' Sophie was obviously very weak after her ordeal but a statement was issued on her behalf from the hospital: 'I am obviously very sad but it was just not meant to be. But there will be other chances. The nurses have been unbelievably fantastic.' Her assertion that there would be other opportunities showed she was not giving up on her ambition to start a family.

While she rested in hospital she was inundated with messages of good will and sympathy, including one from Princess Anne and another from Tiggy Legge-Bourke who was now called Tiggy Pettifer, having married security consultant Charles Pettifer in the same year as Edward and Sophie's wedding. She was still very much part of the Palace family and sent Sophie a box of chocolates.

Sophie was kept in hospital for a few days before being allowed to go home to Bagshot Park with strict instructions to take it easy because recovery was expected to be at least six weeks. Her sadness would take longer to cast aside, and Christmas 2001 was not a jolly affair.

The Queen rallied round her son and daughter-in-law, but she would soon be facing further upsetting news. Just a few weeks into the New Year, Princess Margaret had a fourth stroke and died peacefully in her sleep at the same hospital. She had been a heavy smoker all her life and endured many years of deteriorating health since her first stroke in 1998 in her beloved Mustique.

Sophie was well enough to join Edward for the funeral service, a much more sombre occasion at St George's Chapel than her wedding had been. The Queen openly wept. Unusually for a member of the Royal Family, Margaret was cremated and her ashes returned to rest in the chapel. Her mother, the Queen Mum, a centenarian aged 101, had been flown to Windsor by helicopter from Sandringham where she was recovering from a fall. She was in a wheelchair but was determined not to miss her younger daughter's farewell, which poignantly was on the fiftieth anniversary of the funeral of her husband, King George VI. She insisted that no photographs be taken of her being pushed into the chapel in a wheelchair.

Just six weeks later, Queen Elizabeth the Queen Mother died peacefully in her sleep at the Royal Lodge, Windsor. The Queen had been able to say goodbye at her bedside and this time there were many tears in private. Her coffin lay in state at Westminster Hall before a full state funeral at Westminster Abbey. Some estimates suggested 200,000 people had filed past the coffin to pay their respects. The Queen issued a touching, personal statement: 'Over the years I have met many people who have had to cope with family loss, sometimes in the most tragic of circumstances. So I count myself fortunate that my mother was blessed with a long and happy life. She had an infectious zest for living and this remained with her until the very end.'

On her coffin was a framed sheet of Buckingham Palace notepaper containing the handwritten words: 'In Loving Memory ... Lilibet', which was the affectionate family nickname for the Queen. Her father had started calling her that when she had trouble pronouncing her own name, and it stuck.

Sophie was at the funeral, again supporting Edward but keeping a very low profile. The presence of Camilla Parker Bowles was of wider interest at the time. She did not sit with Charles but was shown quietly to a seat away from the Royal Family. She sat next to her long-time friend Lady Sarah Keswick, the mother-in-law of Samantha Keswick, Sophie's wedding dress maker. Long-standing royal observer Richard

Kay described Camilla's invitation as a 'watershed' moment. She had spent half an hour with the Queen and Charles at the Palace at which it was decided this was the right time for her to be absorbed into things. The private conversation was only the second meeting between the two women – the Queen had been reluctant to acknowledge Camilla officially but had agreed to be seated at the same table for the dinner at Highgrove that celebrated the sixtieth birthday of the exiled King Constantine II of Greece. That had been a huge step forward and this was another.

After the funeral, the Queen Mother was interred at St George's Chapel next to her husband. Camilla travelled to Scotland to be reunited with Charles at Birkhall, which he had inherited on his grandmother's death. Edward and Sophie knew from their honeymoon there that it was the perfect place to get away from it all.

Sophie and Edward went home to Bagshot Park to consider their future. The good news was that the Queen had eased their short-term financial concerns by agreeing to pay them an estimated £250,000 a year from the Civil List. Now known as the Sovereign Grant, this is the money allocated to the monarch every year from government taxation to fund all things royal. This wage would enable the couple to concentrate on official duties assigned by Buckingham Palace. In effect, from being their own bosses they would now be well-paid employees. They both needed to work hard to justify that expense paid for by the Crown, however.

Ironically, Sophie's thoughts about her future role when they became engaged would need to change. Then, she had declared confidently, 'I see my role as a supporting one to Edward rather than rushing off and forging my own path and taking on various charities. The Queen and the rest of the Royal Family do an exceptional job in a public role anyway and I don't see a massive need to go out there and do the same thing.'

Sophie began to realise that she could actually do more than give token support to the charities and services that personally helped her or those that were close to her. Top of that list was the Air Ambulance Service, whose prompt and decisive action had probably saved her life. She and Edward attended a fundraising dinner where she could personally thank the pilot, Andy Busby, and the lead paramedic, Tim Goddard, for their help with her own personal emergency. Her support for air ambulances around the country has not wavered over the years and she was very encouraging as Aunt Sophie to Prince William when he became a pilot for the East Anglian Air Ambulance service in 2015. Her gratitude to the service that had saved her continued over the years, culminating in Sophie becoming patron of the Thames Valley Air Ambulance service in 2019. By then she could share a joke with crew and generally be in good humour, having parked personal experience at home before adopting a royal cloak.

More immediately, she took over one of Princess Margaret's favourite charities by becoming the new president of Girlguiding UK, a position the princess had held for thirty-seven years. The Queen's sister had been a Brownie, Guide and a Ranger, and had been an enthusiastic supporter, as was the Queen and the Queen Mother. Sophie, too, had been a Brownie in Kent, so this was a good choice to start her off in the world of royal patronage.

The Queen was particularly pleased, believing Sophie to be a good choice for continuing her late sister's legacy. The press had never quite conveyed the affection between the Queen and her younger sister, who had grown up together during the nation's bleakest times of the Second World War. Margaret had actually been a Girl Guide during the war while her sister, four years older, served in the Auxiliary Territorial Service (ATS). Sophie was proud to be asked to succeed the princess as president of the Guides, by then called Girlguiding UK, while the Queen remained as royal patron of the association. The four charities that benefited from funeral donations after Margaret's death were the Girl Guides, the National Society for the Prevention of Cruelty to Children, the Royal Ballet and the Royal Opera House. Sophie has long been a supporter of all four and took over as patron of the NSPCC when the Queen stepped down following her ninetieth birthday.

One aspect of royal life that Sophie was becoming used to was that something lamentable or horrid would be followed speedily by a celebration that cheered up the nation. The sad first few months of 2002 were forgotten – or at least put to one side – as celebrations were soon under way for the Queen's Golden Jubilee. The highlight for many was the Party at the Palace, held at Buckingham Palace on a warm evening in early June. Perhaps fortunately, Edward was not asked to organise it. Instead, Sir George Martin, the esteemed Beatles producer, and the equally acknowledged Phil Ramone, who at the age of ten had played violin for the then Princess Elizabeth, were brought in as consultants. The highlight for many of the 12,000 people watching from Buckingham Palace Gardens was Queen guitarist Brian May blasting out the national anthem from the roof of the Palace. It was an unforgettable rock-star moment. Brian recalled he was terrified before he played: 'I thought, if I mess up "God Save the Queen" in front of a billion people on TV then that will be what I am remembered for – the guy who messed up.' He didn't.

Sophie was one of twenty members of the Royal Family who gathered on the Palace balcony to watch a fly-past and acknowledge thousands of flag wavers – never was a jubilee better named. The two princes, William and Harry, stood together, looking youthful and handsome. Sophie was standing a little uncertainly between Harry and Edward.

This was the public face of Sophie. Privately, she had not lost her desire to start a family, and under the expert supervision of Marcus Setchell, the royal gynaecologist, she began IVF treatment. Her ectopic pregnancy may have reduced the chances of a natural conception, so IVF seemed a sensible option for Sophie, now thirty-seven. Charles had two children, so did both Anne and Andrew, so Sophie could be forgiven for thinking she and Edward needed to get cracking. She had also told friends that children had helped both Diana and Fergie cope with the inevitable sense of isolation that being a royal wife might bring – especially as she had stopped going into the office and being sociable every day.

The first two IVF treatments were not successful, but Sophie and Edward did not give up. Perhaps it would be third time lucky?

17

Shock and Delight

L ightning struck for the second time when Edward was in Mauritius. Sophie was at home watching Saturday night television when just after 8pm she started to suffer agonising stomach pains. At least she knew it wasn't an ectopic pregnancy. She only had six weeks to go before the baby was due and everything had gone so well that she didn't mind that Edward had had to go to the beautiful island in the Indian Ocean. She didn't even know the sex of the baby she was expecting. They had both asked not to be told when she had undergone the routine scans and checks over the preceding months.

Marcus Setchell, realised immediately how serious this might be and arranged rapidly for Sophie to be taken by ambulance six miles away to Frimley Park Hospital, just off the M3. Unfortunately, there was some sort of mix-up and the ambulance took half an hour to arrive, but then it was all sirens blaring as an armed police motorcyclist accompanied the vehicle as it hurtled down the motorway. On arrival, Sophie was rushed into theatre for an emergency caesarean to deliver the baby as quickly as possible because she was showing all the signs of acute placental abruption, the medical term for when the placenta has separated from the uterus. The effect on the mother-to-be was a substantial loss of blood. Sophie's condition was so bad that neither she nor the baby might have survived.

Marcus had called the Palace press secretary, Ailsa Anderson, in case disaster struck and she was needed to handle things. She was in the middle of a dinner party but dropped everything when the doctor said he was in a police car on his way to Frimley Park. Ailsa recalled, 'I thought "Crikey!".' When she too arrived at the hospital, there seemed to be more security officers and courtiers patrolling the corridors than nurses.

Edward and Sophie's daughter was born on 8 November 2005 weighing just 4lb 9oz and was hastily taken to a specialist baby unit at St George's Hospital in Tooting. The as-yet-unnamed girl was the first royal baby to be born in an NHS hospital. Sophie had no idea the baby had been taken away as the battle continued to save her life and she slipped in and out of consciousness, this time requiring a transfusion of nine pints of blood. Once again, the newspapers were not being overdramatic when they said Sophie was fifteen minutes from death.

Her parents rushed up from Kent to see her. Afterwards, Christopher reassured everyone that Sophie was 'absolutely fine' after her ordeal. He added, 'She's heavily sedated and rather sleepy but she is perfectly OK. The baby is also fine.' Edward took the first commercial flight out of Mauritius. He wasn't on holiday but was representing the Queen on an official visit to mark Remembrance Day. He arrived back in London via Paris the following evening after more than twelve hours in the air, not yet aware of how close his wife had been to dying. He was shaken to discover the severity of his baby's daughter's birth and that she was in a specialist unit and not with her mother.

A Buckingham Palace spokesman confirmed, 'It was a routine precaution to transfer the baby to a neonatal unit. She is a very small baby.'

After dashing to Sophie's bedside and discovering all that had happened, Edward spoke to the press outside the hospital: 'First of all, I am rather shocked and delighted at the news, obviously very sorry that I was not able to be part of it. I have seen Sophie, she is doing well – she has also had a bit of a fraught time of it.' That was an understatement. He then sped off to see his daughter, a first meeting that left him 'thrilled to bits'.

The Queen and the rest of the Royal Family had taken part that day in the official ceremony at the Cenotaph that marked Remembrance Sunday every year in November. Two days later, Her Majesty unveiled the Australian War Memorial in Hyde Park. Edward was excused from the Royal schedule for a week as he shuttled the thirty-five miles between mother and baby. On the Friday, doctors were happy for baby to travel back to Frimley Park to be reunited with Sophie, whose recovery was progressing slowly.

Edward was very professional in dealing with the enormous interest from reporters and photographers. He was overjoyed that they were all together at last and spent more than three hours at his wife's bedside. He made sure he thanked the staff at both hospitals when he spoke to the media on his way out. He said, 'The important thing is that this has been a fantastic day in our lives, a day of great relief and it's difficult to explain what it is to be together as a family for the first time.' He described the baby proudly as 'cute and cuddly'.

The Queen was sufficiently concerned that she broke with traditional protocol and made a hospital visit to see how Sophie and her latest grandchild were getting along. Zita

West was another who made her way to her bedside to see how mother and baby were doing. Sophie was kept in hospital for sixteen days before she was considered well enough to travel the short distance back to Bagshot Park to continue her recuperation. She posed with Edward, who was holding their daughter carefully in his arms as they left. Sophie smiled for the cameras and looked ready for her close-up, which was remarkable after everything she had been through.

Four days after she returned home, Buckingham Palace announced the baby's names. She had four: Louise, Alice, Elizabeth and Mary. Louise was a favourite name of Sophie's and did have numerous royal connections around Europe. Louise was also the great-grandmother of Prince Philip, who did rather well in the naming of his latest grandchild: Louise was also the female equivalent of Louis, one of his names and also that of the late Lord Mountbatten; Alice was the name of his mother, Princess Alice of Battenberg; Elizabeth was, of course, his wife, the Queen. Mary was chosen to honour Sophie's mum but was also a name with a long regal history. Louise was also the first newborn member of the Royal Family to have the surname of Mountbatten-Windsor.

Sophie was not exactly a changed person when she returned home, but she did become very protective of her baby and her family's privacy as she came to terms with what had happened to her. She could have been forgiven for thinking it was all an injustice because she had been so careful when the third round of IVF had proved successful – giving up horse-riding and official duties for the first few months of pregnancy and making sure she followed the received wisdom for any woman expecting a baby in her late thirties. She had not been feeling poorly at all and just two days before the emergency she had been pictured well and very pregnant in a beige trouser suit when she officially opened the new

City of London headquarters of Childline. Sophie would go on to have a long association with the counselling charity for children founded in 1986 by Esther Rantzen, who was with her to cut the ribbon.

Back home after her hospital ordeal, she needed time to cope with her own exhaustion and to bond with Louise – she barely left her baby's side in the coming weeks – but there was further concerning news three months later. Premature babies may sometimes be at greater risk of eye conditions and Louise was diagnosed with esotropia, a form of strabismus in which one eye, her left, was turning inwards. Sophie was reluctant for her baby to face any treatment so soon and it would be a year or two before her daughter had corrective surgery. Two operations would eventually correct the eye – the first when eighteen months old, was only partially successful but a second, aged ten, dramatically improved things for her. Two years after that Sophie was relieved and confident enough to explain publicly on World Sight Day, 'The squint was quite profound when she was tiny and it takes time to correct it. You've got to make sure one eye doesn't become more dominant than the other, but she's fine now. Her eyesight is perfect.'

One of the key motivations for Sophie over the years has been using personal experience to guide her interest and support as a member of the Royal Family. She quietly lends her patronage to causes that matter to her and her family, both at home and abroad. Her experience with Lady Louise has made her a committed global ambassador for the International Agency for the Prevention of Blindness (IAPB), a role she takes seriously, not wanting to just be a token figurehead, having also visited programmes across the world for sight-saving charities such as Orbis.

The memory of the birth traumas never left Sophie. In

2014, she went back to open a new neonatal ward at Frimley Park Hospital and broke down in tears as she met and thanked the midwives who had helped to save her life. She explained, 'For the first ten years after Louise was born, I found it very hard to go to "prem" wards. It would bring the whole thing back, but I've learned to cope.'

The Queen was hugely sympathetic to everything Sophie and Louise were going through, and made a significant gesture of both public and private welcome to the Royal Family. Her seventh grandchild was just six months old when she was given a historic honour and dressed for her baptism in the Honiton christening gown – commissioned in 1841 by Queen Victoria for her firstborn child, also called Victoria, the Princess Royal, who would later become Queen of Prussia. Sixty-two royal children had worn it, including the Queen herself, her children and her grandchildren. But Louise would be the last. After her christening, the beautiful yet delicate gown was officially retired and a replica made for subsequent arrivals.

Patrick Lichfield took the christening photographs in one of his last commissions before his death the following year. The official portrait showed Edward and Sophie seated at the front with baby Louise on Sophie's lap. The Queen and Prince Philip were on one side while Mary and Christopher Rhys-Jones were on the other. The five godparents standing behind included Lady Sarah Chatto, who is also godmother to Prince Harry. She was a good example of a mum within the Royal Family who kept her children – two sons – well away from the limelight. Sophie was determined to do the same.

Sadly, Sophie's mother, Mary, missed out on seeing her grandchildren grow up – a source of great regret for Sophie. She died before Sophie had given birth a second time. Mary was taken ill in the spring of 2005, when Louise was only eighteen months old, and died in the August. She had been receiving treatment for cancer of the colon. Sophie was by her bedside at the Kent and Sussex Hospital in Tunbridge Wells when she passed.

Her memorial service was held at St George's Parish Church in Benenden, with prayers led by the Rt Revd Peter Nott, who had been in charge at Edward and Sophie's wedding. The turnout at the local church was huge, a tribute to a woman who was a very popular and sociable member of the community for many years. Edward and David Rhys-Jones both gave readings.

As with her feelings towards the air ambulance services and Frimley Park Hospital, it took Sophie a few years to share her deep sense of loss with the public. She would later say of her mum: 'I miss her very much and there are moments where I hear some music she loved or I do something I know she'd have wanted to hear about, which makes her early departure very hard.

'She has missed out on so much and I'm particularly sad that she hasn't seen my children grow up or seen how my work has grown and developed.' Mary had been worried for her daughter's future when she joined the Royal Family, fearing that her marriage might go the same way as Diana's or Fergie's. She needn't have been concerned.

18

A New Arrival

Sophie and Edward hadn't exactly given up but they were certainly taking a break from IVF and the stress and disappointment that came their way. They had a beautiful little girl and she was about to start infant school when Sophie discovered she was pregnant again, this time without any medical help.

As another gesture of thanks, Sophie decided to have the baby – again by caesarean section – at Frimley Park Hospital. He was born on 17 December 2007 and weighed in at 6lb 2oz, which was a relief. At the time of his birth he was eighth in line to the throne, having relegated his elder sister, who had, by then, turned four, into ninth place.

Just five weeks later, the baby was rushed to Great Ormond Street Hospital for Children in Bloomsbury after suffering a nasty allergic reaction. He needed twenty-four hours of tests, which were no fun for him – or his parents – and was diagnosed to be suffering from lactose intolerance. Fortunately, because he had been taken to hospital so quickly, there were no lasting effects. Just as she had done supporting air ambulance and sight charities, Sophie was motivated by personal experience to do as much as she could to help raise funds for Great Ormond Street.

Both Sophie and Edward were discovering that it wasn't at all easy navigating a path to parenthood and beyond. The prince put a brave face on things in public, even keeping up with his busy schedule. He travelled to the Midlands to open a new high school in Bromsgrove. He reassured the head, Paul Copeland, that he wasn't particularly worried and it was being played up a bit in the press. Paul recalled, 'We thought he might not come but when we saw him arrive, we thought it was fantastic.'

The christening again took place at Windsor Castle. This time the Queen, smiling broadly, was standing between Prince Philip and Christopher Rhys-Jones. Sophie had Lady Louise perched on her lap while Edward held his little boy, who they called James Alexander Philip Theo. He would also be styled Viscount Severn, one of Edward's secondary titles that can only be passed down the male line. Louise continued as Lady. She never minded as she obviously doted on her new little brother. One observer noticed: 'She kisses him and cuddles him and is a real little mother to him. It's lovely.'

Prince Andrew was there but Charles and Camilla decided not to travel down from Scotland for the happy occasion, preferring to stay in Birkhall where they were enjoying a break. James was the first royal baby to wear the lovely new replica christening gown that had been made by the Queen's senior dresser Angela Kelly and her dressmaking team.

The following month, pride of place in St George's Chapel was transferred from the Queen's newest grandson to her oldest. Peter Phillips, aged thirty-one, married his Canadian long-time girlfriend Autumn Kelly; she was personal assistant to Sir Michael Parkinson, who had been made a knight in the recent New Year's Honours List. The wedding would prove to be very controversial because the exclusive rights to words and pictures were sold to *Hello!* magazine for a reported £500,000, which was an extraordinary amount of money at that time.

The royal turnout was impressive and an example of how quickly life had moved on since the state funeral of the Queen Mother. This time the front row of the official photograph saw Camilla seated between Charles and Prince Philip. Harry was next to his father while at the end of the row Sophie was placed between her husband and Prince Andrew. Camilla and Charles had married in April 2005 and she was now known as the Duchess of Cornwall. She had jumped above Sophie on the regal ladder. The most newsworthy guest, however, was not in the official photo but was pictured young and carefree on the day. Kate Middleton was there, happy and laughing with Harry's long-standing girlfriend, Chelsy Davy. Sophie was not yet the aunt, sister, friend and mentor to the woman who one day would be Queen Catherine. That would come later when Kate was a married mum and a neighbour in need of a comforting arm around her. Sophie had so much experience of the pitfalls of joining this particular family, but for the moment her number one priority was making sure her small children were all right.

She could certainly have recalled her own experience of meeting the Queen for the first time when she had been too nervous about cutlery to be part of the conversation. The christening was a momentous occasion for Kate because she met the Queen for the first time, although photographers were warned that they could not take 'snaps' of the Royal Family on the day but would have to make do with the official pictures taken, as they were for Sophie and Edward's wedding, by Sir Geoffrey Shakerley.

That arrangement was ignored as the whole day was reduced to farce by photographers taking every opportunity to snatch pictures of the Royals enjoying themselves – particularly Kate and Chelsy, although there was one picture of Sophie 'strutting her stuff' on the dance floor at the reception at Frogmore House, the royal residence in the grounds of Windsor Castle (not to be confused with Frogmore Cottage, which would achieve notoriety when it became the first married home of Prince Harry and Meghan Markle). Prince William was nowhere to be seen. He had flown to Kenya for the wedding of an old friend, an invitation that had been accepted before Peter and Autumn had set the date. He was lucky to avoid the fallout from arguably the most embarrassing group gathering since *It's a Royal Knockout*. The problem was a similar one – exclude certain publications and journalists and they are going to come for you – especially if a politician could be dragged into it. The event was quickly dubbed the '*Hello!*-ification' of the Royal Family. The Labour MP for Norwich North, Dr Ian Gibson, said, 'I think the British public would expect the Queen to rise above being pictured in the pages of *Hello!* She is the Queen, after all, not a footballer's wife', which was being rather unkind to footballers' wives, or WAGs, as they were demeaningly labelled.

Sophie kept quiet about the coverage, not surprisingly considering her own wedding had been featured as a special issue in the same magazine – she hadn't been paid half a million pounds for the privilege, though. She and Edward had taken Lady Louise along to the wedding, so they were a little peeved that their daughter was pictured, especially as they were doing their best to keep her out of the limelight. The Queen let it be quietly understood that no future royal wedding should be sold exclusively in this manner. She liked Autumn and, as with Sophie, had no problem with her background: her mother was a hairdresser and her father a marketing executive. At least Sophie did better than Kate and

Chelsy – there were nineteen photos of the royal girlfriends. The columnist Susie Boniface observed, 'Everybody thought this was just photographers at a wedding and happily posed and grinned away and then were quite amazed a couple of weeks later to see a *Hello!* supplement dedicated to things they thought were private family shots.'

The curse of *Hello!* had the last word, however. Peter and Autumn separated in 2019 and were divorced two years later.

At this stage of her relationship, Kate was experiencing almost exactly the same trial of patience that Sophie had endured the previous decade with Edward. The media attention Kate was being subjected to mirrored the tribulations faced by Sophie. Nobody had yet picked up on the similarities between the two women – a generation apart – but they were examples of the adage that there is nothing new under the royal sun – at least as far as the media are concerned.

They were both privately educated members of the middle-class country set – Kate's parents may have had more money, thanks initially to a family legacy, but life in their rural part of Berkshire was remarkably similar to Kent where Sophie grew up. The atmosphere was calm and welcoming. Like Sophie, Kate was a very accomplished young sportswoman, arguably the best in her junior school. She was also keen on music and the stage, and unlike Sophie she had a lovely singing voice which she used to good effect playing Eliza Doolittle in a school production of *My Fair Lady*. Sophie won a part in that musical at college despite her average singing.

The girls were very different physically as teenagers – Sophie always had beautiful skin and was quite petite, while Kate was unkindly described as a 'beanpole with acne' by schoolmates. The big difference at her first senior school, Downe House, was that Kate was badly bullied. One contemporary told Richard Kay of the *Daily Mail*, 'All the social-climbing girls – and there were lots of them – thought she was not worth bothering with.' She was lonely, homesick and frequently in tears. When they realised what was happening to their eldest daughter, her parents whisked her out in the middle of the academic year and sent her half an hour west to Marlborough College, where she thrived. She left there five years later, a striking, poised young woman.

As with Edward and Sophie, William first noticed Kate in a sporting environment. They weren't actually playing but watching a game of rugby on the touchline at the University of St Andrews. William was very handsome as a teenager and had lots of success with girls. He had one of the best chat-up lines known to man: 'I'm going to be king one day. Are you dancing?' He didn't need it standing next to Kate on a freezing winter's afternoon. She didn't take her top off as Sophie had done when she met Edward. She was wrapped up warm in a fleece jacket and jeans. She had been introduced to him because they were on the same course, history of art, and in the same student block, but had yet to have a chat. That changed when he discovered she knew about rugby and could have a decent conversation about it. She became the only girl in his set of well-to-do public-school types, who always sat together at lunch and dinner.

They started dating in the Christmas holidays and were already a discreet item by the time William publicly commented on how fit she was at the now-famous charity fashion show in which she sashayed down the runway in a transparent dress revealing black underwear. 'She's hot,' declared the prince, which is probably what Edward would have said about Sophie if he had been with his mates at the charity real tennis photocall.

Kate and William actually lived together at St Andrews and, having seen off Ardent Productions, life could proceed quietly and with no fuss. There was no risk of Andrew Morton barrelling up to them in the pub. The genie was out of the bottle, though, when they went skiing together at Klosters with some old Etonian cronies. The *Sun* carried a picture of Kate and William sharing a tender moment on a ski lift with the headline: FINALLY … WILLS GETS A GIRL. William reacted just as Edward would have, by seething at the press, although in retrospect he and Kate were fortunate to have kept their relationship secret for so long. Nothing would be the same for them again.

Kate was readily accepted into the family by Charles and Camilla, and joined William, Harry and their father on another ski trip, this time to the Swiss resort of Verbier. Camilla didn't accompany them because she is not a fan of the winter sport. On this occasion, William started chatting to the *Sun*'s royal reporter, Duncan Larcombe, and told him that he didn't intend to marry until he was 'at least twenty-eight or maybe thirty'. That was not music to Kate's ears – she would have to wait as long as Sophie. William wasn't joking: he was twenty-eight when he finally married her.

Kate wasn't asked to Charles and Camilla's wedding, apparently because it would have breached protocol, although it was never properly explained what that meant. She still hadn't met the Queen by the time of her and William's graduation in June 2005. She did not sit next to her boyfriend when they were awarded their degrees and so, again, missed her introduction to the Queen, who was there to support her grandson.

After a post-degree holiday in Africa with William, Kate moved into her parents' flat in Old Church Street, Chelsea, just a mile from Sophie's old home in Coleherne Court. At first she didn't seem to mind too much being photographed carrying her shopping home, but a picture taken of her on the number 19 bus prompted a dramatic change of mood, not just from Kate herself but from William and his father, who seem to have been consulting the Prince Edward handbook on how to handle such intrusion. They were incensed when the photo was printed the same day in the *Evening Standard*. The response from their lawyers, Harbottle & Lewis, was rapid, claiming this was an unjustified intrusion into her privacy.

Kate had to deal with the same media interest that had plagued Sophie when she set off for work at MCM – especially when she secured her first proper job working for Jigsaw, the luxury high-street chain, as an assistant buyer for children's accessories. Kate had no staff, no PR and no protection to help her through the squabbling, elbowing horde of paparazzi that gathered outside her flat on the morning of her twenty-fifth birthday, 8 January 2007, to go to work. She also didn't have the calming influence of a Brian MacLaurin figure. A rumour had started that the couple would announce their engagement on that day. Again following the Prince Edward set of rules, William issued a statement via the Palace declaring how unhappy he was at the paparazzi harassment of his girlfriend.

Through all this, though, Kate kept her eye firmly on the prize – just as Sophie had done. She was determined to see things through even though the tabloids handed her the unwelcome nickname of 'Waity Katie'. She was not even allowed to sit in the front row next to William at the tribute concert to his mother, the Concert for Diana, at Wembley Stadium in July of that year. Sophie, unsurprisingly perhaps considering her frosty relationship with the princess, wasn't there to lend support, but Kate showed great public decorum that impressed William. At least they had the last dance together at the after-show party.

A few weeks later they enjoyed an idyllic summer trip on

the island of Desroches, one of the Seychelles in the Indian
Ocean. Finally, they were on holiday by themselves and
were able to discuss their future. They returned home with
an understanding that they would be married. It changed
everything for Kate – just as it had done for Sophie when she
came to an unofficial engagement with Edward. Kate now
knew it was her destiny. As a friend observed, 'It's like they
had written it on a piece of paper and stuck it in a drawer
ready to bring out when the time was right. The only thing
missing was the date.'

Kate finally met the Queen at the wedding of Peter and
Autumn, when it was still very much governed by protocol.
Kate was officially representing Prince William and had to
wait her turn for the Queen to come over. She later said, a
little blandly, 'She was very friendly and it was fine.'

Kate coped better than Chelsy Davy with being a royal
girlfriend. When Chelsy complained about Harry having an
eye for a pretty girl in his early twenties, Kate advised her
that it was something they had to put up with and to turn
the other cheek. Just as Sophie had been, she was the centre
of attention at big society weddings when their friends were
getting married. Now that she had met the Queen and had
an unofficial understanding with William, she could be
integrated more easily into the ranks of the Royal Family.
A month after Peter Phillips' wedding she attended the ceremony at which William was invested as a Royal Knight of
the Garter, the world's oldest order of chivalry. This was yet
another event held at St George's Chapel. At least she could
still see the funny side of such ceremony and giggled along
with Harry at the sight of William's traditional costume – a
fetching blue velvet coat and plumed cap with ostrich feathers sticking out the top. Even Sophie had trouble keeping
a straight face as she stood next to Camilla to watch her

nephew arrive. The commentators seemed more interested in what Kate was wearing – a polka-dot skirt and jacket with a matching hat – than William's costume.

The Queen had in mind the perfect person to mentor Kate – Sophie, of course. William's grandmother, who was in her eighties now, had helped guide Sophie through the royal minefield but wanted to pass that particular baton to her daughter-in-law. Sophie was a seasoned professional in the matter of protocol and unassumingly owning a room, so she was the perfect choice. She had also experienced many of the pitfalls that the younger woman, seventeen years her junior, might face. At least, like Sophie, Kate had no embarrassing relations to worry about – or so everyone thought – until, unbelievably, the Fake Sheikh surfaced again. His target this time was Kate's uncle Gary, who was woefully indiscreet to Mazher Mahmood.

Unlike Sophie's rather tame 'old dear' sting, this was good old-fashioned sex and drugs, perfect for the *News of the World*. One could be forgiven for wondering how so many members – or relatives of members – of the Royal Family could be taken in year in, year out. The banner headline said it all: KATE MIDDLETON UNCLE DRUGS AND VICE SHOCK. It was a lurid tale set on the holiday island of Ibiza, where millionaire Gary Goldsmith lived in a luxury villa called Maison de Bang Bang. Most memorable were Gary's first words to the future King William when he and Kate came to stay at his home: 'Oi, you fucker, did you break my glass pyramids?' Gary, apparently, was a keen collector of crystal pyramids.

After the story appeared, nobody seemed quite sure what Gary's biggest crime was – the coke and other assorted substances, the sex, the tattoos or the perception that he was in some way naff. The American media put the 'scandal' in perspective. Mary Jordan of the *Washington Post* observed that the whole discussion centred on class prejudice: 'Class in Britain is roughly equivalent to race in America – despite enormous strides towards equality, social standing simmers never far below the surface.' The renowned royal biographer, Robert Lacey, author of the groundbreaking book *Majesty*, agreed, 'I think class is the primary element in all of this.'

Kate, understandably, was mortified at the exposure and subsequent stories. The Royal Family were well used to this sort of sensationalism by now. Nobody was as outraged as the media would have liked – they were getting used to dealing with the Fake Sheikh. Charles sent her a note telling her to 'try and put it out of your mind'. William was overheard at a polo match reassuring his future bride, 'I want to marry *you*, not your family.'

Her mentor – and soon-to-be aunt – Sophie had literally seen it all before and had the T-shirt. She was able to soothe and reassure her that everyone would soon get over it and that it was best to just move on – bad news flies away on the wind like yesterday's newspapers. Sophie could always be relied on to lend a consoling arm to Kate.

Mahmood was not done with easy targets; the following year he filmed Sarah Ferguson offering access to Prince Andrew for £500,000. Fergie said, 'I can open any door you want.' Cashing in on royal connections, real or perceived, was not a story that ever left the news desks. The reputation of the Fake Sheikh went from strength to strength, with 'investigations' winning him the Sports Journalist Association annual award and also Reporter of the Year for a second time in 2011 after he had exposed some members of the Pakistani cricket team involved in a spot-fixing scandal. When the *News of the World* closed down that year, he featured in the last edition before starting work for the *Sun on Sunday*.

Sophie, Princess Michael, Britney Spears, Sven-Göran Eriksson and Prince Harry were among targets pictured on the front cover of his memoir, *Confessions of a Fake Sheikh: 'The King of the Sting' Reveals All*, which was published in 2008. Maz went from conman to convict in October 2016 when he was jailed for fifteen months for conspiring to pervert the course of justice by changing a statement made to police. He had been accused of tampering with evidence in a case involving the former *X Factor* judge, Tulisa. His driver, Alan Smith, was also found guilty but was given a suspended sentence. News UK, which owned the tabloid newspapers, promptly sacked Maz after twenty-five years. A spokeswoman said, 'It is a source of great regret that his time with the company should end in this manner.'

Neither Sophie nor any other member of the Royal Family commented, although they might have been forgiven for cracking open a bottle of fizz.

Subsequently, Gary kept a much lower profile, although he did resurface in the 2024 series of *Celebrity Big Brother*, in which he was the first housemate voted off before he could reveal anything mischievous. By that time he was not remotely the most embarrassing uncle in the family – that title was unarguably held by Prince Andrew after his squirm-inducing television interview with Emily Maitlis.

19

Being Mum and Dad

Lady Louise had no idea that her grandmother was the Queen until someone told her on the first day of kindergarten; when she arrived home, she announced, puzzled: 'Mummy, people keep telling me that Grandmama is the Queen.' For Sophie and Edward's daughter, the Queen would always be lovely Grandmama who would settle down to watch Mr Tumble on CBeebies with her and her little brother. Sophie proudly observed, 'I guess not everyone's grandparents live in a castle, but where you are going is not the important part, or who they are. When they are with the Queen, she is their grandmother.' It was a two-way street. Sophie and Edward and their two children were the nuclear family the Queen had never been able to enjoy properly because of the demands of being the sovereign when she was younger.

Growing up, both Wessex children were more likely to watch television at Windsor because Sophie rationed the amount they were allowed to watch at home. Edward and Sophie were determined to bring up their children without too much television, which was quite ironic considering his previous career in TV. They did watch DVD box sets, including David Attenborough's award-winning *Planet*

Earth, and *Downton Abbey,* which was much grander than life at Bagshot Park, although they could have filmed it in Sophie's home – it was big enough. At least it meant that the children did not feel left out during the inevitable breaktime discussions at school. A friend gave them *Game of Thrones* as a joke present, but they all loved it and the long-running saga became a must-watch.

Louise was enrolled in St George's School, close to home and one of the oldest schools in the country, originally founded in the fourteenth century to provide choristers for the chapel at which Sophie and Edward were married; its choristers sang at their wedding. Girls were admitted in the mid-1990s with an age range from three to thirteen. All of this was perfect for Sophie and Edward's daughter. The school buildings were situated just below the north wall of the Castle, so it was ideally placed for Louise to pop round to see her grandmother for tea after lessons. The school's official 'vision' is that students become 'Real World Ready', an aim that mirrored Sophie's ambition for her children.

Louise and James had a nanny – at one time they had two – but Sophie was very protective in the early years, wanting everything to be safe and in order at all times. She was the one who made sure that the days at Bagshot Park ran like clockwork. Edward, on the other hand, seemed to be the playful dad, engaging with his children as much as possible. He would leave any telling-off to his wife while he happily pushed the pram or suggested a game of hide and seek in the garden. He also got down on his hands and knees and played horsey. The Queen's lifelong devotion to horses began as a very young girl, when she would sit in her high chair and listen to her grandfather, King George V, talk seriously about his four-legged friends. He was happy to indulge the young princess. On one memorable occasion, the Archbishop of Canterbury arrived for an audience with the King only to find him on all fours, snorting and neighing in a passable imitation of a horse, while his little granddaughter led him along by his beard.

Horses were not an idle pastime for the Queen. The former royal trainer, Ian Balding, was in no doubt that the Queen had the expertise to be a racehorse trainer: 'The Queen is an absolute natural with horses in every way.' She passed on her passion for horses to her daughter Anne. Prince Philip once memorably joked about the princess Royal: 'If it doesn't fart or eat hay then she isn't interested.' Anne won the individual title at the European Eventing Championship in 1971 and was named BBC Sports Personality of the Year; she was presented with the award by the boxing legend Sir Henry Cooper. Her daughter Zara continued the family's equine success, winning the Eventing World Championship in 2006 and that year securing the Sports Personality of the Year trophy too; she was presented with her award by rowing legend Sir Steve Redgrave.

Every member of the Royal Family seemed to be a quite brilliant horseman or woman. Sophie was never going to match such talent – even Princess Margaret had been a very accomplished young rider – but she was determined that one of the first things she was going to do was short-circuit her electric bottom. She had regular lessons so that she could accompany the Queen at least once a week on a ride around Windsor Great Park. When both her children started school, that ride became a morning pleasure if their schedules allowed. This wasn't just a one-way street of deference – the Queen herself was an effective tutor when it came to teaching her grandchildren, Louise and James, how to ride properly, making sure they would soon be better at it than their mother.

Sophie learned far more from the Queen than just the art of horsemanship. Sophie was a practised listener and observer and she absorbed how to be a proper Royal, accepted by everyone, by watching the Queen at work. She explained, 'The art of talking meaningfully is one that has to be learned. It's hard to think that the conversation you've had with them was worthwhile, but the Queen is very good at that – she makes everybody feel very special.' The Queen was also an excellent role model for understanding a sense of duty. 'She would never let anyone down,' explained Sophie.

The Queen was quite willing to ignore the media storm over Sophie's Fake Sheikh, but that did not mean Sophie was able to escape being on the wrong end of 'the look'. She was at a Palace state banquet and was still fussing around trying to find her seat when the Queen rose to speak. The Queen was not amused at having to wait: 'I shan't forget that look,' said her daughter-in-law, who made a mental note never to do that again – always know where you are sitting!

Sophie was astute enough to understand that to be properly accepted as more than Edward's wife she needed to be part of the family and do more than just hang around, smiling and curtsying correctly. She set about embracing the pursuits most enjoyed by the Queen and, just as importantly, by Prince Philip too. She learned to shoot pheasant and grouse and to fish for salmon in the sparkling waters of the Highlands.

Sophie became the model daughter-in-law, so much so that she was routinely referred to in the media as the Queen's second daughter. That was not being unfair in the slightest to Anne, who was immensely hard-working and respected within the family, but the Princess Royal very much had her own life that revolved around her Gatcombe Park Estate near Stroud, in the Cotswolds. She lived only ten minutes down the road from Charles and Camilla at Highgrove but an hour and a half from Windsor. Quietly, and without fuss, the Queen began to rely on Sophie for female company after both Princess Margaret and the Queen Mother died within such a short space of time.

Sophie could pop round to Windsor Castle in ten minutes to watch TV or stay up late discussing history enthusiastically with her mother-in-law. It wasn't a duty. Sophie loved to do it. They would turn the television on and watch historical documentaries together on a Saturday or Sunday evening – or better still, a good old-fashioned British war film – the sort of movie where Richard Todd or John Mills saved the day. Women were a little under-represented in wartime cinema, although the inimitable Thora Hird played a Land Army girl and memorably shot a German soldier in the classic propaganda film *Went the Day Well?* based on a Graham Greene story. The Queen was nineteen when, as Princess Elizabeth, she went out into the streets of London to celebrate with the happy crowds on VE Day with her younger sister; it's easy to think the teenage Sophie would have done exactly the same thing.

One story that did the rounds was that the Queen's favourite film was actually the 1980 comic strip fantasy *Flash Gordon* and that she always watched it at Christmas with the grandchildren – although the source of that inside gossip was the larger-than-life actor Brian Blessed, one of its stars.

If it wasn't television time, the two women could be found poring over the priceless ancient documents preserved in the Royal Archive at Windsor. The Queen found Sophie a most comforting and calm presence and always chose her to share the back seat in the royal car that took the monarch to church in Sandringham – this was a great honour, especially at Christmas.

Sophie also got on very well with her father-in-law. Ingrid Seward, the renowned royal biographer, explained, 'The Queen always found it a bit of a relief, if female members of the family knew how to handle Philip. Sophie was not fazed by his abruptness and would not let him bully her.'

The Queen saw Sophie as the safe pair of hands within the Royal Family – a woman who turned her life around after the initial embarrassments that plagued her in the early years. Crucially, Sophie had a willing partner in Edward – someone who could be stiff and reserved in public but was just Dad when he was at home.

Sophie and Edward both tried to give their children as normal an upbringing as possible within the obvious boundaries of living in a one-hundred-room property. Edward was the man in charge of the barbecue: 'The children love those,' said Sophie. She was, herself, an ace in the kitchen if it was the chef's night off. Whenever she could, Sophie did the school run. And if she was busy with a royal task then Edward would do it. Sophie also made sure they experienced some of the childhood pursuits she had so enjoyed in Brenchley, including sleepovers and children's parties and taking the dogs, Beth and Bluebell, for a walk. They also had a tortoise called Marmite, the most important resident of Bagshot Park.

Penny Mountbatten, a longstanding friend of the Royal Family, observed at the time, 'Sophie went through a lot to have her family and she and Edward have never relied on the nannies. They have always had a rule that when working one of them is at home with the children as far as possible.'

Sophie decided early on that she would let her children make their own mistakes. She didn't forbid the use of social media but was quietly pleased that Louise, the eldest, didn't seem that bothered about it, using it to keep in touch with close friends but not belonging to some noisy big WhatsApp group. The children were introduced to the wider world very gradually. As a result, her children thrived.

Sophie and Edward still saw as much of their long-standing friends as they could. And her father, who stayed in Benenden after his wife died, was always a welcome visitor. The Queen found Christopher charming company and would often invite him to Palace dinner parties, making sure she paired him off with a 'plus one', perhaps a widowed lady-in-waiting or unmarried courtier. It was perhaps the ultimate 'elite' matchmaking service, although Christopher never did find anyone to take the place of his beloved Mary.

While Louise and James (and not forgetting Edward!) remained her number one priority, Sophie was not ignoring patronages where she felt she could make a difference, particularly if they involved children. She was so grateful to finally be a mum after the difficulties she had endured. The year after her ectopic pregnancy she became the first Royal patron of Shooting Star Children's Hospices and opened its Christopher's Children's Hospice in Guildford. In the coming years she would make herself available for many fundraising events, and hosted receptions to increase awareness of this essential charity.

It was one of many charities and causes she would champion in the future. She was just getting started.

PART THREE
A WOMAN OF SUBSTANCE

20

No More Mrs Frump

S ophie might have been forgiven for letting out a long sigh when another tall and graceful young woman entered the ranks of the Royal Family. Back in the 1990s she could not compete with Princess Diana and her superstar wardrobe. And now there was Kate. Sophie was a forty-something mother bringing up two young children, and in comparison to the newest glamorous female on the Palace balcony she felt frumpy and unfit. It was time to do something about it.

For starters she made sure that running, yoga, Pilates and some weight training featured as much as possible in her daily routine. She didn't have to book a class at her local gym – she had all the privacy she needed at home and at Windsor Castle. While an exercise bike at home was a great asset, she still loved to be out pedalling in the fresh air – British weather permitting – and could enjoy the paths of Windsor Great Park without fear of running down a photographer. She could also invite friends over to play tennis and then for a swim, so there was no excuse not to get in shape. She also realised that the quickest way to put on weight was to eat too much at official occasions where there seemed to be a continuous supply of food that did not follow the perceived diet wisdom of the day. Instead, as much as possible, she followed what has become known as a Mediterranean diet, eating nuts, fruit, vegetables and fish – although she could still cook a delicious cake on demand. As with so many aspects of royal life, Sophie would study what the Queen did and follow her lead. The Queen ate four meals a day but kept her portion size under control – although she was keen on chocolate, as was Sophie. They never ordered a take-away.

Getting in better shape was a good start but Sophie still had to dress the part. As a PR executive in the 1990s, she had neither the time nor the inclination to spend an hour or two getting ready. She was always aware, though, that there might be some paparazzi lurking. She had learned that lesson early on as a royal girlfriend when she was caught unawares outside her flat. She had just finished washing her hair when she realised she had left something in the car; there was no one about so she decided to nip down in her dressing gown to fetch it. Sure enough, a photographer jumped out; it was the one and only time Sophie hid her face from the cameras, but it was a lesson learned that she should not take anything for granted as a royal celebrity: never look scruffy.

When she was pictured practically every day going into her Mayfair office, she wasn't on a fashion runway, so the basic uniform of a busy professional woman was enough. Alison Jane Reid observed, 'Her daily work outfit is not very exciting or individual. She would look smart in a trouser suit and sensible shoes but back then she wanted to convey the message that she was out in the big world earning a living. She was keen to eliminate any risk of a wardrobe malfunction that would undermine that image if a camera clicked.'

The wedding of William and Kate in April 2011 was an entirely different affair. She wanted to look her best but she also had a mother's worry about Louise, who had been chosen as a bridesmaid for the ceremony at Westminster

Abbey. She was seven and stepping out in public for the first time in front of a global television audience of 162 million. The viewing figure in the UK alone was 26 million – and then there were the many thousands crammed into The Mall.

Sophie does have a rather tetchy side to her nature, which she usually keeps hidden but it can rise to the surface if her patience is stretched, as it was when she tried her hand at windsurfing during Cowes Week and kept on falling in the water. This time it was after a visit to the Bruce Oldfield boutique in Beauchamp Place, Knightsbridge, just a few days before the wedding. She was pictured in the street by some delighted photographers, jabbing her finger towards her hapless bodyguard, who was keeping his mouth firmly shut. Nobody has ever revealed what triggered Sophie's anger that day, but it was a fraught week and a source did say, 'She happily gives it out with both barrels.'

Sophie had apparently ordered two outfits from the shop so that she could choose which best suited the day. They cost in the region of £3,000 each but Sophie paid for them, not wishing to be seen as some sort of freeloader. Bruce Oldfield had risen to the forefront of British fashion during his association as a favoured designer for Princess Diana. He helped launch a thousand pictures of the iconic figure. He had inherited the mantle of the Queen's favourite dress designers, Norman Hartnell and Hardy Amies. Sophie did not want to copy the late Princess of Wales at all but she did want to promote British designers as much as possible. Bruce was a safe choice, always choosing exquisite fabrics, and has subsequently received much praise for designing Camilla's coronation dress.

Nothing could possibly go wrong in the run-up to the big day; it wasn't her wedding, after all. And then she fell off her horse during her morning ride at Windsor. She was taken to the nearby Princess Margaret Hospital where it was discovered she had broken a rib and was told that all she could do was rest, be patient and take painkillers – of all weeks for this to happen.

She managed to escort Louise to the wedding rehearsal at Westminster Abbey and then had to find something to wear for the glittering pre-wedding gala dinner which the Queen hosted at the Mandarin Oriental Hotel overlooking Hyde Park. This was a black-tie formal affair which was as exclusive as it could possibly be. The guest list was confined to royalty and their families, from both home and abroad. The dress code for the ladies was 'gowns' and Sophie chose a Bruce Oldfield design again. It was Sophie's 'Pretty Woman' moment, observed Alison Jane Reid – a reference to the famous scene from the movie of that name when Julia Roberts is beauty personified in a red dress. Sophie posed happily for photographers in her red creation and didn't grimace once. Wearing her hair longer and looser helped to finally throw off the shackles of Diana comparisons. 'She looked radiant,' added Alison Jane.

The following day was the actual wedding, when hats not gowns were the focus of attention. Sophie's was adorned with feathers that looked as if they might fly away at any moment. Alison Jane enthused, 'It's a very daring hat. It was a head turner, which is rather the point of a good wedding hat. Her beige suit was sublimely tailored and fitted her like a dream, the colour illuminating her blonde hair and pale skin. I loved the embellished sleeve detail that cleverly reinforced the luminous effect of the outfit.'

Everything went well for Louise and the other bridesmaids, who were all shepherded expertly by Kate's sister Pippa, whose rear view actually stole the show. The media and online observers were so obsessed with commenting on her booty that it soon had its own website. Chelsy Davy was there, an acknowledgement that she did not speak out of turn about Harry or members of the Royal Family. She did not, however, join Harry in one of the open-topped carriages that carried the most important Royals over to Buckingham Palace. That seat next to the handsome prince in a smart uniform was taken by Louise, his cousin, who waved happily to the many thousands lining the streets. She also waved to the crowd from the front row of the Palace balcony while William and Kate shared a famous kiss. What a day!

Three months later the wedding of Zara Phillips and rugby star Mike Tindall was a much less formal affair. The ceremony at Canongate Kirk in Edinburgh was a low-key event, although the Queen, aged eighty-five, was there to support another grandchild. Sophie wore Bruce Oldfield again – this time a pleated jacket and skirt in soft ecru. Alison Jane Reid commented, 'The ensemble is pretty, elegant, romantic and jaunty with its shorter ruffle hemline reflecting Sophie in her forties. The colour was perfect for her, again giving a luminous glow to Sophie's complexion. And the hat was carefree and bound to be noticed – a Sophie trademark.'

The event was not televised and much of the publicity centred on it being a public outing for the Duke and Duchess of Cambridge, as the newly married William and Kate were known; it was Sophie, however, who captured the attention of *Hello!* magazine readers, who voted her outfit best of the day. She had said goodbye to the young woman who had once declared airily that fashion wasn't important. Every outfit she chose to wear would be scrutinised in detail by fashion writers and by members of the public, especially in the age of instant online opinion and mobile phones.

One important aspect of royal fashion for Sophie is that she never appeared to be in competition with Kate. Sophie and

Diana had seemed to be pitched against one another in the fashion world right from the start, and it was not a competition that Sophie was going to win as merely a royal girlfriend at that point. They had been practically the same age, but Kate is seventeen years younger than Sophie and very much of a different generation. Alison Jane Reid cast an expert eye on the contrast: 'Physically they are very different. Kate does look good in pretty much everything because she has the body of a catwalk model and possesses that spectacular mane of beautiful hair. She does not, however, have Sophie's naturally vivacious personality or smile. Sophie is shorter and more athletic in build and needs to choose fashion that accentuates her colouring and beautiful eyes, and that doesn't cut her body in half.

'Sophie looks best in bespoke and couture fashion that is designed for her petite body, to elongate, give her a tiny waist, erase the hips and always look regal, yet utterly modern. That's the true art of couture – to flatter the female form and create a fabulous silhouette that looks good from all angles, especially if the wearer is going to be scrutinised by fashion editors, photographers and, basically, every woman!'

Sophie and Kate shared similar tastes in that they both wore the same designers and labels. Sophie would even order a second outfit in Kate's size if she thought the one she had chosen would suit her new niece. They both liked the New Zealand-born designer Emilia Wickstead, who was much admired among leading ladies and first ladies, including Lady Gaga and Melania Trump. Alison Jane observed, 'She creates refined, elegant, ladylike clothing in bold colour palettes.' Unsurprisingly, considering her celebrity popularity, Emilia was named Red Carpet Designer of the Year in 2014.

Other favourites of the two royal women were Suzannah London (the label of Suzannah Crabb), Erdem, Alexander

McQueen and, a new name at the top table, Victoria Beckham, whose designs for Sophie are praised by Alison Jane: 'Victoria excels at the miracle dress with a bit of stretch to smooth, shape, flatter and define the female form.'

The two royal wives have grown closer over the years. As the old cliché goes, Sophie had seen it all before and was able to lend a reassuring word to Kate when the going got tough – and that wasn't just dealing with the fallout from a Fake Sheikh exposé. The next slice of déjà vu occurred when the French glossy magazine *Closer* published topless photos of Kate taken while she and William were on holiday in the South of France in September 2012. She was relaxing by the pool at Viscount Linley's villa in Provence wearing just her bikini bottoms. William reacted with all Palace guns blazing, ensuring the pictures did not find their way into the British tabloids – as Sophie's had distressingly done – and instructed lawyers to sue for invasion of privacy. They ended up winning £92,000 in damages. At least it wasn't a couple of weeks before her wedding, but Sophie was able to lend some words of sympathy and understanding.

Kate's presence sparked an interest in fashion for Sophie that had seemed less important with two young children. James started school when he was three, as a day pupil at Eagle House, a co-educational preparatory near Sandhurst, just a few miles from Bagshot Park. That gave Sophie a little more time to devote to the causes and projects that mattered to her. She was able to combine her relatively new interest in fashion with doing something a little more than showing up in an eye-catching frock. She became the first royal patron of the London College of Fashion, attracted by its Better Lives programme, which used fashion to tackle issues around equality, diversity, social mobility and sustainability. Sophie was always looking to give an extra edge to something she was doing – her blossoming interest in fashion gave her a chance to do more than be a walking advertisement for top designers. She did not appreciate the view that fashion was just red-carpet frivolity. She became a keen supporter of Making for Change, which was just about to get under way. The groundbreaking initiative aimed to teach women in prison the vocational seamstress skills that would give them a better chance of finding employment when they had finished their sentence; that strategy would reduce the prospect of reoffending.

As the project was linked to women's prisons, Sophie started off by making an unpublicised visit to HMP Holloway, in north London, to support the launch of a new fashion training unit. She has also hosted receptions at Buckingham Palace to increase awareness of the programme, as well as visiting Downview Prison in Sutton, Surrey, to chat to women offenders in the easy Sophie manner; that was her style and she was making it her own.

21

The Bike Ride

Sophie had several big advantages when it came to functioning as a full-time Royal. She had been an accomplished writer at school and that had carried on professionally when she composed a hundred and more press releases. She was also a skilled interviewee, having held the hand of many celebrities while guiding them through interviews with journalists looking for a story. Most tellingly, she discovered she was good at speaking in public and to the public. She wasn't constrained by being too posh, strangling her words and sounding as if her vowels were stuck in her front teeth.

Sophie had a voice and she was determined to use it. She had demonstrated that winningly when she had articulated the difficulties faced by those with sight problems. Her first major solo trip abroad came in 2013 when she travelled to India and Qatar in support of the Orbis sight-saving charity. Her first stop was Kolkata, where she visited an eye hospital and watched cataract surgery being performed. She even had a go herself – with a simulator, not the real thing.

The press seemed more interested in what she was wearing than in what she was actually doing. The *Daily Mail* reported that on the visit she had to put hygiene ahead of style and wore blue shoe coverings. Apparently she chose a palm-tree-print dress with a silver jacket and matching clutch bag and had a purple pashmina draped around her neck. She also saw the specially converted DC-10 plane known as the Orbis Flying Hospital that enabled specialists to reach sufferers, particularly children, in poverty-stricken areas of developing countries. The eye surgeons, anaesthetists and nurses were all volunteers and would happily pass on their expertise to local staff to carry on their work after they moved on. For an evening reception she changed into a silk patterned dress and black heels.

Sophie was passionate about sight because of her ongoing concern about Louise's condition. She articulated this in a speech to a medical training symposium at the Swabhumi Conference Centre in the city. *Hello!* noted that she was wearing a smart white blazer over a matching dress. She flew on from Kolkata to Qatar in the Middle East, where she hoped to raise awareness and funds for Orbis and other essential programmes worldwide. She was given a tour of the Museum of Islamic Art and was officially greeted by the Prime Minister Sheikh Abdullah bin Nasser bin Khalifa Al Thani, a member of the ruling Al Thani family, at the Doha Palace. This was nine years before the oil-rich Arab state hosted the football World Cup, so a visit from a member of the British Royal Family was a big deal.

On her return to the UK, Sophie marked World Sight Day by writing her first article for a national newspaper, the *Daily Telegraph*, in which she talked about her trip, pointing out that 90 per cent of the world's blind people live in developing countries. She also wrote that there were 285 million blind and visually impaired people throughout the world. Sophie's account was moving, especially when she recalled watching children whose sight had been restored after an operation the previous day: 'They could not have been more excited as they showed off how many fingers they could count and how they could now colour in pictures without going over the lines.'

The purpose of the article was to increase awareness of the extent of the problem worldwide and also to raise money for Orbis and the two charities with which Sophie had a particular connection: VISION 2020: The Right to Sight and the International Agency for the Prevention of Blindness (IAPB). Sight was a cause that she returned to many times. She wanted to create a world where 'no one is needlessly blind and where everyone with unavoidable vision loss can live to their full potential'.

During her trip to Qatar, Sophie had come into constant contact with the burka worn by Muslim women in the state. She had plenty of positive things to say about the garment the following year: she hosted a reception at Windsor Castle on behalf of the Duke of Edinburgh's International Award where she met representatives from the Islamic Fashion Festival. She risked controversy in a subsequent interview with *Harper's Bazaar* magazine: 'One of the aims is to try and use fashion to break down barriers and dispel the myths about Muslim women. It's very evident that Muslim women can be fashionable while retaining their modesty. And it's a great way of bringing people together and saying, "Look, this is what we're really like." And what people forget is that underneath the burka and everything else, there is somebody who is probably wearing something really quite fashionable. But you don't have to show a lot of flesh in order to be beautiful.'

Sophie was clearly trying to support women while still showing respect to the men who controlled the purse strings. But not everyone saw it that way. Celia Walden, writing in the *Daily Telegraph*, called it Sophie's 'Marie Antoinette' moment, a reference to the famous 'Let them eat cake' quote attributed to the French queen that displayed her obliviousness to the harsh conditions that poor people suffered while she enjoyed privilege and pampering. Celia observed, 'Would the one-time PR girl feel as enamoured with the burka if her step-father, Prince Philip, had insisted she wear one not once, for fun or effect, but every day for the rest of her life?'

What might have seemed a little clumsy struck exactly the right note in Qatar. On World Sight Day in 2015 Sophie returned to the state and this time the Qatar Development Fund (QDF) pledged an investment of eight million dollars to the Qatar Creating Vision initiative that had been set up after Sophie's first visit. On her return to London she was at Buckingham Palace to greet the Qatar foreign minister, another member of the Al Thani family, after the QDF had signed the framework agreement with Orbis UK. This really was a case of job well done for Sophie. Over the next four years, the plan was that the money would deliver more than five and a half million eye screenings and treatments for children, concentrating first on India and Bangladesh.

She could make a difference.

The Duke of Edinburgh's Award, both at home and internationally, was something Sophie and Edward embraced enthusiastically. Edward, in particular, had devoted much of his royal work to promoting the charity and making sure that his father's brainchild would continue to thrive.

Prince Philip had wanted a legacy that would outlive him, so in 1956 he founded the Duke of Edinburgh's Award. He didn't just lend his name to something that landed on his desk on a Monday morning. He thought of the original idea and then was one of three men responsible for framing an award that has involved more than six million boys and girls in the UK alone. The other two founding fathers were Lord Hunt, who as Colonel John Hunt had led the famous expedition that conquered Everest three years previously. He became the scheme's first director, a post he held for ten years. The other key figure was Kurt Hahn, the founder of Gordonstoun School, who had remained an inspiring figure to Philip. Their shared vision was to devise a programme that would provide young men in the post-war era with a sense of purpose, promote self-confidence and develop new interests: it was motivational. The four sections were voluntary service, physical recreation, skills and adventure. You needed an extra one – a residential project – if you wanted to reach the summit of the Gold Award. After the first pilot proved so successful, girls were invited to take part as well.

Sophie was a huge fan, especially as the scheme was enthusiastically embraced by the Girlguiding Association. She was echoing the passion that her husband had for the scheme. He had achieved his own Gold Award in 1986, starting his five sections at Gordonstoun and finishing at Cambridge. He had completed a four-day trek in the Cairngorms, helped run the Air Training Corps squadron at school, taken part in building a sailing hydrofoil, taken a flying course in which he secured his pilot's licence and while at university took up real tennis, which counted as his physical recreation element. His father was immensely proud when he presented him with his award at St James's Palace in London.

When Sophie and Edward became full-time Royals after the demise of their companies, one of their first public engagements together was a trip to Tyneside to present Bronze Awards to pupils of Firfield Community School in Blakelaw. Edward told them, 'When I was at school it was never really academic lessons that inspired me.' He and Sophie would have to wait more than twenty years to become the Duke and Duchess of Edinburgh, but this was the first clue that they were aware of the responsibilities that title might bring.

The sections of the DofE scheme were a reflection of the way Sophie lived her life and she was particularly keen to broaden its appeal worldwide. In June 2013 she became the global ambassador for its International Award Foundation, which basically meant she would travel around the world encouraging young people to take up the challenge of the award. She joined Edward for a trip to South Africa to promote the DofE, then made her first solo trip as the global ambassador to Hong Kong, where she visited a school for young people with educational needs including ADHD, autism and obsessive-compulsive disorder. The intention was that the students would benefit from their involvement in the scheme. She also founded and was the first chair of the Duke of Edinburgh's Award Women's Network Forum. Her objective was to improve gender equality and gender balance in the workplace. She explained the goal to a group of young female students, 'I want you to go home thinking, WOW, I am inspired to learn more and to pursue my dream job, but also keep my options open.'

Sophie wanted to do something extra special for the DofE's Diamond Jubilee. She hadn't taken part in the scheme at school so she was keen to make up for that. Kate had achieved her Gold Award at Marlborough and had been very enthusiastic when talking about the experience. It had become such an important part of Sophie's family's lives but required public generosity to keep the charity going. She decided on a bike ride – not just once or twice up and down The Mall but a 445-mile seven-day marathon from Edinburgh to London. She may have been a fit, working mother of two who ran five miles most days – provided it wasn't pouring with rain – but she was not in shape for such a commitment. Both the Queen and Prince Philip thought she was mad: 'There are certain members of the family who think I am crazy,' she confessed.

Just the training took six months and was 'pure hell', particularly in the early days when, among other disasters, she had to pick herself out of a hedge or two. She revealed, 'Every incline was like the north face of the Eiger and I prayed for the end of every ride. I confess I even shed a tear or two of desperation and frustration.' She enlisted the help of Rachel McKenzie, one of the physical training instructors at Sandhurst, and was given advice and encouragement from the two 'professionals' in the Royal Family – Mike Tindall and Zara Phillips. She also received plenty of 'advice' from impatient motorists.

Having turned fifty the previous year, she admitted happily that she was fitter than she had ever been: 'The more time passed the more I believed in myself. I have been surprised by how much I enjoy cycling.' She even made sure she took the bike up to Balmoral with her so she could continue her daily regime during the annual holiday in the Highlands. She estimated that she had managed 176 hours of training, pedalling some 3,000 miles in preparation for the ride. Her Just Giving page had already raised close to £100,000. She was ready.

Her husband and father-in-law were there to wish her luck and a safe journey when she set off from the Palace of Holyroodhouse, in Edinburgh, on a bright September morning. Louise and James were at school but would be at Buckingham Palace to welcome their mother if she managed the whole journey. They were well used to seeing Mum leave the comfort of Bagshot Park in her turquoise Lycra for her daily training, so it was no big deal to them. Rachel was there in Scotland, too, and they were also joined by cyclists

from the four Royal regiments that Sophie represented: RAF
Wittering, Queen Alexandra's Royal Army Nursing Corps,
5th Battalion The Rifles and the Corps of Army Music.

All went swimmingly for the first half hour and then her
chain broke. Fortunately, they were already out of sight, so
no embarrassing pictures were taken to poke fun at her in the
newspapers. In keeping with modern times, she wrote a blog
describing her trip day by day, including lunches in 'salubri-
ous' car parks and munching through coconut and fruit cake
thoughtfully provided by supporting members of the public.
After all that training, the hills were not as daunting as she'd
feared: 'I had built them up in my head into walls of doom,
but they have not been nearly as brutal as I had imagined.'

Along the route through Northumberland, Yorkshire,
Lincolnshire and down the country towards London her
peloton was greeted by schools, military bases and just members of the public wishing them well. It had captured the
imagination just as the legendary walks of Ian Botham had
done in the 1980s. She found the time – and the breath – to
explain to local press along the way what they were doing
and to articulate why the Duke of Edinburgh's Award
scheme was so important. Crucially, she said, the DofE
made an impact whatever the background of the participant:
'For those for whom life hasn't dealt the kindest of cards, it
represents a real opportunity to turn things around. How it
achieves this is simple; the young people are shown the way,
but every achievement is their own, therefore they own the
outcome.'

And then on the seventh day, Sophie's outcome came into
view – Buckingham Palace. She wrote eloquently, 'I felt a
huge sense of sadness and an enormous amount of emotion
that this great adventure was coming to an end.' The Band
of the Coldstream Guards was there to provide a rousing

rendition of 'Congratulations', a touch that had Prince Edward written all over it. He was there to hug her, along with Louise, James and her own father, who had made the journey from Benenden. The final figure raised for the DofE was more than £180,000. She had earned her Diamond Award – specially designed for the jubilee – and she proudly showed it off to photographers. But, as she concluded in her blog, 'What on earth am I going to do now?'

22

Horse and Carriage

While Sophie was keen to give her children a sheltered, publicity-free upbringing she did want to prepare them for a life outside a royal one, if they needed it. She was anxious that they should know something of the outside world. She and Edward took them on a private visit abroad when they travelled to South Africa to visit the Ubunye Foundation in the Eastern Cape province. They saw first-hand the important work being done for underprivileged, mainly Black, children, particularly in rural areas. She wanted Louise and James, then aged eleven and seven, to see for themselves that Africa was not just about fantastic animals in the most amazing landscape. 'There is a huge need to support, protect and nurture the communities that live within and around these beautiful surroundings,' declared Sophie, who was developing a strong voice for the issues that mattered in the world – and one that would become more powerful as the years passed.

For the most part Louise and James were kept well away from photographers. They were included in just one or two photos on the trip but mostly it was Sophie, as royal patron of the foundation, who was pictured. Happy family snaps for us to see were very much rationed. Sophie smiling and laughing at Buckingham Palace after her epic bike ride and posing happily with her children was a rarity. Away from the cameras they were growing up. They still saw lots of Grandma and Grandpa, mainly at weekends or at Sandringham and Balmoral for proper holidays.

They were looked after by their grandparents on the Palace balcony during the Trooping of the Colour annual ceremony in 2015. James stood between the two of them with his elder sister on the other side of Prince Philip; they were very much centre stage, although it was Prince George, the eldest son of William and Kate, who took most of the media and public attention. Sophie and Edward were missing. They were in Sweden representing the Queen at yet another royal wedding – this time of Prince Carl Philip to the model Sofia Hellqvist. Over the years Edward and Sophie were the go-to couple for these events, and it must have been like meeting up with old friends when they arrived. All the princesses, queens, duchesses and countesses in the world seemed to be there, wearing flowing gowns and a lot of jewellery. When they stopped for their photo outside the Royal Palace in Stockholm, Edward said, 'We've caused a traffic jam.' For once Sophie was not wearing a dress by a London designer but a bespoke, lilac, cap-sleeved gown by the internationally acclaimed Czech designer Tatiana Kováříková, a gift on a recent visit to Prague. She paired it with her favourite aquamarine tiara. Sophie and Edward enjoyed a waltz on the dance floor, safe in the knowledge that their children were being well looked after by Grandma and Grandpa. Back on the Palace balcony, the Queen's face was all smiles and she was clearly enjoying her morning and, touchingly, the company of her grandchildren. Every so often James would ask the Queen a question and she made sure to answer him even if a noisy plane was flying overhead.

James, who was doing well at Eagle House School, had developed a love of fly fishing – something he could enjoy quietly with Prince Philip and his mother – or simply by himself, watched by a helpful gamekeeper, a ghillie as they are called in the Highlands. He was carrying on a family tradition because the late Queen Mother was a lifelong devotee of the pursuit, finding it a welcome diversion from her daily royal diary. She had always enjoyed fishing trips with her husband, King George VI, and continued to do so for as long as she could.

Fortunately, Sophie much enjoyed these hours spent with her son, in waders up to their armpits. Edward enjoyed shooting but lacked the patience to spend hours standing in the River Dee. He much preferred a morning ride with his mother or his daughter, who had become a very accomplished horsewoman. She was also showing great promise in the family sport of carriage driving. Sophie had demonstrated an aptitude for it, taking part alongside Prince Philip, but Louise was displaying a proper championship talent, much to the delight of her grandfather.

She had been sitting next to him in one of his favourite carriages during a drive around Sandringham when, out of the blue, he asked if she would like to try and just handed her the reins. She showed a natural ability right from the start, although she did find it rather intimidating being tutored by a master of the sport. She recalled, 'It was slightly scary because he invented the sport pretty much, but it's also incredible to have learned first-hand from him and definitely made us closer.'

That 'invention' took place when Prince Philip had to give up polo because of an injured wrist and worsening arthritis. He had only just turned fifty and was looking for a new pastime to enjoy away from his public engagements. He didn't fancy golf. He recalled, 'I suddenly thought, well, we've got horses and carriages so why don't I have a go? So I borrowed four horses from the stables in London, took them to Norfolk and practised and thought – why not?' Having decided he loved it, the prince put together a committee to devise a set of rules for international competitions. Carriage driving is a form of competitive horse driving in harness in which the driver and horses need to complete dressage, marathon and obstacle driving.

Prince Philip may not have *actually* invented carriage driving but he made it much more than just a parade of pretty ponies. He gave it kudos and made it popular. He gave the sport a competitive edge. Emily Viller, a member of the Great Britain Carriage Driving Team, observed, 'He's been very supportive over the years of drivers of all abilities, particular of younger drivers.' He was certainly supportive of Louise, who was soon better at it than her mother. 'I trail in her wake,' said Sophie, proudly. 'It's a lovely thing to do and she is so good at it!'

After learning from the master, Louise was able to make her debut, aged fourteen, at the Royal Windsor Horse Show when she led a parade of the British Driving Society. She drove a carriage that had been steered by the Queen herself at the very first Windsor Horse Show in 1943. She looked poised and comfortable as her picture was taken many times. For someone so in control of a carriage, Louise could be a little accident-prone: she ended up on crutches after a fall during a skiing holiday with her parents to St Moritz in the Swiss Alps and had broken her arm when she fell off a horse – pleading with her parents not to blame the horse.

Prince Philip had retired from competition, so he was delighted when Louise literally took up the family reins and proved to be exceptionally good at it. He would always ask her how she fared in a competition. She recalled, 'His eyes would light up because he just gets so excited when he talks about it.' Just after his ninety-sixth birthday in the summer of 2017, she was the reserve champion in the young driver classes at the British Driving Society Annual Show that was held at Smith's Lawn in Windsor Great Park.

Sophie would turn up and watch if engagements allowed, happily snapping pictures for the sideboard and making sure her daughter's olive-green jacket and matching hat that she liked to wear for competitions remained immaculate through the day. Sometimes the Queen would be there too, and she was in great spirits in 2019 when Louise finished third in the Private Driving Singles at the Royal Windsor Horse Show. Her husband arrived flanked by two aides but still steering his two-horse carriage. He was thrilled that Louise had done so well and would carry on his family tradition. He had actually won the competition back in the 1980s. One of the most amusing sights of the day was Prince Philip putting his fingers in his ears to block out the noise from the cannons of the Royal Horse Artillery. He was prone to doing this, having famously done the same during a performance of Alicia Keys at the *Royal Variety Performance* a few years earlier.

The horse show was one of the understated social events of the year, attracting visitors from all over the world taking advantage of the only day on which members of the public could enjoy the castle grounds. It began in 1943, originally as a wartime fundraising event, and has grown to become the biggest event of its kind in the country; the Queen made sure it was in her diary every year, even competing herself in the early days. Latterly, her own home-bred horses always did well in the showing class competitions. Royal observers liked to point out that Louise had the air of the young Queen about her – conscientious, straightforward and mad about horses.

Louise was now attending St Mary's School Ascot, which she had joined in Year 9, an all-girls Catholic school that promoted the original prediction of its founder, Mary Ward, that 'Women in time will come to do much' – a sentiment that greatly appealed to Sophie. Non-Catholic pupils were admitted based on exam results and it was one of the top girls' schools in the country based on A-Level results.

In addition to her studies, her mother and father were keen for her to continue the family tradition in participating in the Duke of Edinburgh's Award, believing it would be a welcome distraction. Edward was pleased because, he observed, it had made her more confident, and said: 'It's just broadened her horizons. I think she's probably got a little focused on … the academics.' Sophie echoed the view that the DofE had given Louise a huge amount of confidence, revealing 'She's taken up fencing again as her skill, which she has really loved.' Unsurprisingly, Louise stayed the course to secure her Gold Award.

23

Harry and Meghan

Sophie and Edward hadn't seen much of Harry over the years. He was always cheerful company at the functions and dinners they all had to attend but he was of a different generation and was much more likely to be seen laughing and joking with Kate and William – or Willy, as his brother called him. He was very popular with the public, an enduring legacy of the heartbreaking sight at the funeral of his mother Diana when, aged twelve, he had walked solemnly, head bowed, behind her coffin while trying not to cry.

Both Harry and his elder brother were consumed by what Tony Blair's press secretary Alastair Campbell described as a 'total hatred of the media'. They believed, as many did, that the paparazzi had caused their mother's death by pursuing her car through the Paris streets. He later put those feelings into words, 'One of the hardest things to come to terms with is the fact that the people that chased her into the tunnel were the same people that were taking photographs of her while she was still dying in the back seat.'

Harry wasn't given an easy time by the media, who would, it seemed, always put the boot into a member of the Royal Family because it was easy pickings, especially if they were headstrong teenagers who invited tabloid headlines, including

'Harry's Drug Shame' and countless stories about a notorious fancy dress party. Two terms fighting in Afghanistan did much to turn the boy into a better man.

Harry's acts of kindness are often left unknown or unreported, such as the time when, as a tank commander, he stood up for an openly gay colleague and gave a proper military telling-off to a group of ignorant soldiers who were taunting the man. They never insulted their comrade-in-arms again. His second tour of duty ended in 2012, and he returned to London as a staff officer with responsibility for helping injured soldiers with their recovery. In this role he founded the world-famous Invictus Games in 2014.

One of the nine sports featured in the first competition was wheelchair basketball, and it wasn't reported at the time but Sophie had actually beaten him to it. She had been made patron of British Wheelchair Basketball a year earlier. She had become enthusiastic about the sport when she had seen it played at the London 2012 Paralympic Games and gave it a tremendous boost by handing it a royal patronage. She continued to support it enthusiastically over the years and took part in the 'Inspire a Generation' session outdoors in Finsbury Park in 2021, when she proved very adept at the sport herself. Clearly playing with the kids in the garden at Bagshot Park had paid off. Sophie was not a fair-weather supporter of her charities and associations; she was an advocate, determined to inspire at home and abroad.

If their paths had crossed more often, then Sophie and Harry would have had much to talk about. When he turned thirty, Sophie was already fifty with two children, who were her priority. He was ready to settle down. His two most serious relationships had been with Chelsy Davy, who he had been with on and off for seven years, and Cressida Bonas, another dazzling blonde who, a little ironically, forged a successful acting career after they split up in 2014. His father and brother both liked Cressida, and Charles was even said to have referred to her as 'the one that got away'. Both young women hated the attention that came with being a royal girl-friend. Kate just about coped, with some telling intervention from William. Sophie managed with the powerful support of the Queen and the Duke of Edinburgh.

And then Harry met Meghan Markle and nothing in the Royal Family was ever the same again – not because she took a wrecking ball to its traditions but because her arrival coincided with the global obsession of social media and any mention of Meghan, particularly if it was a negative one, snowballed around the world in a moment. As Mark Twain is credited with saying, 'A lie can travel halfway around the world while the truth is still putting on its boots.'

Harry had no idea who Meghan was before he met her on a blind date at the Dean Street Townhouse in Soho: 'I'd never watched *Suits* and I'd never heard of Meghan.' He should have been paying attention. Just two months earlier in New York she had been a guest on Comedy Central's satirical *The Nightly Show with Larry Wilmore* and described Donald Trump as 'divisive' and 'misogynistic'. This was a woman who was already a millionaire and, while not an Oscar winner, was earning a reported $50,000 an episode on the television legal drama. She was about to turn thirty-five and was divorced. Kate Middleton was nineteen when she met William Wales. Sophie was twenty-eight when she first came into contact with Prince Edward. Crucially, Meghan already had a voice in the world before that became a royal voice.

As a biracial woman, Meghan faced racist barbs on Twitter, backed the Erase the Hate campaign against racism, had been part of a Hollywood group cheering up the US troops in service abroad at Christmas time and seen for herself the hardship endured at the Gihembe Refugee Camp in Rwanda. She also wrote a famous essay for *Elle* magazine entitled, 'I'm More Than An "Other"', about finding her voice as a biracial woman.

Her CV away from acting and before she met Harry was quite formidable. She had addressed a UN Women's Conference and stressed the need for greater female representation in politics worldwide. She had been back to Rwanda to raise awareness and money for the Clean Water Campaign; and she had been named a global ambassador for World Vision Canada, which was not a sight-related charity but one similar to the Ubunye Foundation that aimed to help boys and girls around the world to overcome their terrible poverty.

If Meghan had realised how her endeavours away from acting would be ignored when she became Harry's girlfriend, she might have stayed in to wash her hair instead of going out for a glass of wine. Instead, all hell was let loose when she was revealed as the prince's latest love three months after they met. That was about the same amount of time Sophie had before her friendship with Edward was revealed in the papers. The *Sun*, which had carried the topless picture of Sophie nearly twenty years earlier, devoted its front page this time to HARRY'S GIRL ON PORNHUB and wrote of her stripping off and groaning in *Suits*. The journalist Tamara Khandaker, writing for *Vice News*, based in Toronto, where Meghan lived, put the revelation into perspective when she observed, 'The clips on the website are of Markle's appearance on *Suits* and wouldn't even fit into your religious grandmother's idea of pornography.'

The *Sun* apologised, as the newspaper had done when it so upset Sophie: 'We would like to make it clear that Miss Markle has never been involved in such content and had no idea that the video clip had been published on this website. We appreciate that this has caused hurt and upset to Miss Markle and the Prince and apologise to both.'

Once more, there was really nothing new under the royal sun except for the fact that Meghan was biracial. The respected writer and broadcaster Afua Hirsch neatly drew attention to a newspaper article that declared Meghan was a 'departure from Prince Harry's usual type' and 'not in the society blonde style of previous girlfriends'. Afua noted drily, 'I think what they are trying to say is that Markle, actor, global development ambassador and lifestyle blogger is Black.'

Meghan travelled to India a couple of months later to highlight her role as a promoter of development around the world, particularly where women were concerned. She saw for herself the plight of teenage girls whose education was being sorely affected by the stigma surrounding menstrual health and the lack of proper sanitation. She wrote an article for *Time* magazine entitled 'How Periods Affect Potential'.

On her return, it was time to meet Grandmother. Sophie had first met the Queen at a Windsor Castle lunch. Kate had been presented at the wedding of Peter Phillips. Now it was Meghan's turn, and she was invited for a traditional English tea at Windsor with the Queen. Earlier in the year she had popped into an old-fashioned tea room in Pasadena while visiting her mother, Doria, so she had some idea of what to expect. During a very friendly chat the Queen suggested that Sophie would be a good person for Meghan to talk to about finding her feet. In the Queen's opinion, she had done brilliantly well mentoring Kate so it was a logical step that she might help Meghan. The Queen was now a ninety-one-year-old great-grandmother, so she could not be expected to help very much with personal advice.

Sophie responded promptly by inviting Meghan for tea at

Bagshot Park, and while they enjoyed a cordial time it did not develop into the fun friendship she had with Kate. The problem for Sophie was deciding what she could actually do to help. She could have said to Meghan to try not to be the centre of attention when she entered a room, but that is not something the reporters and photographers inevitably gathered would have supported or allowed. Kate was different in that she was a blank canvas not just in terms of entering the Royal Family but also in making her mark on the world. Meghan had already done that.

The former MP and broadcaster Gyles Brandreth launched a thousand stories that Meghan wasn't interested in receiving help from Sophie. He suggested that she thought it would be enough that she had Harry to guide and advise her. That soon became interpreted by others as a firm quote from Meghan that she had made the blunt response to Sophie: 'I've got Harry.' After all, she was already a self-made millionaire. At least she wouldn't have to face a sting from the Fake Sheikh. He went to jail the very same month that she was revealed in the press as being Harry's new girlfriend. It would have been interesting to see which member of her family he might have considered a target.

Meghan and Harry didn't have an unofficial engagement as Sophie and Edward had done or an 'understanding' as William and Kate had reached. Harry was in love and didn't want to waste any time being cautious. He ignored his elder brother's reported advice to take as much time as he needed to 'get to know this girl'. Instead, they were engaged in November 2017, a little more than a year after they met. They were married six months later in St George's Chapel, as Sophie and Edward had been.

The wedding itself was the spectacle of the year, with 100,000 people lining the streets of Windsor. Inside the chapel, Sophie and Edward and their children were seated in the same row as the Queen and Prince Philip. As always with a royal wedding, much of the focus was on the wedding dress as Meghan walked down the aisle with Prince Charles standing in for her absent father, Thomas Markle. Meghan's bridal gown was designed by Clare Waight Keller, the first female director of the French fashion house, Givenchy. The dress was a triumph of unfussy haute couture that took seasoned observers back to the golden Hollywood age of Audrey Hepburn. Fashion commentator Alison Jane Reid thought it sublime: 'It's not about being overly ostentatious; it's about ravishing craftsmanship and extraordinary attention to detail.'

Alison Jane was also impressed with Sophie's outfit. She had mastered the art of dressing as a guest – not too flashy to take attention away from the bride but wearing something that might garner an admiring glance or two. She had chosen a luxurious 'duchess satin' skirt with an embroidered grey bodice, designed by Suzannah London, and a matching Jane Taylor bijou hat. 'It was a gorgeous fabric – perfect for a royal wedding,' observed Alison Jane. 'It was simple, regal and unfussy, which is a style that works best for Sophie.'

As she always did, Sophie followed the Queen's lead and did not show any emotion during the uplifting sermon entitled 'The Power of Love', delivered by the Most Reverend Michael Curry, a Black American bishop, originally from Chicago. Other members of the Royal Family, including Camilla, Kate – who had given birth to her third child the previous month – Zara Tindall and the Princesses Beatrice and Eugenie battled to control guffaws, smirks and side-eye glances. Charles, meanwhile, found the order of service absolutely riveting.

The honeymoon of the royal newly-weds was kept a

secret. They could have slipped away for peace and quiet to the Highlands as so many had done, including Sophie and Edward, the then Princess Elizabeth and Prince Philip, and Charles and Camilla. Both Harry and Meghan were worried at the prospect of their trip being spoiled by photographers. Harry revealed in his book *Spare* that they made their escape from London in a removals van with the windows covered in cardboard. They ended up sailing around the Mediterranean for ten days. Disappointingly Harry recalled, 'We were also sick. The build-up to the wedding had worn us down.'

They were back in time to go to Royal Ascot and take part in the traditional procession down the course in an open-topped carriage. This was one of the Queen's favourite weeks of the year. Prince Philip would happily wave to the racegoers and then disappear into the Royal Box to watch the cricket on television. On this occasion Meghan was seated in a carriage next to Sophie, and she chatted amiably until she was dive-bombed by a flying insect.

Sophie loves Ascot week, and not just because the Queen enjoyed it so much. In 2018, she and Edward went four times, including on their wedding anniversary, while Meghan attended just on the first day. It's the only time so far that Meghan has been. By October, Meghan was pregnant and the news was announced officially by the Palace. She did travel to give a speech on female empowerment in Fiji and another on women's suffrage in Wellington, New Zealand.

She was back in the UK the same month for the next royal wedding at St George's Chapel. The centre of attention this time round was Lady Louise, who was to be a bridesmaid at her cousin Princess Eugenie's wedding to businessman Jack Brooksbank. Generally, Sophie did her best to keep her children well away from public scrutiny. One mention on social media or in the press was likely to generate a thousand posts.

She didn't want happy snaps of a family smiling together or any suggestion that she and Edward were using their children as a distraction from the more troublesome discussions about the Royal Family. She was happy, though, to agree when the princess asked if Louise could be a bridesmaid at her October wedding.

Louise had been chosen as a special attendant, which meant that at the age of fifteen she was responsible for ushering eight small pageboys and bridesmaids from their limousine into the service. She clung on tightly to the hands of the pageboys, one of whom was Prince George, the eldest son of William and Kate, but another, Louis de Givenchy, fell over as a strong gust of wind blew down the chapel steps. Louise had to haul him smartly to his feet. Then, Princess Charlotte, George's sister, took a tumble as well. Louise had to ignore the wind blowing her striking blue Claudie Pierlot-designed dress all over the place. She kept her head, staying focused as Sophie had told her to do. When she took her seat, slightly flushed, next to the Tindalls, Zara put her hand reassuringly on her wrist while Mike murmured a quiet 'well done'.

After the service, Kate's bold, fuchsia-coloured dress, designed by Alexander McQueen, also blew up in the wind just as the photographers started snapping away as the Royal party gathered outside the chapel; it was described as her Marilyn Monroe moment, recalling how the screen legend's dress famously billowed up over a subway grate in the film *The Seven Year Itch*. Fortunately for Kate she was standing next to Sophie, who placed a hand strategically to keep the dress down and then positioned herself close to her so that it wouldn't happen a second time. She had forgotten the Queen's old trick of making sure a little weight or two was sewn into the hem of her dresses. Panic over, the two women were soon giggling away at what had happened.

As a reward for being such a star on the day and to celebrate her fifteenth birthday, Sophie took Louise to a live recording of their favourite television programme – they didn't watch much TV together but they never missed *Strictly Come Dancing*. Often, they would make the trek over to Windsor Castle and watch it with the Queen, who was also a fan. Camilla and Charles, too, watched it every Saturday. Host Tess Daly gave Sophie and Louise a backstage tour before showing them to their front-row seats. Louise told Tess, 'This is such a treat.' They smiled and clapped happily along with the rest of the audience when cricketer Graeme Swann and professional dancer Oti Mabuse opened the show with a quickstep to the classic swing track 'Sing, Sing, Sing'.

Meghan, understandably, had practically vanished from public view during the last months of her pregnancy. By the time her son Archie was born in the spring of 2019, Sophie had delivered the biggest speech of her royal career.

24

The Unjust Stigma

Sophie patted her companion on the arm as they chatted happily yet intensely. This was not a fellow member of the Royal Family but one of the most glamorous women in the world – the Oscar-winning actress Angelina Jolie, who would become an unlikely mentor and role model for the Countess of Wessex. The two were the star guests at a special festival in 2018 at the British Film Institute (BFI) in London that proposed to use the power of film to help in the fight against discrimination faced by women survivors of wars and conflicts.

The festival, entitled Fighting Stigma Through Film, was supporting the Preventing Sexual Violence in Conflict Initiative (PSVI) that Angelina had helped set up in 2012 alongside the then Foreign Secretary William Hague. An astonishing total of thirty-eight films and documentaries were shown over two days, sharing the stories of survivors and inspiring those who watched to make a difference in the future.

Angelina was already on good terms with the Royal Family, and earlier in the year had appeared in the documentary *The Queen's Green Planet*, which promoted a project called the Queen's Green Canopy. The idea was to encourage the preservation of forests in each of the fifty-six Commonwealth countries. The Queen approved of Angelina, who was made an honorary dame in 2014 for her campaigning work against sexual violence in war zones.

At the time, the actress explained, 'It is a myth that rape is an inevitable part of conflict. There is nothing inevitable about it. It is a weapon of war aimed at civilians. It has nothing to do with sex, everything to do with power.'

At the Palace, the Queen was introduced to Angelina's then husband Brad Pitt and their six children, who all called the monarch 'Your Majesty' and bowed and curtsied as they had practised. The Queen clearly liked and admired Angelina. That was good enough for Sophie. She would also have approved of the star's words of advice to her children: 'What sets you apart is what you are willing to do for others. Anyone can put on a dress and make-up. It's your mind that will define you. Find out who you are, what you think, and what you stand for. And fight for others to have those same freedoms. A life of service is worth living.'

They are words that resonated with Sophie. When she met Angelina, it was not an occasion for designer outfits and cheeky hats, although the Hollywood actress still looked a million dollars and the glossy magazines noted that Sophie was stylish and gorgeous in a chic navy coat. Sophie had clearly dressed in a low-key manner for an evening that was dealing with such a serious subject; this was not a celebrity or showbusiness outing.

This was the day on which Sophie started to save the Royal Family.

She went away, convinced that she could and would do something meaningful for the cause herself. She decided to stand with Angelina to help women affected by sexual violence, including in the Democratic Republic of the Congo and South Sudan. She chose International Women's Day the following March to speak out about the consequences of conflict and to reveal that she would be taking an active role in the future.

Sophie wrote a moving piece for the *Daily Telegraph* under the headline: 'Why I'm joining the fight to end the silence around women in conflict'. She starkly identified the global problem: 'The consequences of conflict do not go away when the guns are laid down.' While Sophie was already a supporter of women, this was a frontline agenda. Sophie promised that she would be taking an active role in championing the cause of the PSVI and also the UK's work on 'Women, Peace and Security'.

She highlighted the efforts already being made around the world, including in Syria, where local projects were training doctors to provide expert forensic medical reports for court evidence of sexual violence. 'More needs to be done,' she said, simply. Sophie ended her thought-provoking observation: 'Only when women and men work alongside each other as equals will the world see sustained improvement in conflict resolution and a reduction in sexual violence in conflict.'

A couple of days later Sophie was in New York giving a speech that she wrote herself to the United Nations General Assembly. Her contribution was part of the UN's 'Women in Power' event that was discussing, as Sophie put it, 'the crucial issues of gender equality and women's empowerment'. She spoke eloquently and confidently as she promoted the need for women to have a seat at the table of power. She emphasised, 'If all the seats at the table are full, you just need to pull up an extra chair. There is no excuse not to include women.'

Sophie recalled her conversation at the PSVI International Film Festival with Nobel Peace Prize laureate, Dr Denis Mukwege, a gynaecologist in the Democratic Republic of the Congo, who had treated hundreds of victims of rape and abuse. She had been struck by his words about silence: 'He considers the silence to be an enemy of survivors of sexual violence and a crime in itself; the silence that prevents survivors, their families and communities from reporting these crimes and seeking justice – and makes complicit those who deliberately enable such a situation. Here at the UN we can give survivors a voice, we can break down the stigma they face.'

Sophie was sensible enough not to fill the room with empty rhetoric. Instead, she issued a rallying call for everyone present to listen to those women on the ground, whether they were leaders or victims. She concluded by confirming her determination to use her position to 'break down the silence around sexual violence and to champion women's full and meaningful participation in peace.'

It was a powerful speech, well made and well meant.

You might have thought that Sophie had a willing partner for this work just a mile or two down the road at home. Like Angelina Jolie, Meghan Markle was a beautiful Hollywood actress who had supported important issues affecting women around the world; she and Harry had only just moved into Frogmore Cottage, a property that briefly had been under consideration as a home for Sophie and Edward. Meghan was also very pregnant and was being criticised unfairly in the tabloid press for cradling her baby bump and for eating avocado on toast, a snack that apparently fuelled drought and murder.

Sophie was back home when Meghan gave birth to a baby boy at the Portland Hospital in London in May 2019. The proud parents did not pose for photographers when they left to take their son home; nor did they reveal his name. Sophie was the first member of the Royal Family to pop round – she was the nearest – to see how the new mum was doing and to meet the sixth in line to the throne who had shoved her husband and children down one place in the order of succession.

A couple of days later their son's name, Archie Harrison (*Harry's son*) Mountbatten Windsor was released on Instagram, and Harry, Meghan and Archie took part in an official photocall at St George's Hall, Windsor, where the Queen met and posed with her great-grandson.

The daily media pursuit of Meghan and Harry continued throughout the year, prompting the prince to say, 'I lost my mother and now I watch my wife falling victim to the same powerful forces.' Seventy-two women MPs signed a letter expressing solidarity with the duchess against national newspaper coverage, calling out the 'outdated colonial undertones' of some of the stories. The attention continued when the family travelled to South Africa and Archie was introduced to the legendary figure Archbishop Desmond Tutu. The next month the television documentary *Meghan and Harry: An African Journey* was broadcast in which Meghan, filled with emotion, memorably said, 'You've got to thrive. You've got to be happy.'

Understandably, there was only one royal story in town, and it wasn't Sophie following up on her promise and visiting women victims of war. She went to the state of Kosovo in south-eastern Europe to meet survivors of the brutal war there that had devastated the country just before the millennium. An estimated 20,000 rapes of Kosovar women were carried out by Serbian soldiers and police during the conflict.

She met survivors of sexual violence, religious leaders and British NATO soldiers helping to keep the peace. She also visited the Heroinat Memorial in the capital, Pristina. The statue is of a woman's face made up of thousands of pins to represent the thousands of women affected by the conflict.

Sophie was visibly moved as she embraced survivors and joined hands; she has never been able to disguise sadness – you can see it in her eyes. She gave another thoughtful speech, in which she praised the women she had met: 'Their stories are harrowing and their pain is still so evident, but it is their courage and determination not to be defined by their dreadful experiences that is so very impressive.'

Once more, she challenged the stigma associated with these crimes: 'We must shift the blame from the victim to the perpetrator. Conflict leaves many wounds, but the biggest wound of all, I believe, is the unjust stigma that so many survivors are confronted with, not only here in Kosovo, but around the world.

'If the stigma goes unchallenged we are merely perpetuating the offence, over and over again. So I say there is no place for stigma in our world today ... no one should have to feel ashamed again.'

Truly, Sophie had found her voice.

Back at home in the UK, Sophie could only watch with the rest of the country as Prince Andrew torpedoed his own royal status with the now infamous Emily Maitlis interview about his connection with the notorious Jeffrey Epstein. As Emily herself observed, he lost the respect of the nation. Sophie followed the behind-the-scenes instruction never to comment on what had happened, but there would be one family member fewer carrying out royal engagements. Within a very few months, that number would increase to three.

It was business as usual for the rest of the Royal Family. Sophie enjoyed a sunny Christmas Day walk with Edward and the children to the annual church service in Sandringham. Sophie wore the usual suspects – an Emilia Wickstead blouse and a Suzannah London coat topped off with a Jane Taylor deep-red headband. Most noticeably for fashion commentators, she had lent – or given – an outfit to Louise, including a Stella McCartney coat that seemed to fit her perfectly.

Harry and Meghan were in Vancouver, Canada, for a private Christmas. Nobody quite realised it at the time but that was the start of the 'short goodbye' for the Sussexes. They announced after New Year that they would be dividing their time between North America and the UK and stepping back as 'senior' members of the Royal Family. They intended to 'work to become financially independent'.

Nobody suggested it, but Edward and Sophie had already shown many years before that it was impossible to be half in and half out of the Royal Family. After the fiasco of Ardent and R-JH, they had been faced with a choice and decided to be fully in. Part of Sophie had always missed that independence, but she was now showing that you could have a public face – and voice – as well as a private one in the Royal Family.

Understandably, all the headlines and conjecture were about what Harry and Meghan were actually going to do. Sophie did not capture the attention when she flew to Sierra Leone in the same month. The West African country, which the Queen had visited before Sophie was born, was the location for her next step towards countering the stigma of sexual violence in conflict. The figures for war rape were overwhelming – UN agencies estimated that more than 60,000 women were raped during the civil war in Sierra Leone between 1991 and 1992. Again, Sophie met with survivors of the violence and saw the archives that recorded their suffering for future generations. She attended a learning club that increased awareness of gender-based violence. She was also told about a programme distributing menstrual hygiene products and educating girls about their menstrual health. Once more, Sophie was keen to hear about progress in meeting the challenge of bringing perpetrators of sexual and gender-based violence to justice, as a result of the stigma that prevented many cases from being reported. In many depressing areas of gender concern, Sophie and Meghan were singing from the same hymn sheet.

Meghan made a deft farewell to the UK during International Women's Week in the first week of March 2020, bowing out with a visit to a school in Dagenham where she urged the boys there to value and appreciate the women in their lives. Sophie was in South Sudan, perhaps at the time the country worst affected by conflict rape. She was accompanied on the trip by Christina Lamb of the *Sunday Times*, who subsequently wrote a feature that captured Sophie as a person and not just as a royal wearer of designer dresses.

Christina was very amusing in quoting the Court Circular of 3 March: 'The Queen held an Investiture at Buckingham Palace this morning. The Prince of Wales, President, visited the Royal College of Music. The Countess of Wessex arrived at Juba International Airport, South Sudan.' Anyone following the news would know that South Sudan in north-east Africa was one of the most dangerous countries in the world to visit.

The grim conditions that the two women witnessed surprised even a seasoned war correspondent like Christina. Sophie told her, 'I didn't expect my first visit to the Nile to be like this. I thought it would be in Egypt by some temples.' In a camp run by UN peacekeepers they were told that victims even fear going to hospital as they might be seen. 'People will say she is a dirty woman rather than castigating the man with a gun who raped her. There is no justice or rehab centre.'

Sophie was not turning into the Mother Teresa of Bagshot Park. She would be back home at the weekend, popping over to Windsor to tell the Queen about her trip abroad, as she always did. Quite often, the Queen had visited the country in question at some point, but not South Sudan, which had been in existence only since 2011. Sophie summed it up to Christina, 'I have to compartmentalise.'

Before they left, Sophie gave another impassioned speech. She again called for an end to the stigma that survivors face and called for them to achieve justice. On this occasion she called for investment to ensure that every girl – and boy – was given a quality education.

At the weekend, she joined Edward and other members of the Royal Family for the annual Commonwealth Day Service at Westminster Abbey, which was one of the must-attend events of the year. This time it was the last public occasion for Meghan and Harry as full-time working Royals. Meghan wore a sunny smile the whole time while her green Emilia Wickstead dress launched a thousand photographs. They sat in the same row as Edward and Sophie, who didn't seem to have much to say and was clearly very tired after her distressing trip. Edward was more chatty, as always at such events. Afterwards, Meghan wasted little time in catching a flight back to Vancouver. She just beat lockdown. All Sophie had to say about her former neighbours was, 'I just hope they will be happy.'

25

Lockdown Support

Most days, Sophie, Edward, Louise and James would try to make it round to Windsor Castle when Covid lockdown began in late March 2020. These were lonely times for everyone and that included the Queen and Prince Philip, deprived of the family contact that they so enjoyed. The Wessex four had to stay outside, waving to the elderly couple on the balcony, twenty feet up in the air. They would have to shout their hellos and how-are-yous. Sophie explained, 'It always seemed to be so windy so we could barely hear.'

The Queen, her husband and some essential staff were in what had been nicknamed HMS *Bubble*. The whole country, it seemed, was in separate bubbles, checking on nearest and dearest through the letterboxes of the land. To begin with, the Queen did not even have the distraction of a corgi because she had been adamant that at her age she did not want any more dogs. She thought she was too old to give them the attention and the walks a pet would need.

That changed when Covid arrived and she welcomed a new corgi called Muick, named after one of her favourite spots in the Highlands where Sophie had taken a happy photograph many years before. She couldn't wait to go back there. Sophie was pleased with the Queen's decision: 'Dogs have to be exercised and that's always a good motivator. It forces you to go outside.'

At Bagshot Park they had two dogs that needed walking around the grounds at least twice a day. Edward, in particular, doted on the dogs – a black Labrador called Teal and a cocker spaniel they had named Mole. They would be joined later by Teasel, a sweet black Labrador puppy.

Sophie had no intention of sitting around catching up on box sets – although she did love *Line of Duty* and was later pleased with herself for correctly guessing the identity of chief villain 'H'. She was determined to help in the Covid effort and join thousands of people up and down the country doing their bit to help those less fortunate. Her first task was to send a handwritten letter of encouragement to Amanda McLean, who was in charge of the Thames Valley Air Ambulance, a service that remained close to her heart. She told Amanda, 'Please look after yourselves and each other as we make our way through this period.'

She thought it important that the Royal Family be seen to contribute. Kind words were a good start; so was joining in the nationwide weekly clapping for the doctors, nurses, carers and other underappreciated health workers. Every Thursday at 8pm they stood outside the back door of Bagshot to applaud. Sophie did not want to stay trapped behind the gates of Bagshot Park, so she sprung into action as soon as lockdown came into effect by driving over to Camberley to volunteer at the Hope Hub charity, where she helped to pack up meals and essentials for the homeless and vulnerable. She later delivered Easter eggs to cheer up those housed in temporary accommodation during the pandemic. A couple of days after that she was in the London kitchens of Rhubarb, a company that provided catering for many key events throughout the year, including private boxes at Royal

Ascot. Sophie put on mask and gloves to prepare vast vats of spaghetti to be taken to beleaguered NHS workers. The following week she drove to Frimley Park Hospital to help pack up meals. She was usually photographed doing these good works, with the expectation that it would encourage others to follow suit.

Edward was keeping busy with a mountain of Zoom calls to personally congratulate DofE Gold Award winners. He did join Sophie in June 2020 to help prepare meals at the London Irish Rugby Football Club in Brentford and then deliver them to the hospital. Sophie was filmed making a video call to an air ambulance team from a corner of her kitchen – the first time anyone had seen inside the home where she had lived for more than twenty years. The crew were surrounded by cardboard boxes while Sophie had three vintage fine china tea sets behind her. Her camouflage blouse was more in keeping with the difficult times.

The children had to continue their studies at home. Louise was now in her GCSE year and was doing well in academic pursuits as well as sporting ones. She had opted to study English, history, politics and drama at A Level and was hoping to go to university – something her mother had missed out on. James, meanwhile, would be moving to senior school the following year. Edward and Sophie had opted for Radley College, a private school in Oxfordshire where he would board, if Covid allowed. Inevitably there were family quarrels between a brother and sister spending so much time together at home. Sophie would break up the bickering by encouraging Louise to go out for a cycle ride, something her daughter found very soothing, and she would arrive back home calm, having forgotten the argument. Just like her mother, she preferred to be outdoors.

Restrictions eased enough in the summer for the Queen

and Prince Philip to travel to Scotland as usual to begin their annual holiday at Balmoral. The Wessexes were the first family guests to arrive. They had waited at Bagshot for Louise's GCSE results – they were good despite the national controversy about grades based on estimates and algorithms – before speeding up to the Highlands and enjoying the fresh air and country walks with the grandparents.

They were the last to leave but they were soon out and about again as a family. This time they drove seventy miles to Portsmouth to spend the day cleaning up Southsea Beach. The event was labelled the Great British Beach Clean. The Royal presence gave the day a huge publicity boost at a difficult time. The day met the government guidelines and provided a double-edged benefit for Sophie. First, her children could experience the pleasure and satisfaction of volunteering for something worthwhile, and second, it was important for the environment. They all put on gloves and picked up plastic bottles, broken fishing lines, wet wipes and other litter that had been left by careless visitors at a beautiful spot. This particular year saw a nationwide crisis over the amount of discarded PPE that was a constant reminder of Covid. The prospect of discovering a valuable Roman coin in a face mask was an incentive, but they had to make do with collecting empty beer bottles.

At all times the Royal Family had to meticulously follow government guidelines. That was an essential requirement for being a national figurehead.

On 4 October 2020, Sophie ran in the Virtual London Marathon, postponed from its usual April spot on the sporting calendar. She did not complete the whole 26.2 miles, although she probably could have managed it with enough training. Instead, she ran one and a half miles in the rain – not her favourite pastime – in Windsor Great Park, as part of Team Mencap's participation in a virtual version of the annual event. She had been the charity's patron since 2004. She ran alongside a man with learning disabilities who was competing in his first marathon. She called him an inspiration but so was she for, quite simply, getting stuck in.

Shortly afterwards, on 9 October, Sophie found she needed to self-isolate having come into contact with someone who tested positive for Covid the next day. She didn't show any symptoms but, like so many others, had to stay indoors. She could not pop over to visit the Queen, although the rest of the family were still able to come and go because, thankfully, Sophie did not have a dark line on a test so was the only one at Bagshot Park who had to isolate.

Although the Queen and Prince Philip were back at Windsor Castle, for the first time in more than thirty years they decided to miss the family's traditional Christmas gathering at Sandringham. The omicron strain of the virus had produced a surge of cases and greater concerns once more about the winter threat of Covid. Edward and Sophie travelled up to Norfolk with Louise and James and the four of them, in masks, were the only members of the Royal Family to attend the Christmas Day service.

Kate and William were in Norfolk, staying at Anmer Hall, their residence about three miles from the Sandringham Estate. The two families did meet up briefly at the Luminate light trail, a Christmas-themed after-dark woodland walk on the estate. The children did mingle together a little, which caused some question of whether the two-tier lockdown rules that were in force at the time were being obeyed properly. Louise was very popular with the young children, especially Charlotte. She had been the ideal babysitter during Balmoral holidays, patiently spending time showing the young princess how to draw pictures of rabbits and deer.

The Queen's traditional Christmas message, which had been broadcast every year of her reign, reflected what a difficult year it had been for everyone: 'For many, this time of year will be tinged with sadness – some mourning the loss of those dear to them, and others missing friends and family members distanced for safety when all they'd really want for Christmas is a simple hug or a squeeze of the hand. If you are among them, you are not alone.'

Surely 2021 would be a better year for everyone. But then, in April, Prince Philip passed away peacefully in his sleep.

On the morning Prince Philip died, Lady Louise took out his carriage and gave his two favourite ponies a spin in Windsor Great Park. It was her personal mark of respect to her beloved grandfather. He had ensured he bequeathed his granddaughter the two horses, Balmoral Nevis and Notlaw Storm, as well as his green carriage that he had designed and in which he had spent so many happy hours. She always made him very proud and, undoubtedly, he would have asked her how the day's drive had gone if he had seen her afterwards.

Prince Philip died at Windsor Castle just two months shy of his one-hundredth birthday, when he would have been eligible for a congratulatory telegram from his dear wife. They had been married for seventy-three years. He was also the longest-serving consort – husband or wife – of a British monarch in history. Sophie described his last moments: 'It was so gentle. It was just like somebody took him by the hand and off he went – very, very peaceful, and that's all you want for somebody, isn't it?' She was clearly struck with grief – and would be for some time – when she attended a church service at Windsor with the family two days after he died. Edward gallantly put into words for the media what everyone was feeling: 'However much one prepares oneself for something like this, it's still a dreadful shock. And we're still trying to come to terms with that. And it's so very sad.'

The Queen released the treasured photograph that had been taken by Sophie while she was pregnant with Louise in 2003. The picture showed the Queen and her husband happy, relaxed and smiling while seated on a tartan rug on the hillside known as the Coyles of Muick, a favourite beauty spot near Balmoral. They were just a couple enjoying a day out with their daughter-in-law. It was a perfect memory.

The Duke of Edinburgh would have a proper ceremonial funeral – not a state one – in St George's Chapel. On the day, the nation witnessed probably the most iconic and certainly the saddest image of the whole Covid crisis. The Queen, a frail but dignified figure in black, obeying the social-distancing rules and sitting by herself; completely by herself. Her lonely image would resonate with everyone who had lost someone in those unforgiving times. Sophie observed, 'It was very poignant.' The sombreness of the occasion was heightened by the limit on the number of people allowed to attend – just thirty – so there were many rows of empty pews. Edward was one of those walking behind the coffin and was taken aback to walk into the Chapel and realise just how few people were there. Everyone wore black clothing and a black mask – there were no military uniforms. Sophie was so upset that at one point she had to remove her mask to wipe her teary eyes and blow her nose. She was seated between her two children in the same row as Camilla and Charles. James was just thirteen but Louise, at seventeen, had accompanied her parents on the official outings they had undertaken in connection with acknowledging Philip's passing.

Prince Harry had flown in from the US, although Meghan remained in California, as she was expecting her second child. The funeral took place a month after the broadcast of their controversial interview with Oprah Winfrey in which they spoke candidly about their mental health challenges and the racism Meghan had faced. Sophie and Edward were asked about the Oprah interview a few weeks later by Camilla Tominey when they invited the royal journalist for a rare chat inside Bagshot Park for the *Telegraph Magazine*. They shut down the discussion quickly and lightly. Edward answered, 'Oprah who?' while Sophie chuckled, 'Yes, what interview?' The days of them blundering into things and generating unwelcome headlines had long gone.

While the Oprah interview was a talking point for many months, it later emerged that the biggest controversy surrounding the funeral happened the night before, at 10 Downing Street, where there were two raucous leaving parties. The *Daily Telegraph* put the number of people socialising at about thirty, matching the number who were allowed to attend the funeral the following day. One partygoer said that a staff member made the short walk to the local Co-op on The Strand with a suitcase and returned with it brimming with bottles of wine.

After the full extent of what went on had been revealed, Sir Ed Davey, the leader of the Liberal Democrats, observed, 'The Queen sitting alone, mourning the loss of her husband, was the defining image of lockdown. Not because she is the Queen, but because she was just another person, mourning alone like too many others. Whilst she mourned, Number 10 partied.' Following an investigation, the police issued fines to some of those who attended.

After the funeral, everyone went back to the Palace and Sophie was able to catch up with Harry and hear his news. Then she and Edward went back to Bagshot Park to watch the day on TV.

*

Surprisingly, considering it was Prince Philip's long-term and well-known wish, the title Duke of Edinburgh was not granted immediately to Edward. The rules meant that it was passed first of all to Charles, the eldest son and heir, and he seemed in no hurry to give it to his younger brother. The Queen was still technically the Duchess of Edinburgh, so he might have thought it more fitting to wait while she was still alive. Edward would have to make do with being the Earl of Forfar, a title that he had been granted when he turned fifty-five in 2019. The title had appeal for Edward because of the town's association with his grandmother, the Queen Mother, whose famous home, Glamis Castle, is only ten minutes away in the car.

Sophie went back to business as usual after Prince Philip's funeral, although she made sure she checked in daily with her mother-in-law. Every couple of days she would drive over for a socially distanced chat and a cup of tea. The Queen was still in official mourning for her husband when she passed the age of ninety-five just four days after the funeral; nobody was in the mood for a celebration.

Sophie continued to be busy. She became patron of the Wellbeing of Women charity, very much the kind of organisation she liked to support both at home and internationally. She wanted to add her voice to the need for discussions about issues, predominantly periods and the menopause, that affected every woman. She explained, 'We've all been there, and it's about time we had a grown-up conversation about it.'

Encouraging grown-up conversations was one of the characteristics that distinguished Sophie's work within the Royal Family; it didn't stop her getting licked by sweet dogs when she took over as patron of Guide Dogs for the Blind. She succeeded Princess Alexandra, who had fulfilled the role for sixty years but was now eighty-four. Sophie was already committed to supporting the organisation because of her determination to help those with sight problems after what had happened to Louise at birth. The two Royal ladies were together to open a new Guide Dogs Regional Centre when the transition was announced. Popping into the Guide Dogs Scotland HQ in Forfar made Sophie's trips up there particularly enjoyable.

The death of her father-in-law was still obviously very raw for Sophie when she agreed to a wide-ranging interview with Naga Munchetty for Radio 5 Live to coincide with what would have been Prince Philip's one hundredth birthday. She invited the *BBC Breakfast* presenter to Bagshot Park and told her that the loss of Prince Philip had left a 'giant-sized hole' in the lives of the Royal Family. She was fighting back the tears when she spoke of him, describing it as an 'Oh my goodness moment'.

She came across as being entirely sensible about the things that mattered to her, taking the opportunity to rekindle her campaign to increase awareness about rape in war. She did not want the issue to 'drop off the agenda'. She thought there was a case for teaching the subject in schools. She also promised to be an advocate for all those women who did not have a voice.

Sophie had pointed out to Naga that during lockdown they had all become adept at managing disappointment. Perhaps things were looking a little sunnier as the year wore on, but a major concern was the deterioration in the Queen's physical wellbeing. She was ninety-five, after all, and needed a walking stick for the first time at an important official function – the centenary in October of the Royal British Legion at Westminster Abbey. A week later she spent a rare night in hospital, King Edward VII's in Marylebone, for what an official statement said was for 'preliminary tests', whatever that meant. For the second year running she wasn't up to travelling to Norfolk for the traditional family gathering at Sandringham; in any case it wouldn't be the same without Philip.

Sophie and her family also decided to stay home at Bagshot Park so that they could celebrate with the Queen at Windsor. They went to a Christmas service in St George's Chapel, but the Queen did not attend. Her annual Christmas broadcast began with a lovely tribute to her 'beloved' Philip and his ability to 'squeeze the fun out of any situation'. She also mentioned that 2022 would be her Platinum Jubilee, marking seventy years since she succeeded her father as monarch.

26

The Trailblazer

In March 2022 Sophie quietly slipped out of the country to address a United Nations event in New York. There, she let the Taliban have it in no uncertain terms. She was the keynote speaker at a meeting highlighting the struggles of women in Afghanistan. The troops might have left but the crisis had not. In an emotional speech, Sophie said, 'The effects are worsening daily. The Taliban would have us believe that they are allowing citizens to go about their daily activities. We know this is not true.'

Afghanistan was facing a humanitarian and economic crisis as well as food shortages. 'It is hard to imagine how much life has changed for so many in so little time – where once there was hope, with women playing a central role in society, there is now hunger, destitution and violence.' Sophie delivered one stark message that summed up the prevalent attitude in so many of the issues she considered the most important in the world: 'We need to ask why men are so afraid of having women in the room.'

The event was called simply 'Upholding Women's Rights in Afghanistan'. Listening to Sophie's powerful words, it was clear they didn't have many rights at all. The evening was hosted by three important organisations: UN Women, the

Georgetown Institute for Women, Peace and Security, and a third called the Group of Friends of Women in Afghanistan that aimed to promote collective, international action to safeguard and strengthen the human rights of women and girls in the aftermath of the ruinous conflict in that country.

Sophie didn't just wake up one morning and think it was a good idea. Her dedication to similar agendas throughout the world was getting her noticed. During the frustrations of the Covid lockdown she had been a guest at international virtual events raising the issue. While her Afghanistan speech was the centre point of her trip to New York, she also attended a UN briefing about Ukraine and the effects of the Russian invasion on the female population.

She was only in the US for four days, but she dashed around making sure she did not ignore the other issues that mattered most to her. She met with international eye health leaders from UN Women, UNICEF and the World Health Organization to celebrate the adoption of the United Nations 'Vision for Everyone Resolution', as part of her role as Global Ambassador for the International Agency for the Prevention of Blindness (IAPB). The agreement, which had been passed unanimously in July 2021, set down eye health as part of the UN's Sustainable Development Goals in support of the 1.1 *billion* people living with preventable sight loss worldwide.

She did not forget another of her global ambassador roles, joining the 100 Women in Finance organisation for lunch to discuss the greater need for gender equality in the workplace, especially when it came to promotion and pay. As ever, the reporting of her visit to New York was torn between what she wore and what she said, but her powerful message about women victims of war resonated with the Georgetown Institute based in Washington and she was awarded the Hillary Rodham Clinton Award for her work concerning sexual violence. She could look forward to receiving the accolade later in the year from the former secretary of state herself.

Sophie had one very familiar royal task to complete while in New York – she planted a tree. The Queen planted her first tree in 1937 and planted more than 1,500 over the years since. Sophie picked up a spade and placed a rosemary bush into the ground at the Queen Elizabeth II September 11th Garden, a small welcoming space in Hanover Square, Lower Manhattan, that is dedicated to the memory of the people of the Commonwealth who lost their lives in the 9/11 attacks on the World Trade Center.

Sophie had to make sure she was back home in the UK for the first big ceremonial event of the year – the memorial service for Prince Philip at Westminster Abbey on 29 March. Thirty people had been at his original funeral because of Covid; 1,800 attended this tribute. While the occasion was packed full of European royalty, the most notable attendees were some of the Duke of Edinburgh's Gold Award winners that he had specifically asked to be at his funeral. They lined up on either side of the Abbey entrance. The scheme truly was his life's work.

The official Platinum Jubilee celebrations began on 2 June with an open-topped carriage parade down The Mall for the Trooping of the Colour. The Queen was in attendance to begin the celebrations, but she was not well enough to attend several of the other planned events, including the State Opening of Parliament. Sophie shared a carriage with her two children and Prince Edward, who looked slightly self-conscious in full military dress. Sophie appeared far more comfortable in a pink gingham coat dress that had been designed by Suzannah London using sustainable cloth. She waved happily to the cheering crowds; this was a good way to get the bank holiday weekend started. Fashion experts noticed that Lady Louise's hat was borrowed from her mother, who had worn the Philip Treacy creation to the same ceremony thirteen years before in 2009.

The Palace balcony was limited to working members of the Royal Family, which was a neat way of making sure the headlines were not about shamed Prince Andrew, who the Queen had stripped of his military titles and royal patronages in January of that year, or Harry and Meghan, who had flown in from California with their young children, Lilibet and Archie. Lilibet, who had been born the previous June in Santa Barbara, California, would turn one during the jubilee celebrations and was taken by her parents to meet the Queen in person for the first time at Buckingham Palace; there were no pictures.

Harry and Meghan were at the thanksgiving service in St Paul's Cathedral the following day but were placed in the row behind Sophie and her family. They were late to arrive and the Princesses Eugenie and Beatrice, and their husbands, had to stand up to let them pass along as if it was a screening at the Odeon on a Saturday night. The Queen did not attend, nor was she fit enough to make the trip to Epsom for the Derby the next day. She watched Desert Crown win the race on television. Sophie and Edward also missed the race because they had travelled over to Belfast and Bangor to make sure Northern Ireland was included in the celebrations. They were a good choice for meeting the public – pouring pints of Guinness, making omelettes with Michelin Star chef Jean-Christophe Novelli and tucking into a Belfast Bap, basically a big fry-up in a roll that they were told was a favourite cure for a hangover. As always, Sophie was good with the excited children and joined in with some craft classes.

They were back in London in time for the jubilee concert,

the Platinum Party at the Palace. Once more, disappointingly, the Queen was not well enough to attend but she did steal the show for the 22,000 people in The Mall with a delightful video clip that opened proceedings, in which she co-starred with Paddington Bear. She had filmed the sketch back in March but had kept it a secret as much as possible from the rest of the family. She was seen having tea with Paddington, voiced by Ben Whishaw, at the Palace. She revealed that she kept a marmalade sandwich in the royal handbag. Simon Farnaby, who directed the clip, suggested to the Queen that she should say her lines as if she was talking to her grandchildren. He told Richard Herring's *Leicester Square Theatre* podcast that he had congratulated her after filming: 'Ma'am, that was fantastic. You're a very good actress.' She replied, 'Well, of course, I do it all the time.'

Sophie stayed for the whole concert. Meghan and Harry, who would have attracted much comment and attention, stayed away. Brian May was not on the roof this time around but Queen did open proceedings with 'We Will Rock You'. Sophie was on her best royal form for the final day of celebrations on 5 June, when she and Edward walked down the very long row of almost 500 picnic tables for 3,000 people that had been set up on the Long Walk at Windsor for the Big Jubilee Lunch. The Wessexes chatted to as many diners as possible, reminiscing about the Queen's reign and answering questions about how the monarch was feeling. Nine days later Sophie was at Royal Ascot every day, but the Queen missed the entire meeting for the first time since her coronation.

A month later, though, the Queen looked on happily as Sophie proudly took pictures of Lady Louise leading the parade of fell ponies at the Royal Windsor Horse Show, driving Philip's carriage as she always did. The Queen didn't want to miss her favourite horse show.

Her daughters-in-law stood in for her at the Commonwealth Games at the end of the month, which gave Sophie the chance to quiz Kate about the University of St Andrews, which was the first choice for Louise – it seemed a secure location for a royal student. Sophie was very keen that Louise should lead a normal life at uni – something that Kate had seemed to do even if her boyfriend was a prince. Louise's A-Level grades were kept a secret but were good enough, probably the required three A grades, to secure her a place to read English at St Andrews, the subject Sophie would have chosen if she had continued her education after leaving school. Kate was a fan of her alma mater, especially now that an Ardent Productions film crew would not be hiding in the bushes to bother Louise – perhaps she too would find a long-term love there.

Covid had scuppered many school-leavers' plans for a gap year, so Louise spent part of the summer holiday working in a garden centre near home and saving up for her first car. She greeted customers with a sunny hello, helped out on the tills and watered the plants. As one shopper memorably put it, 'It's not every day you buy your begonias from a Royal.' At the time the national minimum wage was £6.83 an hour.

When the A-Level results were announced Louise was with her mum and dad at Balmoral for the annual August holiday in the Highlands, but everyone was back at Bagshot Park by the end of the month. It was business as usual for Sophie; Thursday 8 September began normally with a visit to a school in Caterham, followed after lunch with chatting to elderly residents at the Woodhouse Centre in Oxted, a workshop that taught new skills to retired men and women and those with disabilities. And then Sophie received the call that Mama was fading.

She dropped everything and dashed to a waiting RAF

plane to travel to Scotland with her husband, Prince Andrew and Prince William. They landed in Aberdeen at 4pm and William drove them to Balmoral to join the vigil at the Queen's bedside where Charles, Camilla, Anne and Tim Laurence had already gathered. They were too late – the Queen had already passed.

Her death was announced to the nation at 6.30pm. She was ninety-six. Her biographer Gyles Brandreth wrote that she had been suffering from bone marrow cancer, which would have been a cause of her painful mobility problems. Officially, she died of old age, but it would be easy to speculate that she never recovered her spark after the death of her great love, Prince Philip. The crowds that had cheered the Platinum Party just three months earlier, now wept.

At Balmoral, Sophie and the other members of the family began a period of traditional royal mourning. Lady Louise arrived and joined her mother and father at a church service in Crathie Kirk. Afterwards she held her mother's hand as Sophie chatted with the line of well-wishers outside the church. They read some of the messages left on floral tributes before going back to the castle.

Amid all the protocols and nationwide condolences, two images stood out as the nation prepared for the state funeral. The first was when the Queen's coffin arrived at the Palace of Holyroodhouse in Edinburgh after a six-and-a-half-hour journey in a hearse from Balmoral. Princess Anne was clearly upset and Sophie put a comforting hand on her back; it would not be the last time she would make that gesture to a member of the Royal Family, but not many realised that Sophie and Anne had developed a very good relationship over the years.

The second was of Sophie and Edward's fourteen-year-old son, James, head bowed, standing vigil with his cousins by the coffin lying in state at Westminster Hall. He was the youngest of the grandchildren group that comprised William, Harry, Beatrice, Eugenie, Louise, Zara and Peter that stood guard for fifteen minutes. Sophie and Edward looked on, a little nervously, from the Gallery. Sophie later told the *Telegraph* that James had been 'really keen' to take part even though he was the youngest: 'I was slightly holding my breath, wanting them to feel they had done it well more than anything else.'

The Times estimated that one million people had descended on the capital for the funeral on 19 September. The newspaper's writer Ben McIntyre described it as 'the grandest the world had seen', but it was also a time for private grief. Sophie arrived at Westminster Abbey in a car with Meghan. She sat with Edward at the end of the front row for the service and both were in tears. Sophie wiped her eyes with a tissue. On the way out, she put a consoling arm around Prince George, who would be king one day. In the car ride back to Windsor, both she and Edward were still very upset. They said their final goodbyes at a private committal service before Mama was interred in the vault of the King George VI Memorial Chapel, the final resting place of her closest family.

Sophie resumed her working life with gusto. She was the first member of the Royal Family to travel to the Democratic Republic of the Congo to lend her voice to those within the country who had suffered sexual violence in the fighting that had engulfed the country in recent years. Her campaigning was clearly getting somewhere because she had been asked to make the trip by the Foreign Office. She was able to speak of her visit at the International Conference for Preventing Sexual Violence in Conflict that was held in London the following month. Sophie had found a willing international partner highlighting the global problem in Olena Zelenska, First Lady of Ukraine.

Olena would be with her once more before the end of the year when Sophie travelled to Georgetown University in Washington to receive the Hillary Rodham Clinton Award from the former US first lady, who called her a 'trailblazer'. Sophie delivered a powerful speech which confirmed that description. She declared, 'My work with women activists and peace builders is one in which I hold huge pride. I listen to their voices and I hear courage and commitment in every word. They work tirelessly without seeking recognition or accolade, moving heaven and earth to protect and support those in need.'

She had to pause and move away from the microphone during the speech to grab a tissue but, this time, it wasn't to wipe away a tear. She had a sniffle. She told the audience, 'That's a first for me, but you don't want me to carry on sniffing throughout.'

27

The Show Must Go On

Sophie was still waiting to become a duchess. King Charles III continued to drag his feet about making his youngest brother the next Duke of Edinburgh. As the Prince of Wales, Charles had inherited the title on his father's death and so, technically, he was the second Duke of Edinburgh. The timing of passing it on to Edward was entirely at his discretion, and while his mother would certainly have wanted him to do this, it seemed it was not top of Charles's agenda. Edward – and Sophie – stayed patient, fingers firmly crossed that the promise made public on their wedding day would eventually be fulfilled. The Queen's youngest son remained the first royal prince since Tudor times not to be created a duke.

We will never know what horse-trading went on behind Palace doors that caused the Queen in her last months to suddenly announce that she endorsed Camilla's future role as Queen Consort: 'When, in the fullness of time, my son becomes King, I know you will give him and his wife Camilla the same support you have given me. And it is my sincere wish that, when the time comes, Camilla will be known as Queen Consort as she continues her own loyal service.'

Whether Camilla ever actually wanted to become queen is another matter. Her biographer, Christopher Wilson, explained, 'There's a theory that she never wanted to marry Charles. Camilla and Andrew had divorced in early 1995, the same year as the controversial *Panorama* in which Diana had discussed Charles and Camilla's affair. Despite it all, Camilla remained devoted to Andrew Parker Bowles, was happy with her home life, and seemed to friends perfectly content for her unusual love triangle to continue.

'I don't think she ever envisaged becoming queen – but the decision was out of her hands. What Charles wants, Charles gets, and he wanted Camilla all to himself. The Queen was against the marriage but in the end, rather than risk a family rift which could stain her otherwise flawless reign, she gave in to her son's demands. The wedding was on.'

The suggestion from royal courtiers before Charles and Camilla were married in 2005 was that when the time came, the new royal wife 'intended' to be known as Princess Consort – a title that had never been used before in British history. This was Charles's idea, to appease public opinion following the death of Diana. According to Christopher Wilson, it was well known in royal circles that he had every intention of making Camilla his queen and that she would be crowned alongside him: 'Queen Elizabeth knew it was a lie and she was deeply uncomfortable with the subterfuge.'

In fairness to Camilla, she has never provoked controversy in her time as a royal partner – unlike Sophie with the Fake Sheikh and topless photos furore – but she wasn't close to the late queen. Sophie was, and she would have reflected the Queen's view of Camilla. Personally, she never had a problem with her but they had little in common other than coping with the corridors and courtiers of royal life. She and Edward are not part of the new king's inner circle and were never turning left from Bagshot Park towards Highgrove.

Sophie was brought up in a comfortable middle-class

existence but Camilla Shand, as she was born, was very much upper crust. Her family tree connects her with at least seven dukes, six marquesses, fifteen earls, seven viscounts and eight barons. She descends directly from kings and queens including Mary, Queen of Scots (1542–87) and King Charles II (1630–85). Ironically, the previous King Charles had the most famous royal mistress before Camilla, but Nell Gwyn was never queen. She did, however, live in Sophie's home village of Brenchley in a sprawling, half-timbered building called the Old Palace.

Camilla went to the prestigious Queen's Gate School in Kensington, followed by finishing school in Switzerland and then Paris. Her parents hosted her debutante 'coming out' party for 150 guests, then she enjoyed the 'season' full of balls and dances, tiaras and top hats. She was happy to let everyone know that her great-grandmother, Alice Keppel, was best known for being the mistress of King Edward VII. She did have something in common with Sophie, however. Her first job was as a secretary for various firms in the West End before being hired as a receptionist at a Mayfair decorating firm. She was fired after arriving late for work following a night on the town.

When the Queen died, Camilla was instantly placed at the top of the brigade of royal women, ahead of both Kate and Sophie, although the former will also be queen one day. Sophie, meanwhile, remained a mere countess despite she and Edward putting in the long years of official engagements. She would have to wait another six months after Mama's death to be elevated in the ranks. One theory among experts is that Charles wanted to save the title for his younger grandson, Prince Louis, who was born in 2018, and did not want him to wait until Edward died – after all, there was a fifteen-year age gap between the two brothers.

In the end, Charles did the right thing and Edward was made Duke of Edinburgh on his fifty-ninth birthday on 10 March 2023. The granting of the title had therefore seemed like a lovely birthday gift, rather than fulfilling the strong wishes of Prince Philip. Christopher Wilson observed, 'It's hard to get past the idea that Charles never fully appreciated the work Edward has done over the years in keeping their father's name alive with his work for the Duke of Edinburgh's Award Scheme.' Christopher could have added Sophie to that compliment, especially recalling her bike ride from Edinburgh to London.

In the short term, the decision meant that Edward and Sophie could now attend the coronation as Duke and Duchess on an equal footing with the other thirty or so odd dukes, although technically a royal duke ranked above a hereditary one. Edward's title is a peerage for life and when he dies it will revert back to the Crown – probably King William – to pass on as he wishes. The date of the coronation had been announced in the previous October, so Edward could be excused for thinking that as a mere Earl he and Sophie would be sat behind the wash pipes.

On the big day itself, Saturday 6 May 2023, Sophie and Edward had a front-row seat, literally. In the royal pecking order they were now right up there. The seating plan was Sophie, Edward and Kate, and then her children. William, who was needed for ceremonial duties, stood to the side. Prince George, too, had official duties in his role as a Page of Honour. Both ladies looked their most regal. Sophie wore a white, bridal-style, floor-length Suzannah London dress with a specially designed Jane Taylor headpiece that featured handmade satin leaves. Suzannah explained, 'The dress features a beautiful hand-embroidered train inspired by gowns and regalia from the Queen's coronation in 1953.' Kate wore

Alexander McQueen. Neither lady sported a tiara, perhaps avoiding headlines that would have called Kate the Queen-to-be. But they did both wear very grand, rich-blue mantles, trimmed in scarlet – the uniform of a Dame Grand Cross of the Royal Victorian Order. Camilla had chosen a Bruce Oldfield-designed dress, so it was very much the best of British for the three royal ladies.

Edward and Sophie had arrived with James, who was now the Earl of Wessex, and Louise, who was still Lady Louise, wearing a full-length Suzannah London silk dress that bore the hallmarks of one of the gowns that her mother would have loved. Sophie looked serious beforehand, wanting to make sure it went well for the family, a moment of history for them all. They entered the Abbey together and the children were sat in the second row next to the Duke of Gloucester. They were immediately in front of Prince Andrew, who had to make do with the third row, as did Prince Harry. His wife Meghan was a notable absentee, staying in California with her young children. She would have been the centre of so much media attention, not to mention photographic clamour, that it seemed like a wise decision not to attend. Fergie was also missing, although Princesses Beatrice and Eugenie were there.

Afterwards, Edward and Sophie, James and Louise were part of the troupe on the Palace balcony for the fly-past, again alongside Kate and William, Charlotte and Louis. Tim Laurence and the Princess Royal were there too, although Anne was almost hidden from view behind the much taller Princess of Wales. On the day, Anne had been given an important ceremonial role as the 'Gold Stick in Waiting', responsible for the monarch's safety during proceedings. She might have also been called a 'good stick' as she rode next to the new King's carriage on the way from the Abbey to the Palace. Charles, seventy-four, stayed safe, although many onlookers thought he looked tired during the day.

One of the more ironic afterthoughts about the big day is, what is going to be done with the archive footage? The BBC commentary was provided by the subsequently disgraced Huw Edwards, who was given a suspended jail sentence for possessing indecent images of children in September 2024. The crown was placed on the new King's head by the Archbishop of Canterbury, Justin Welby, who resigned two months later over his failure to properly report a prolific child abuser. You could change the voiceover, but it would be difficult not to have Welby doing the actual crowning. One of the other central figures was the Lord President of the Council, Penny Mordaunt, who cut a striking figure carrying the heavy Sword of State throughout the ceremony. She later confessed that she had taken painkillers to help her stay strong. The following year the former defence secretary lost her Portsmouth North seat at the general election.

Now was the time for everyone to breathe. The next day would see more celebrations, including street parties, but nothing that was going to be watched by 16 million people worldwide. Sophie and Edward drove thirty miles to the village of Cranleigh in Surrey for one of the community Big Lunches that were held throughout the country. Much closer to home they popped along to the grounds of Windsor Castle for the Coronation Concert, the first time such an event had been held there. Apparently, some well-known British acts had turned down the invitation to perform, although Take That closed the evening with 'Greatest Day', 'Shine' and 'Never Forget'. Sophie was there, again in the front row with Edward, Louise and James. She loved it and was clearly in her element, dancing and swaying to Lionel Ritchie's classic 'All Night Long', a hit in 1983 when Sophie was eighteen and enjoying discos and parties around Brenchley and the West End.

Sophie had spent most of the day within touching distance of Kate, which was reassuring for both of them but particularly for the new Princess of Wales. They were standing next to each other for the official coronation portraits that will be part of history in years to come. Even though Sophie was seventeen years older, the two women had developed an unshakeable bond ever since the Queen had put them together all those years before. They shared a similar taste in clothes and would chat about what they would be wearing, often selecting matching colours. They had both chosen bold red for the concert. They clearly had a conversation before the garden party at Buckingham Palace two days later when they wore striking, carefully coordinated blue outfits that had a queenly look that would have appealed to the late Queen.

And now they were neighbours, too. Kate and William had chosen to move into Adelaide Cottage in the Windsor Castle grounds, a much more private place to live than Kensington Palace. Kate was keen to make sure her children were brought up away from the limelight as much as possible, just as Sophie and Edward had managed to do with Louise and James. All three – George, Charlotte and Louis – currently attend Lambrook School, a ten-minute drive from home. When the family moved in late 2022 much was made of the fact that they were downsizing but, while it's true that their new home only has four bedrooms, they still have other homes dotted around the country. They have places in Wales, the Balmoral Estate and their main country retreat, the imposing mansion Anmer Hall on the Sandringham Estate. None of them can remotely match the size of Bagshot Park, however.

A tragic postscript to the coronation celebrations occurred

in West London. The day after attending the garden party, Sophie was being driven in an official car back to Windsor when one of her motorcycle outriders struck an elderly lady crossing the Cromwell Road near Earls Court. It may have surprised many that Sophie had a motorcycle guard. According to eyewitnesses, eighty-one-year-old Helen Holland sustained multiple injuries. Sophie's limousine was not involved. The Palace issued a brief statement: 'The Duchess's heartfelt thoughts and prayers are with the injured lady and her family.' Helen lost her fight for life two weeks after the accident and the Palace said that Sophie was 'deeply saddened'.

Sophie was out of the country when Helen Holland died. Her trip had been kept secret for security reasons. She had flown to Iraq, her first solo foreign visit as the Duchess of Edinburgh, to continue her efforts to promote the Women, Peace and Security (WPS) agenda and see the ongoing problems faced by women survivors in the country that had been ravaged by war in the first decade of the twenty-first century; it was hard to believe that it was twenty years since Saddam Hussein had been captured. Sophie was the first Royal to visit Baghdad, an illustration of the high regard in which she was held around the world. Increasingly, it seemed, she was the member of the Royal Family best equipped to deal with the serious issues of the day. She visited a school and a family planning centre, and attended a forum of female business leaders in Iraq trying to secure a fair wage for women.

She continued to promote global concern for these causes during her visit to Ethiopia later in the year when she witnessed the work that UNICEF was doing to help women in the country. She also visited a camp for internally displaced persons – mainly women and girls – which was like a small town, with 16,000 people living there. Sophie joined in playing table tennis, a game at which she was rather good. She marked World Sight Day, one of the most important in her annual calendar, by giving the keynote speech at a conference concerning plans to combat trachoma, the horrid eye disease in which sufferers find it excruciatingly painful to even blink and which can lead to blindness if left untreated. The aim was to eliminate trachoma by 2030.

Already it seemed it was business as usual, continuing to embrace the traditional events that had been an essential and enjoyable part of the late Queen's year: the Royal Windsor Horse Show in which Louise competed in the Coaching Marathon and acted as an official on the day; Royal Ascot, where Sophie cheered on the horses, laughing and joking with Kate and Camilla; the summer holiday with the royal gang in Balmoral; and the festive break at Sandringham that included the Christmas Day service at St Mary Magdalene Church.

Louise had reached her twentieth birthday in November, although Sophie missed the actual day because she was on a five-day solo visit to Toronto and Niagara, in Canada. She did manage to toast her daughter when she visited a winery and tasted the local wine. The main purpose of the trip was what was now called the Duchess of Edinburgh Cup, in which her military affiliations would go up against each other in a series of tough challenges. Sophie presented the winners with a trophy and later was the guest of honour at a dinner hosted by the Lincoln and Welland Regiment Foundation in Toronto. She was its Colonel-in-Chief, one of the military roles she had assumed, as all the senior Royals did.

Now that Louise had reached twenty and James would soon be thinking about his future after school, Sophie could be more relaxed about her family being out in the big world. The need for secrecy in order to protect them from the public gaze had reduced; it was time to be more open about her life.

28

The Brilliant Rock

Sophie had given so many moving speeches in the past few years, but arguably nothing had brought a tear to the eye more than what she said at Headingley Stadium in Leeds two days before 'my darling Edward' celebrated his sixtieth birthday in early March 2024: 'He is the best of fathers, the most loving of husbands and still my best friend.'

She was speaking at the Community Sport and Recreation Awards but took the opportunity to praise the man who had been the most important person in her life for more than thirty years. The trophies were being presented by Edward in his role as President of the Sport and Recreation Alliance. He was more than a little surprised when Sophie turned her speech into an appreciation of her husband. She had joined him to mark International Women's Day but had turned it into Edward Day.

She wanted to give the world an insight into the man to whom she was 'so proud to be married'. She began by saying that Edward would be horrified at what she was about to say about him and would look rather like his father had when she'd made a speech praising Prince Philip – eyes narrowed and arms folded. She had only spoken about the late Duke of Edinburgh in his presence twice: 'On both occasions feeling like I was about to launch myself out of an airplane without a parachute, but holding on to the vague hope of a soft landing.'

She wanted to point out some of the affiliations that Edward spent hours doing his best to support, from art and culture, to sport, charities helping people with disabilities, the environment and, of course, the DofE itself, which certainly owed a huge debt to Edward, as it did to his dad. Sophie insisted, 'He is not just a name on a piece of paper, but he commits of himself to them all and cares deeply for each of them.'

Edward was like an iceberg, she explained – what is seen above the water or in public is only a small proportion of what goes on behind the scenes: 'What is never seen or can ever be quantified is the effort spent on ensuring good governance for his patronages, encouraging people to support worthwhile causes, chairing committees, meeting chief executives and think tanks, writing papers, speeches, forewords, introductions, the list goes on.'

Sophie declared that he had been her guide and shown her the (Royal) way over the years. She confided that they usually shared speech notes but had not today. He would have put a line through most of the compliments.

Edward was not horrified at listening to his wife sing loudly his praises. Instead, he was clearly moved and quietly wiped his eye. Afterwards, she put her arms around him as they gazed into each other's eyes as if they were the only couple on their personal desert island.

The day was a welcome tonic for the couple as they absorbed the grim news that had beset the Royal Family yet again since the start of the year. Charles had been admitted to the London Clinic in Marylebone for a planned procedure for an enlarged prostate, a benign condition. He was said to be 'doing well' when he was allowed home after a couple of days; only he wasn't. Diagnostic tests carried out had revealed he had cancer. He told his closest family first, including Edward and Sophie, before announcing it publicly, just a week after he had left the hospital. The Palace did not say what cancer he had, although did state it was not prostate. Clearly, it was serious enough for Prince Harry to take a flight from California to see 'Pa'.

Charles stopped all public engagements while he received treatment. He would not be the only key member of the Royal Family who had to do this. Kate had been admitted to the same hospital the previous month for abdominal surgery and was kept in for two weeks. She was visited by the King just before he went to a different part of the clinic for his operation. It was said that her condition was not cancerous but she would need to stop public engagements until Easter at the earliest. At the end of February the Palace announced that Kate was 'doing well'; only she wasn't either. Two weeks after Sophie's speech in Leeds, Kate revealed that tests after the operation revealed she did have cancer after all. With considerable understatement, she added, 'This has come as a huge shock.' She had started preventative chemotherapy.

While public attention and concern were understandably focused on Charles and Kate, Sophie had left the country on a top-secret mission. She was on her way to Kyiv to be the first Royal to visit the war-stricken country of Ukraine. After a flight to Warsaw, accompanied by a small team of helpers and security, she boarded the night train that bounced and rattled its way across 500 miles. She didn't sleep.

Sophie kept a diary of her trip, which she shared with the *Sunday Times* on her return to the UK. Her words were informative, gripping and passionate as, once more, she became a voice for women who had become the silent and ignored victims of 'heinous crimes'. Sophie strongly believed that women were not casualties or symptoms of combat but were being used as a deliberate tactic to over-power nations: 'It is a weapon requiring no training, no investment, and it is deployed globally.'

Estimated figures in the two years before her visit suggested there had been 169 cases of conflict-related sexual violence in Ukraine, but Sophie believed this was likely to be 'only the tip of the iceberg'. She met with one woman who had been subjected to three weeks of suffering at the hands of Russian soldiers but had escaped with her husband and taken with them a boy from a local orphanage, who had a serious disability. She visited a mass grave in the city of Bucha where 500 victims of the invasion were buried, and was shown a distressing photograph of a local priest whose body lay 'crumpled and riddled with bullets'. And she met again with Ukraine's First Lady, Olena Zelenska, a true friend and ally in this personal fight. This time, she also spoke with President Zelenskyy and passed on a message from King Charles, who was hoping to meet him personally in the not-too-distant future. In reality, Sophie's meeting with the president was more of a photo opportunity than anything else, but it did reveal how important she had become internationally.

Sophie understood well and with considerable foresight that those in positions of leadership would engage in the politics of war while it was left to her and others to amplify the voices of survivors. She was clear that she was not being brave or courageous by visiting the ravaged country: she declared, 'The brave people are those who have endured extreme violence and survived. The courageous are those who have reported the crimes committed against them.'

The images of what she had seen would stay with her, just as they had done following her visits to other countries facing the consequences of war.

The ability to compartmentalise was a precious gift that she had learned from the late Queen and copied successfully over the years, although the former monarch was unlikely to have been photographed skipping across the famous pedestrian crossing outside the Abbey Road recording studios in north London. Sophie was recreating the famous cover of the Beatles' *Abbey Road* album, something every holidaymaker had done when visiting that part of St John's Wood. She was attending a reception for Orbis Visionaries in connection with her ongoing work with sight charities. She could not resist popping outside to copy the Fab Four.

She was closer to home for the Royal Windsor Horse Show, arriving in a carriage next to Louise, who was acting as an official at the event. Sophie was clearly going to keep up the royal tradition of attending every year if she could. James was there too, and this time Charles was well enough to join everyone and was in good spirits. Kate wasn't with them but she did make her first public appearance of 2024 at the Trooping of the Colour ceremony, although she admitted she was still undergoing treatment and was not out of the woods yet. Lady Louise was on the Palace balcony between her father and Princess Anne, although her mother did her best to be the centre of camera attention in dazzling yellow. As everyone left, Sophie placed a comforting hand on William's shoulder, the simple gesture that had become a trademark of her love and support.

She and Edward also took time off from royal business to pose in the gardens of Bagshot Park for some official photographs. They were pictured happy and relaxed in each other's company through the warm lens of photographer Chris Jelf. Sophie's sure fashion touch was clearly on show as they mirrored each other's homely country attire. Sophie makes Edward more chilled, especially at Bagshot, which is enormous, but of course day to day they only use a few of the hundred-plus rooms. Sophie is always fighting against the house being a bit gloomy and Victorian inside, with dark wooden tables and antique clocks, especially without the happy sound of their children's laughter, although there are plenty of framed photographs of them growing up. Fortunately, both of the Edinburghs enjoy spending as much time as possible in the garden playing with the dogs; if it's raining there's always the light and bright conservatory with a view over the lawns. The house is never going to be open to the public or be the mystery property on *Through the Keyhole*.

They decided to spend their silver wedding anniversary in June at Royal Ascot. The day also coincided with Sophie's father Christopher's ninety-third birthday and he joined them, having come over from Benenden to stay at Bagshot Park. He had his arm around Sophie as they looked at the horses in the paddock, a simple gesture that showed the unshakeable closeness of father and daughter. He had never embarrassed her.

Louise was the star attraction at the Sandringham Horse Driving Trials at the end of the month, winning a silver medal. Sophie's driving skills, however, reduced everyone to fits of giggles when she competed in a carriage-driving drinking game. As part of the course, she had to pick up a wine glass, have a drink of the sparkling water it contained and put it back at the next table. She missed the chance and had to hold the glass in her mouth as she went around again for a second go. This time she made it, but she probably wished the glass contained something a great deal stronger than water.

Standing next to Louise was her boyfriend from St Andrews, Felix da Silva-Clamp, who was trying not to laugh too hard at Sophie, especially as she had just been named President of the Trials. The event was the first time Louise and Felix had been seen together in public. They had met at St Andrews, not at an academic lecture but as members of an amateur dramatic group called Mermaids. They were in the cast of an original, student-written play called *Dragon Fever* at the university's Byre Theatre. Louise, billed as Louise Mountbatten-Windsor, played a powerful and cynical witch called Nilvana. The student newspaper, *The Saint*, thought she displayed impressive physicality and gave a compelling performance. Felix, who boasted striking red hair and a winning smile, was cast as a young squire called Grant and won approval for his stage presence. They also played opposite one another in the perennial favourite *School for Scandal* by R.B. Sheridan and Oscar Wilde's *An Ideal Husband*. Edward applauded and approved of their theatrical endeavours.

Felix also worked at Jannettas Gelateria, an ice cream parlour in the town, as a 'gelato artist', which is the term for a Mr Whippy in the modern barista vernacular. A fellow employee described him as a 'lovely person'. Sophie approved of him taking a job to earn some spending money at college. Felix was born in London, where his father is a solicitor, but spent much of his childhood in Melbourne with his Australian-born mother, so it remains to be seen if Louise travels around that country as Sophie did as a young woman.

More immediately, Louise was in military uniform for the Royal Edinburgh Military Tattoo in August, where she fulfilled the role of Salute Taker, something that took the guest of honour, Princess Anne, by surprise – her face broke into delighted smiles when she realised it really was her niece, Louise, in uniform. The event on the Esplanade outside Edinburgh Castle was the first attended by Aunt Anne since she had suffered a head injury in June in a nasty incident with a horse which left her badly concussed. She spent five days in hospital afterwards. Louise was very keen on the military and joined St Andrews' Officers' Training Corps. She wrote on her Instagram page, 'I am interested in pursuing a career in the military, diplomacy or law.' While Anne, Kate and her mother Sophie have many military titles between them, none of them has actually served in the armed forces. Anne and Sophie had grown much closer since the death of 'Mama'; they were united in grief but also in their joint philosophy of just getting on with things. They had, for instance, jointly hosted a reception for the first time when they welcomed Korean war veterans to Buckingham Palace. The two women stood in for King Charles, who was not well enough to attend. They were in Paris for the Olympics, but not at the same time. Sophie was in the stands cheering excitedly the Team GB women cyclists, who won gold in the sprint. After the summer holiday in Balmoral, she and Edward went back to the French capital to watch the Paralympics.

Sophie was solo again when she travelled to Tanzania in September to continue her work as a global ambassador for the International Agency for the Prevention of Blindness (IAPB) as part of her campaign to eliminate trachoma. As usual she did not shirk comforting those badly affected by the disease. She adopted a children-friendly look for World Sight Day, held every year on the second Thursday in October. She chose to read a CBeebies Bedtime Story entitled *Specs for Rex*, an enchanting tale by the Irish-born illustrator, Yasmeen Ismail. Rex hates his new glasses and keeps on trying to hide them when he goes to school, but they are big and round and red. Sophie put on a large pair of specs to pose with a cuddly-toy version of Rex, a mini lion.

Kate had read a CBeebies story a few years before, but she was still keeping a low profile, although she did release a statement saying that she had finished her chemotherapy and was focusing on staying cancer-free. Sophie had been a huge support popping over to Adelaide Cottage when her schedule allowed, or joining Kate and William in Norfolk when she and Edward were staying at Sandringham. The royal wives stood together on the balcony of the Foreign Office to watch solemnly as wreaths were placed on the Cenotaph war memorial on Remembrance Sunday. Kate was clearly emotional at what was her first major royal event since her diagnosis at the beginning of the year. She turned and whispered to Sophie, 'You're never quite ready for this.' Sophie kept her spirits up and placed the reassuring and comforting Sophie hand on her back as they left. One body language expert observed that the gesture offered a form of 'maternal affection, care and reassurance'. Sophie was again by her side for Together at Christmas, the annual carol concert hosted by the Princess of Wales at Westminster Abbey. Kate looked the brightest and happiest she had done all year as she gave Aunt Sophie a hug and a kiss.

Kate was also a guest at the black-tie dinner and dance that Sophie held at Bagshot Park to mark her sixtieth birthday. The celebration on 18 January 2025 came just four days after Kate had announced that her cancer was in remission, so it was a happier start to a year for the Royal Family. Christopher Rhys-Jones arrived from Kent, and Sophie's elder brother David was there with his wife Zara. They were both funeral directors in East Sussex, having started a new career when their pub business in Kent ran into financial difficulties and closed. Only those who had been discreet about Edward and Sophie were invited, and that included Andrew Lloyd Webber and his wife Madeleine, who came over from their Hampshire estate. They were very enthusiastic owners and breeders in the horse-racing world and so always had plenty to chat about with the Royal Family.

One advantage of living so close to Windsor Castle was that staff from there could be diverted over to Bagshot Park to help cater and run special occasions. The grounds of the castle were also ideal for the pheasant shoot that Sophie had wanted for her birthday morning – although this was not a pursuit she wished to be advertised in these more enlightened times.

Following on from her anniversary photo shoot, Sophie posed for more landmark pictures, this time taken by Christina Ebenezer, an acclaimed young photographer she much admired. Sophie had liked two of Christina's pictures of Black actors Letitia Wright and Michaela Coel – that were hanging in the National Portrait Gallery. She was keen to promote a rising young female photographer and so contacted Christina, who was born in Nigeria, explaining that she wanted to be captured in a different light to mark this new chapter in her life.

She invited Christina over to Bagshot for a relaxing day. The photographer recalled, 'My favourite part was definitely working together on outfit choices.' They chose well. Sophie was dressed in a chic, dark polo-neck sweater and white pleated skirt. The radiant photograph of Sophie taken in a window at the house was joyful and carefree. As fashion expert Alison Jane Reid observed, 'I couldn't help thinking they reminded me of the celebrated pictures of a laughing Princess Diana taken by Patrick Demarchelier that appeared on the cover of *Vogue*. She smiles and looks confidently into the camera wearing a black polo neck.'

In some ways that is a fitting observation, because Sophie's passion about things that matter to anyone with a conscience in the world reflects the concerns that Diana had for the important issues of her day. The days when Sophie's appearance was compared to Diana's have long gone, however. Alison Jane said, 'She no longer bears a resemblance to Diana. She just looks like Sophie. She wears her hair up in a bun for formal royal occasions and down with a side ponytail for charity events and more relaxed public appearances. She is like a Hollywood star of the 1950s.

'Sophie looks fabulous at sixty. She is definitely the poster girl for the idea that royal women and women at sixty can be dynamic, radiantly beautiful, fashionable and ageless. She looks better now than she did in her thirties.'

Sophie doesn't seek praise, she just gets on with it, but Edward paid her a heartfelt compliment in response to her lovely remarks about him: 'She's been an absolutely brilliant rock and I'm incredibly lucky that I found Sophie and that she found me.'

Conclusion:
Bridging the Generation Gap

Sophie must be sick of being described as the King's secret weapon. In the Royal Family's recent troubled times she has stood out like a beacon where for years she flew pretty much under the radar. 'I don't know what people thought we were doing beforehand,' she has said with good humour and a hint of exasperation.

Looking at her progress during the past twenty-five years it became very apparent that both the late Queen and Prince Philip had a protective arm around Sophie, happy that their youngest son had found a genuinely nice woman with whom he could share his life, raise a family and continue the best of the traditions they had nurtured.

The Queen once famously said that you wouldn't notice her in a room. That was actually a compliment. Early on, Sophie learned the art of *not* being the centre of attention everywhere she went, ensuring that the event was always more important than the shoes she was wearing.

She was the perfect choice to stand in for Charles at the emotional and poignant ceremony that marked the fifti-eth anniversary of the Birmingham pub bombings on 21 November 2024. Twenty-one people had lost their lives and nearly two hundred others were maimed or wounded in the terrible explosions. Sophie read out a message from the King that made his words seem real and not just going through the motions. That is the gift that Sophie brings to the Royal table – she is relatable.

Sophie was suitably solemn and understated as she ended, 'My thoughts, prayers and very best wishes remain with you as you mark this saddest of days.' Who else among the working members of the Royal Family could have delivered the lines that brought tears to the eyes of so many in the crowd that had gathered by the memorial in New Street?

Three days later Sophie was revealed as the new royal patron of the international organisation Plan International UK. The global children's charity aims to 'Build an Equal World for Girls'; it works in more than eighty countries to ensure every child is safe and receives an education – a world where 'all girls are free from violence, in control of their own body and know their rights'.

The goal chimed perfectly with Sophie's own ideals that she had voiced powerfully many times – except now everyone was paying more attention. The announcement featured a picture of Sophie in Chad, the country she had visited a few weeks before. The media had been full of her visit to Ukraine because that country was a distressing story on a daily basis. But now that Sophie was getting properly noticed, her visit to Central Africa was on the news agenda as well. She was in tears and admitted to feeling 'quite wobbly' when she met and talked with women refugees from neighbouring Sudan. Many had been forced to exchange sex for food and water – a bargaining tool of conflict that infuriated and upset Sophie in equal measure.

Survival for victimised women was on the agenda for Sophie again a couple of days after the Plan International announcement when she attended the opening of 'The Women Who Beat ISIS' photographic exhibition in Durbar Court, part of the Foreign Office building in Whitehall. The exhibition told the harrowing story of the survivors of the Yazidi genocide in Iraq and Sudan.

And the very next day she was off to Cheshire to open a new college building at the David Lewis Centre in Alderley Edge. The charity focused on improving the lives and prospects of young people over nineteen who had special educational needs.

That was just one week, but it was pretty much like that every week for Sophie and has been for some time. Ten years earlier, in November 2014, in seven days she travelled to the north-east to open a mental health hospital in Sunderland, visit a children's hospice in Stockton and meet the Tynemouth Volunteer Life Brigade. Then she joined the rest of the gang for Remembrance Sunday at the Cenotaph before jetting off to Zambia to represent the Queen at the state funeral of the country's president, Michael Sata. I wasn't aware that she had done any of those things and had to look them up.

When she first became a full-time working Royal, Sophie understood quickly that she was the icing on the cake at many charity events and couldn't really change anything. As the years have gone by, she has realised that she does have a voice and has been prepared to use it. Her guiding principle is that she believes in 'equality for everyone'. That's probably a view that's easier to express outside the Royal Family than within it, where there are so many protocols that have little relevance in the modern world.

One of the more amusing aspects that the media, both social and newspaper-based, focus on is the dreaded curtsy. It's easy to understand the 'protocol' that dictated a curtsy to the Queen – after all she had started her reign so long ago – and who could forget Princess Anne's curtsy to her mother's coffin, a heartfelt gesture of love and respect – but to Charles? My understanding from a royal source is that every woman would have to do a quick curtsy (the men a bow) if he was in an official room where he was the King and not father, brother or uncle. That would be much more pronounced at a big event like the coronation. If, however, it was just a family occasion then nobody bothered because they would be there all day before getting stuck into the sherry. All the stories about Sophie having to curtsy to Meghan were just nonsense. No royal woman curtsies to Kate, either.

Sophie is relatable for many women because of the experiences she has been through that have so strongly influenced the causes she has embraced: IVF, ectopic pregnancy, difficult birth – to put it mildly – concern and worry for a child born with a problematic health condition, which in Louise's case was esotropia. Her patronage of charities that strive to improve sight throughout the world has been in tandem with her passionate support of women suffering as a result of war and conflict throughout the world. She always seems to be breaking new ground for the Royal Family, talking openly, for instance, about her experience of the menopause. In doing so she was backing an initiative from the Wellbeing of Women charity of which she was patron. The campaign called for employers to sign a pledge to support women in the workplace going through the menopause. Sophie took part in a video call with the charity's chair, Dame Lesley Regan, in which she was refreshingly candid about her own experience: 'You suddenly can't remember what on earth it was you were talking about. Try being on an engagement when that happens; your words just go. And you're standing there going, "Hang on, I thought I was a reasonably intelligent person. What has just happened to me?"'

One of the gifts Sophie possesses is being able to be pitch-perfect when moving from personal to official at any function. That ability was observed by Janet Lindsay, the charity's CEO, who witnessed Sophie in action at their events: 'She's totally natural. Women's issues and rights are very much one of her key areas, and she just has a natural empathy with everybody she's talking to, whether they have baked and run and jumped for us, or are esteemed experts from the research advisory committee.'

One of Sophie's best quotes came in her conversation with Dame Lesley, in which she delivered a rallying call for women everywhere: 'We are fabulous in our forties, and we are even more fabulous in our fifties, sixties and seventies, and we need to celebrate that and keep opportunities going for women.'

The whole world seemed to notice how fabulous Sophie was when she turned sixty in January 2025. Alison Jane Reid, editor of the *Luminaries Magazine*, observed that she had become 'very much her own woman'. Fashion, and the way she presents herself, is something Sophie takes very seriously. She absolutely has to do that because whatever she decides to wear will be written about in the minutest detail – not just the outfits and the wonderful hats but also the jewellery she has chosen for the occasion. She seems to love it all though.

Top antique jeweller Zuleika Gerrish, at Parkin and Gerrish, noted that Sophie's jewellery choices reflect her elegant yet approachable style. 'She favours modern diamond suites, including several impressive necklaces inherited from the late Queen. Sophie honours royal heritage while incorporating contemporary elegance.'

Alison Jane sums up Sophie's fashion: 'Sophie is definitely the poster girl for the idea that royal women at sixty can be dynamic, radiantly beautiful, fashionable and ageless. I think she looks better now than she did in her thirties.'

Sophie spends a lot of money on looking as good as she does – although it may not be as much as Diana used to spend. One of the few members of household staff she relies on looks after the clothes, the hats and the jewellery. Fortunately, Bagshot Park is so large that it could have a walk-in-wardrobe in ten rooms and nobody would notice.

It's not easy being relatable when you live in such a grand manner. Bagshot Park is an enormous home, with extensive gardens that stretch to more than fifty acres; it is truly idyllic and beyond the imagination of practically everyone. Both she and Edward have always kept quiet about any staff they employ but they can call on the household servants at Windsor Castle as they did for Sophie's sixtieth birthday.

Sophie and Edward warned their children that they will probably have to earn a living when they grow up. That may or may not be the case. Sophie is not a secret weapon, but Louise and James may be. There's talk of Louise joining the military when she leaves university, which is exactly what would have been proposed if she had been male. Perhaps it is a sign of modern times that she will follow that path before becoming a full-time working Royal. She is the only young woman of her age in the Royal Family.

The question of age is Sophie's biggest asset for the Royal Family moving forward. At sixty, she is placed almost exactly in the middle of Kate and both Anne and Camilla – she bridges the gap between the generations. None of these other royal women enjoyed the best of health in 2024. There's talk that Sophie will fulfil a more important role when William becomes King, and it has been whispered quietly that Charles has not announced as yet that he is in remission from his cancer diagnosis. Camilla is likely to adopt a low profile as his widow, the Queen Dowager Camilla. Kate and Sophie are the best of friends, always laughing together. Nothing portrayed that relationship better than Royal Ascot in 2017, when they travelled together down the course in the same open-topped carriage. Sophie was attempting to change places when she fell on top of Kate, reducing both women to a shriek of giggles – it was a truly happy moment. The Princess of Wales, however, has three young children to occupy her attention, but Sophie is there to help and support when she can. Meghan has gone for ever, which is a pity because she and Sophie would have made a great team standing up for the empowerment of women and articulating that concern.

In my biography of Meghan, I wrote that the Queen was the glue that binds the institution together and 'Goodness knows what will happen to the Royal Family when she passes.' I'm still not too sure. Sophie has become the figure within the family who is the comforter to its members and a reassuring and inspiring presence for the country. She is a modern woman and yet a throwback to happier Royal times. She is now the 'glue that binds'.

Sophie Rhys-Jones; Sophie, HRH Countess of Wessex; Sophie, HRH Countess of Wessex and Forfar; Sophie, HRH Duchess of Edinburgh – it's a pity she can never be queen because she would have made a real good one.

Life and Times

20 Jan 1965: Sophie Helen Rhys-Jones is born at the Nuffield Maternity Home in Oxford. She has an elder brother, David, who is two. Her father Christopher works for a tyre importer. He met his Irish-born wife, Mary O'Sullivan, on a trip to Gibraltar.

Sept 1969: Starts at Nash House, the junior part of Dulwich College Preparatory School in Cranbrook, nine miles from the Kent village of Brenchley, where the family had moved the previous year. Her home is Homestead Farmhouse, a comfortable, four-bedroom thatched property. At school she develops a lifelong love of water by splashing around with the other children in the shallow pool.

Sept 1972: Moves to a girls-only building called Little Stream, where she wears a school uniform for the first time. She has her own gang of friends with whom she shares sleepovers and parties. Outside school, she takes ballet lessons and reaches Grade 4 in dance. It is an idyllic world.

Sept 1974: Moves to Coursehorn, a more senior mixed part of the school at which exams become important. She takes confirmation classes from the school chaplain, Trevor Vickery, who also teaches her to box. Sophie is proving to be good at all sports, especially hockey.

Sept 1976: Having passed her entrance exams, starts senior school at Kent College for Girls in nearby Pembury, where she becomes friends with the Olympic swimmer Suki Brownsdon. She would go on to pass eight O Levels, including English, her strongest subject. Meets her first boyfriend, David Kinder, at a theatre workshop when she is fifteen.

Sept 1981: Decides not to stay on at school but starts a two-year secretarial course at West Kent College of Further Education in Tonbridge. She can also study for A Levels there. Goes to college every day with best buddy Jo Last, who drives them in her old Citroën called 'Matilda'. To pay for nights out, she takes her first job as a waitress, at the Halfway House pub in Brenchley.

July 1983: Moves to London and shares a flat in Kensington with childhood friend Sarah Sienesi, who some years later would become her first lady-in-waiting. Within a month Sophie secures her first job as secretary to the managing director of the Quentin Bell PR organisation in Covent Garden. Enjoys the 'Sloane' social life in Chelsea and Fulham.

Jan 1986: Holds her twenty-first birthday party as a black-tie event in a marquee in the garden at Homestead Farmhouse. Her father thanks 'the Disco Johnny for providing the music'. Shortly afterwards, Sophie lands a job in the press and promotions department of Capital Radio, where she is responsible for organising diaries and events for the well-known DJs.

Dec 1989: Leaves Capital Radio and trains as a ski rep with Bladon Lines in Putney, south-west London. Sophie is posted to the fashionable Swiss resort of Crans-Montana. She is in charge of Chalet Isabella and earns £50 a week. She meets Michael O'Neill, a good-looking Australian ski instructor, and they become a couple.

April 1990: Travels to Sydney, Australia, to be with Michael, but their relationship does not last. Decides to stay in Australia and takes a job as a personal assistant in the city before moving on to see as much of the country as she can.

June 1991: Now twenty-six, she returns home to Brenchley via Thailand in time for her father's sixtieth birthday party in the garden, where she tells guests all about her Australian adventure. It pours with rain.

Dec 1991: Becomes a promotions assistant at the Cancer Relief Macmillan Fund in Chelsea. She moves into a flat in West Kensington, which she shares with an air hostess friend.

May 1993: Joins Brian MacLaurin's PR company MCM, which moves to offices in Hammersmith close to her home. She meets up again with Chris Tarrant, a colleague from Capital Radio days, who is a client. She does marketing work for *Thomas the Tank Engine*, Mr Blobby and the American singer Gene Pitney.

June 1993: Meets Prince Edward for the first time at a photocall at Queen's Club in West London to publicise his real tennis day, part of the Prince Edward Summer Challenge, which is raising money for charity. She takes the place of Sue Barker, who had to pull out at the last minute, and changes into a number of T-shirts with the names of different radio stations across the front.

Sept 1993: Edward calls out of the blue to ask her out. He had been waiting until the challenge had been completed. They go on a first date at Queen's Club and on to dinner at Buckingham Palace.

Nov 1993: Edward flies to Swaziland for the Duke of Edinburgh's Award scheme. He phones Sophie constantly at all hours and, on his return, goes straight round to her flat to pick her up. She meets the Queen for the first time, at lunch in Windsor Castle.

Dec 1993: Biographer Andrew Morton strides into the MCM office, walks up to Sophie and declares, 'May I be the first to call you Her Royal Highness?' The whole world will soon know she is Edward's girlfriend and she becomes of immediate interest to the paparazzi. Spends Christmas in Brenchley but travels for the first time to Sandringham to see in the New Year.

Jan 1994: Edward throws a surprise party at his Buckingham Palace apartment to celebrate Sophie's twenty-ninth birthday. A skiing holiday is cancelled when they realise Princess Diana would be at a nearby resort and the place would be swarming with photographers. Instead, they get away to Craigowan Lodge next to Balmoral.

June 1994: The *Daily Mirror* declares IT'S OFF, announcing that her romance with Edward is over. It is not true.

July 1994: Avoids being photographed next to Diana at the wedding of Princess Margaret's daughter Sarah at the St Stephen Walbrook church in the City of London. She attends her first official event with Edward when she is a guest at the Royal Tournament at the Earls Court Exhibition Centre. Sophie is given a police escort.

Nov 1995: Two days after Diana's notorious *Panorama* interview, Sophie hands in her notice to Brian MacLaurin, having agreed with Edward not to be as publicly visible as a PR. Her leaving do at a restaurant close to the office is ruined when the paparazzi burst in and start taking pictures.

Jan 1996: A planned engagement party at Buckingham Palace goes ahead as just a party because Edward had not proposed. He did not want to be used as the good news after the *Panorama* storm.

Feb 1997: Decides to set up her own PR company, R-JH, with fellow London-based PR Murray Harkin. They move into upmarket premises in Mayfair with an impressive starting list of clients.

Aug 1997: Becomes the cover girl of *Hello!* magazine for the first time when she 'speaks candidly about her life and how she sees her future'. The Sophie words and pictures run to thirteen pages, which is great publicity for R-JH and for her client, the Haven Trust cancer charity – to whom the magazine makes a substantial donation. Diana is killed in a car crash in Paris.

Sept 1997: Does not attend Diana's funeral at Westminster Abbey. She reportedly has decided she looks too like the princess from a distance and that would be upsetting to the vast crowd. Any engagement is once more put on hold.

March 1998: Edward acquires a fifty-year lease from the Crown Estates for Bagshot Park, a magnificent country house close to Windsor Castle. The property, boasting more than a hundred rooms, requires nearly £3 million of renovation before they can move in.

Dec 1998: During a beachside vacation in the Bahamas Edward finally drops to one knee and asks Sophie to marry him. She replies, 'Yes, please!'

Jan 1999: It's official! Buckingham Palace makes the announcement. The happy couple pose for photographs in front of St James's Palace. Sophie wears a tailored suit designed by Tomasz Starzewski and shows off her diamond engagement ring that was estimated to have cost £105,000. Edward places a gentle kiss on Sophie's cheek.

May 1999: Less than a month before the wedding, the *Sun* publishes a topless photo of Sophie with Chris Tarrant. Buckingham Palace describes it as 'premeditated cruelty'. The newspaper and its editor apologise. The DJ who sold the photo is fired by radio station Heart.

June 1999: Sophie and Edward marry at St George's Chapel, Windsor. She does not want to be known as Princess Sophie so instead becomes HRH The Countess of Wessex, or as she prefers, Sophie Wessex. It is agreed that at some point in the future Edward will become Duke of Edinburgh, a title his father was given on his wedding day. Sophie wears a wedding gown designed by Samantha Shaw. They honeymoon at Birkhall on the Balmoral Estate.

Sept 1999: Provokes a 'royals for hire' controversy by posing next to a new Rover 75 car at the Frankfurt Motor Show, having reportedly secured a £250,000 contract for RJ-H to publicise it.

July 2000: Fittingly, their first official foreign visit together is to Prince Edward Island off the eastern coast of Canada. They mix easily with local residents, including a young girl who lets Sophie pat her pet guinea pig's nose.

April 2001: Is the subject of a famous sting by the Fake Sheikh, *News of the World* journalist Mazher Mahmood. He had taped their conversation at the Dorchester Hotel in which she thought she was securing a lucrative contract for her company. She chats freely about the Blairs, William Hague, John Major, Charles and Camilla. She calls the Queen an 'old dear'.

Dec 2001: Suffering from serious stomach pains, Sophie is rushed by air ambulance from Bagshot Park to the King Edward VII Hospital in Marylebone. She has life-saving surgery for an ectopic pregnancy. She is in theatre for three hours and requires five pints of blood.

Jan 2002: Joins Edward for the funeral of Princess Margaret, a less-happy occasion at St George's Chapel. The Queen openly weeps for her sister. The Queen Mother, aged 101, is pushed into the chapel in a wheelchair. She herself will die six weeks later.

March 2002: Announces that she is standing down from her role at RJ-H. She will no longer draw a salary and becomes a non-executive director for now. At the same time Edward gives up his TV company, Ardent Productions. They both intend to concentrate on the Queen's Silver Jubilee, but the moves are permanent. They become working members of the Royal Family.

Nov 2003: Six weeks before she is due to give birth, Sophie is rushed to Frimley Park Hospital, six miles from home, for an emergency caesarean to save mother and baby. She is fifteen minutes from death and requires a transfusion of nine pints of blood. Her daughter weighs just 4lb 9oz and is taken immediately to a specialist baby unit. Edward is on an official visit to Mauritius but takes the first flight home. The Queen visits Sophie in hospital, where she recovers for sixteen days.

April 2004: At her christening, Sophie's daughter is given a historic honour by the Queen when she is dressed in the Hamilton christening gown, commissioned by Queen Victoria in 1841. Sixty-two Royal children, including the Queen herself, have worn it. Lady Louise will be the last before it is officially retired, owing to its delicate state.

April 2005: Attends the wedding of Charles and Camilla at St George's Chapel. Sits in the same row as the Queen, Prince Philip, Prince Andrew, her husband and Princess Anne.

Aug 2005: Her mother Mary dies in hospital in Tunbridge

Wells. She had been receiving treatment for cancer of the colon. Sophie is at her bedside when she passes. Mary will never meet her grandson, and many years later Sophie reveals how much she misses her.

Dec 2007: Edward and Sophie's son James is born at Frimley Park Hospital. He is styled Viscount Severn, one of his father's lesser titles that can only be passed down the male line. At five weeks old he is rushed to Great Ormond Street Hospital in London after suffering a severe allergic reaction. He is found to have lactose intolerance.

Sept 2008: Mazher Mahmood's book *Confessions of a Fake Sheikh* is published and features a picture of Sophie on the front cover alongside, among others, Britney Spears, Sven-Göran Eriksson, Princess Michael and Prince Harry.

Feb 2010: Acts as president of the Royal Bath & West Show, reflecting her interest in farming. The following year she becomes the annual event's royal patron.

April 2011: Dazzles in a Bruce Oldfield-designed red evening gown, despite nursing a broken rib, at the pre-wedding gala dinner for Kate and William at the Mandarin Oriental Hotel. The following day, Louise, seven, is a bridesmaid at Westminster Abbey.

July 2011: Readers of *Hello!* magazine vote her outfit, a Bruce Oldfield-designed pleated jacket and skirt, the best of the day at the Edinburgh wedding of Zara Phillips and Mike Tindall.

March 2013: Becomes the first ever patron of the London College of Fashion. She is keen to promote its Better Lives campaign, which aims to use fashion to tackle issues such as equality, diversity, social mobility and sustainability.

Sept 2013: Undertakes first major solo trip abroad when she visits India and Qatar in support of the Orbis sight-saving charity. Sight is a cause she returns to many times following her anxiety over her daughter's eye condition, esotropia, which will require two operations.

March 2014: The Queen approves the title of the Countess of Wessex's String Orchestra for the new twenty-four-member string band from the Royal Corps of Army Music. Sophie opens a new neonatal unit at Frimley Park Hospital and breaks down in tears as she meets and thanks the midwives who saved her life.

Dec 2014: Gives an interview to *Harper's Bazaar* magazine in which she says Muslim women can be fashionable while retaining their modesty. She observes that underneath the burka there is probably a woman wearing something quite fashionable.

April 2015: Edward and Sophie take their children on their first official visit overseas to the Ubunye Foundation in South Africa to witness the work being done to help underprivileged, mainly Black, children in poor, rural areas.

Sept 2016: After training for six months, embarks on a seven-day, 445-mile bike ride from Edinburgh to Buckingham Palace. Edward, her children and her father are at the Palace finish line to greet her and say well done. She raises more than £180,000 for the Duke of Edinburgh's Award Diamond Jubilee appeal.

June 2017: Riding in an open-topped carriage with Kate on the first day of Royal Ascot, Sophie almost falls in her lap. The two royal women dissolve into a fit of giggles.

Nov 2018: Meets Angelina Jolie at a festival in London entitled Fighting Stigma Through Film. The Oscar-winning actress is a kindred spirit in providing a voice for women victims of conflict rape. As a fifteenth-birthday present, Sophie treats Louise to an evening in the audience of *Strictly Come Dancing*, one of their favourite TV shows. They meet host Tess Daly and cheer on the contestants.

March 2019: Writes an article for the *Daily Telegraph* entitled, 'Why I'm joining the fight to end the silence around women in conflict'. Gives a powerful speech to the United Nations General Assembly as part of a UN 'Women in Power' event, in which she says, 'If all the seats at the table are full, you just need to pull up an extra chair. There is no excuse not to include women.' Becomes the Countess of Forfar when Edward is granted the title Earl of Forfar by the Queen.

May 2019: Is the first member of the Royal Family to pop round to see how Meghan is doing after giving birth to her son Archie.

Oct 2019: Visits Kosovo in south-eastern Europe, where she meets survivors of sexual violence during the war there just before the millennium. She praises the women for the courage they have shown. Makes a speech at a reception at Buckingham Palace for the Diamond Jubilee Trust, in which she calls the Queen 'Mama'.

Jan 2020: Travels to Sierra Leone, where an estimated 60,000 women were raped during the civil war of 1991/2. Meets survivors and also hears of a programme aimed at providing menstrual period products for girls so that their education is not disrupted.

March 2020: Just before the Covid lockdown she visits South Sudan, a country where women victims fear going to hospital in case they are seen. Arrives home in time for the Commonwealth Day Service at Westminster Abbey, at which she and Edward sit next to Harry and Meghan, who are making their last appearance as full-time working Royals.

April 2020: Volunteers at the Hope Hub charity in Camberley, Surrey, to help pack food packages for the homeless. Cooks spaghetti at the London kitchen of the catering company Rhubarb, to help provide meals for NHS workers during the pandemic.

Sept 2020: The Wessex family spend the day helping to clear rubbish from Southsea Beach, Hampshire, as part of the Great British Beach Clean.

April 2021: Prince Philip dies in his sleep at Windsor Castle. The Queen releases a private photo that Sophie had taken in 2003 while pregnant with Louise. It shows the monarch and her husband looking happy and relaxed at a favourite beauty spot in the Highlands. At the funeral, the Queen sits by herself, dressed in black. Sophie takes off her mask to wipe away a tear.

July 2021: Succeeds Princess Alexandra as patron of the Guide Dogs for the Blind Association.

March 2022: Gives the keynote speech at a UN event in New York highlighting the struggles of women in Afghanistan. She declares, 'The Taliban would have us believe they are allowing citizens to go about their daily activities. We know this is not true.'

June 2022: Joins Edward in Belfast and Bangor, Northern Ireland, as part of the Platinum Jubilee celebrations. Pours pints of Guinness, makes an omelette or two and munches on a Belfast Bap. Watches the stars perform at the Platinum Party at the Palace.

Sept 2022: Dashes to a waiting RAF plane to join Edward, Prince Andrew and Prince William to fly to Balmoral to see the dying Queen, but they arrive just too late. The Queen has already passed. James, now fourteen, stands vigil with his cousins by the coffin as it lies in state at Westminster Abbey. Sophie arrives for the funeral in a car with Meghan. Both she and Edward are in tears during the service.

Dec 2022: Receives the Hillary Rodham Clinton Award in Washington for her work campaigning against sexual violence in conflict zones. The former US first lady and secretary of state describes Sophie as a 'trailblazer'.

March 2023: King Charles finally grants Edward the title of Duke of Edinburgh, so Sophie is now HRH The Duchess of Edinburgh. Their son James is now the Earl of Wessex. Their daughter remains Lady Louise.

May 2023: Sophie and Edward have a front-row seat at King Charles's coronation in Westminster Abbey alongside Kate and her children. Afterwards they are part of the select troupe on the balcony at Buckingham Palace. Stands next to Kate for the official coronation pictures. Attends the Coronation Concert, where she dances and sways to the Lionel Richie classic 'All Night Long'. Becomes the first Royal to visit Iraq to promote the Women, Peace and Security (WPS) agenda – an indication of her growing international reputation.

Oct 2023: Marks World Sight Day by visiting Ethiopia to draw attention to the fight against the disease trachoma, which makes it painful for sufferers to even blink.

March 2024: Pays tribute to her husband on his sixtieth birthday in a speech in Leeds, when she says, 'He is the best of fathers, the most loving of husbands and still my best friend.'

April 2024: Becomes the first Royal to visit Ukraine and meets President Zelenskyy. Visits a mass grave in the city of Bucha where 500 victims of the war are buried. Writes a diary of her trip for the *Sunday Times* in which she describes how the invading Russian soldiers are murdering women, men and children as they flee the conflict in cars or on foot. Recreates the famous Beatles' album cover by dancing over the zebra crossing at Abbey Road.

June 2024: Spends the afternoon at Royal Ascot celebrating her silver wedding anniversary with her husband and her father, who is ninety-three the same day. Takes part in a carriage-driving drinking game at the Royal Windsor show.

Oct 2024: Wears a large pair of bright red spectacles and reads a CBeebies Bedtime Story called *Specs for Rex* to mark World Sight Day.

Nov 2024: Supports Kate on the balcony of the Foreign Office in Whitehall as they watch the wreaths being laid on the Cenotaph war memorial as part of Remembrance Sunday. Places a comforting hand on her back as they leave.

Jan 2025: Sophie is sixty.

Acknowledgements

The other morning over a strong coffee I worked out how many books I have written. This is the twenty-ninth! I'm including in that total the two biographies I've done about Robbie Williams, Kylie Minogue and Britney Spears. I hadn't realised it was that many and I certainly need a lie down.

I'm often asked, especially in interviews, which of my subjects is my favourite and my reply is always the same. It's the one I am currently working on – so Sophie is my number one at the moment. Many of my books have been about music superstars and I always collect all their records and play them constantly to get in the mood; so I have shelves of Adele, Ed Sheeran, Harry Styles and many more. The one I keep going back to is the wonderful George Michael, so if I was pushed to name a favourite it would be the much-missed Georgios.

Sophie admits to having no singing voice so, hopefully, she won't release a Christmas song any time soon. Seriously, George is a classic example of there being two sides to a celebrity – the one we see in the public eye and the one we don't. That's also true to some extent with the Royal Family. I hope I have conveyed just how much fun Sophie is, while still promoting the serious issues that she cares about deeply.

We first noticed Sophie when she was revealed as Edward's

girlfriend by my old friend Andrew Morton. We've known each other for years, ever since we played in the same cricket team on Ham Common, Richmond, every weekend. We weren't much good, but the teas were always delicious and the company the best, especially when we adjourned to the pub afterwards to discuss how the umpire had been completely wrong. Thanks, Andrew, for checking I got things right.

Another old friend, Christopher Wilson, has been of great help on all things royal. He knows far more than I do and his book on Camilla and Charles is highly recommended. Wearing another hat, he is the novelist TP Fielden, whose Guy Harford mysteries are set in Buckingham Palace during wartime. I am also grateful to royal expert Claudia Joseph, who has always been happy to pass on much-needed advice and guidance. My fashion guru, Alison Jane Reid, has helped me so much over the years, including with my first book on Sophie, written before she married Edward. AJ is a superb writer and I heartily recommend the *Luminaries Magazine*, which she runs online.

Many thanks as always to Gordon Wise, my agent at Curtis Brown, who has looked after my interests so well for many years. Gordon has stuck with me for about eighteen years now and our Christmas lunch remains one of the highlights of my year. Last Christmas (sorry George!), we were joined by his assistant, Elliot Prior, who does so much to calm the day-to-day author panic. I'm already looking forward to this year's celebration.

This is my first book for Sphere Non-Fiction, so thanks to publisher Kelly Ellis for commissioning *Sophie: Saving the Royal Family*. Thanks also to Nithya Rae, the managing editor on the project; Marie Hrynczak, production manager; Charlotte Stroomer, senior designer; Brionee Fenlon, marketing manager; Ellen Turner, publicity manager; and Linda Silverman, picture research manager.

I've been lucky once again to have Helena Caldon looking after the words and doing a superb job copy-editing my original manuscript. Jo Westaway has been brilliant organising the research and dealing with all things technical. I'm never going to get any better at that!

I well recall the good time I had visiting Brenchley and surrounding villages with my much-missed pal, Garth Gibbs, one of the great men of Fleet Street. He made the first biography of Sophie so much fun to do. He was most famous, of course, for not finding Lord Lucan in some of the nicest places to visit in the world – Cape Town, Macao, Hong Kong and the Bahamas, where, incidentally, Sophie became engaged. Garth once wrote, 'I regard not finding Lord Lucan as my most spectacular success in journalism.'

Garth died in 2011 and I dedicated my biography of Kate Middleton to him when it was published that year. He didn't 'find' Lord Lucan in Sophie's home village of Brenchley, but we came across many friendly people in the pubs and cafés around that lovely area of Kent. A long list of people who talked kindly of Sophie includes Brian MacLaurin, Janie Stewart, Leanne Tritton-Jones, Nick Skeens, Peter Brown, Neil Fox, Graham Dene, Marino Franchi, Andrew Parkinson, Mike Whitehill, Alice de Smith, Jayne Fincher, Gareth Crump, Andrew Murray, Trevor Vickery, Jayne Fincher, and Tim and Eileen Graham. The veteran royal expert Judy Wade, who died in 2020, was always a great help to me over the years.

Team Sean seems to get bigger every year. I am just the icing on the cake, which is something Sophie might have said about her early days as the Royal Apprentice. She has become much more than that.

You can read more about my books at seansmithceleb.com or follow me on X and Facebook: @seansmithceleb. That's also my new imprint for republishing some of the earlier books as part of my *Path To Fame* series, available on Amazon and in bookstores.

I began these acknowledgements by mentioning that *Sophie: Saving the Royal Family* is my twenty-ninth book. I want to make thirty, so I had better get cracking.

Select Bibliography

Brandreth, Gyles, *Elizabeth: An Intimate Portrait*, Michael Joseph, 2023

Eggar, Robin, *Commando, Survival of the Fittest*, John Murray, 1994

Hutchins, Chris and Thompson, Peter, *Diana's Nightmare: The Family*, Neville Ness House Ltd, 2015

James, Paul, *Prince Edward: A Life in the Spotlight*, Piatkus Books, 1992

Seward, Ingrid, *Prince Edward, A Biography*, Century, 1995

Seward, Ingrid, *Prince Philip Revealed: A Man of His Century*, Simon & Schuster UK, 2022

Wilson, Christopher, *A Greater Love: Charles and Camilla*, Headline, 1995

Wilson, Christopher, *The Windsor Knot – Charles, Camilla and the Legacy of Diana*, Citadel, 2003